PSYCHIATRY FOR THE RICH

THE WELLCOME INSTITUTE SERIES IN THE HISTORY OF MEDICINE

Edited by W. F. Bynum and Roy Porter
The Wellcome Institute

Florence Nightingale and the Nursing Legacy
Monica Baly

Vivisection in Historical Perspective
Nicholaas A. Rupke

Abortion in England, 1900–1967
Barbara Brookes

The Hospital in History
Edited by Lindsay Granshaw and Roy Porter

Women as Mothers in Pre-industrial England
Valerie Fildes

Birth Control in Germany, 1871–1933
James Woycke

The Charitable Imperative
Colin Jones

Medicine at the Courts of Europe, 1500–1837
Vivian Nutton

Mad Tales from the Raj
Waltraud Ernst

British Medicine in an Age of Reform
Roger French and Andrew Wear

Doctor of Society
Roy Porter

Medical Journals and Medical Knowledge
W.F. Bynum, Stephen Lock and Roy Porter

Medical Theory, Surgical Practice
Christopher Lawrence

The Popularization of Medicine, 1650–1850
Roy Porter

Women and Children First
Valerie Fildes, Lara Marks and Hilary Marland

PSYCHIATRY FOR THE RICH
A HISTORY OF TICEHURST PRIVATE ASYLUM, 1792-1917

Charlotte MacKenzie

London and New York

First published 1992
by Routledge
11 New Fetter Lane, London EC4P 4EE

Simultaneously published in the USA and Canada
by Routledge
a division of Routledge, Chapman and Hall, Inc.
29 West 35th Street, New York, NY 10001

© 1992 Charlotte MacKenzie

Typeset in 10/12 point Baskerville
by NWL Editorial Services, Langport, Somerset, England

Printed and bound in Great Britain by
Biddles Ltd, Guildford and King's Lynn

All rights reserved. No part of this book may be reprinted or reproduced
or utilized in any form or by any electronic, mechanical, or other means,
now known or hereafter invented, including photocopying and
recording, or in any information storage or retrieval system, without
permission in writing from the publishers.

British Library Cataloguing in Publication Data
A catalogue record for this book is available from the British Library

Library of Congress Cataloging-in-Publication Data
MacKenzie, Charlotte
Psychiatry for the rich: a history of Ticehurst private asylum, 1792-1917 /
Charlotte MacKenzie.
p.   cm. – (The Wellcome Institute series in the history of medicine)
Includes bibliographical references and index.
1. Ticehurst Private Asylum (Sussex, England) – History.
2. Psychiatric hospitals – England – Ticehurst – History.
3. Psychiatric hospitals – England – Ticehurst – Sociological aspects.
4. Psychiatric hospital care – England – Ticehurst – History.
I. Title   II. Series.
[DNLM: 1. Hospitals, Proprietary – history – England.   2. Hospitals,
Psychiatric – history – England.   3. Mental Disorders – history –
England.   4. Social Class.   WM 28 FE5 M15p]
RC450.G752T535   1992
362.2'1'094225–dc20
DNLM/DLC   92–49160
For Library of Congress   CIP

ISBN 0–415–08891–7

For my parents

Contents

	List of plates, figures and tables	viii
	Acknowledgements	x
	Introduction	1
1.	The commercialization of care	6
2.	Starting a family business	35
3.	The asylum and moral reform	61
4.	Madness and the Victorian family	97
5.	Mid-Victorian prosperity	128
6.	The fourth generation	163
7.	The protection of private care	193
	Conclusion	214
	Bibliography	218
	Index	226

Plates, figures and tables

Plates

1	A south-east view of the asylum at Ticehurst, Sussex	68
2	A view of the pleasure grounds and aviary	69
3	The moss-house and part of the pleasure grounds	72
4	A map of the vineyard, asylum and Highlands with the pleasure grounds, Ticehurst, Sussex	73

Figures

2.1	Newington family tree: Joseph Newington and Mary Tompsett	36
2.2	Newington family tree: Samuel Newington and Martha Playsted	38
2.3	Place of origin of first admissions to Ticehurst, 1792–1817	46
2.4	Place of origin of first admissions to Ticehurst in five-year periods, 1792–1817	48
2.5	Towns and villages from which nine or more patients were admitted to Ticehurst, 1792–1817	49
2.6	Newington family tree: Charles Newington and Eliza Hayes	54
3.1	Place of origin of first admissions to the asylum, 1817–42	78
3.2	Towns and villages from which seven or more patients were admitted to the asylum, 1817–42	80
4.1	Outcome of stay: profiles, 1845–1915	120
4.2	Outcome of stay of first admissions, 1845–1915	123
5.1	Place of origin of first admissions from within the United Kingdom, 1845–85	131
6.1	Newington family tree: Charles Edmund Hayes Newington and Eleanora Wetherell	164
6.2	Newington family tree: Samuel Newington and Georgiana Oakeley Malcolm Beatson	165
6.3	Place of origin of first admissions from within the United Kingdom, 1885–1915	168

Plates, figures and tables

Tables

2.1	Number of patients resident, 1795–1815	40
2.2	Pauper admissions, 1792–1817	41
2.3	Admissions, 1792–1817	45
2.4	Length of stay of first admissions, 1792–1817	51
2.5	Length of stay of patients resident, 1795–1815	52
2.6	Outcome of stay for patients resident, 1795–1815	52
3.1	Admissions to the asylum, 1817–42	65
3.2	Number of patients resident in the asylum, 1820–40	65
3.3	Pauper admissions to the asylum, 1817–42	66
3.4	Former occupations of first admissions to the asylum, 1 August, 1827 to 31 July 1832	76
3.5	Former occupations of first admissions to the asylum, 1 August 1832 to 31 July 1845	76
3.6	Length of stay of first admissions to the asylum, 1817–42	77
3.7	Length of stay of patients resident in the asylum, 1820–40	77
3.8	Outcome of stay for first admissions to the asylum, 1817–42	88
3.9	Outcome of stay for patients resident in the asylum, 1820–40	88
4.1	Number of patients in private asylums, 1850–80	97
4.2	Percentage of private patients in private asylums, 1850–1890	115
4.3	Length of stay of patients resident in Ticehurst, 1845–1915	118
4.4	Length of stay of admissions to Ticehurst, 1845–1915	122
5.1	Admissions to Ticehurst, 1845–1915	129
5.2	Number of patients resident in Ticehurst, 1845–1915	129
5.3	Former occupations of admissions to Ticehurst, 1845–85	132
5.4	Supposed causes of insanity in first admissions to Ticehurst, 1845–1915	151
5.5	Diagnoses of first admissions to Ticehurst, 1845–85	154
6.1	Former occupations of admissions to Ticehurst, 1885–1915	170
6.2	Diagnoses of first admissions, 1885–1915	184
7.1	Distribution of private patients, 1890–1910	205
7.2	Voluntary boarders admitted to Ticehurst, 1890–1914	206

Acknowledgements

The Ticehurst archives held at the Wellcome Institute for the History of Medicine in London were made available by kind permission of Nestor Medical Services Ltd. The engravings on the jacket and pages 68–9 and 72–3 of this book are reproduced from the 1828 prospectus for Ticehurst which forms part of this collection, and appear with their permission. I am deeply grateful to Nestor Medical Services Ltd for agreeing to follow the Ministry of Health's directive on confidentiality of patient records, HC(89)20, and giving permission for patients' identities to be revealed for the first one hundred years of Ticehurst's history.

The Wellcome Trust provided financial support for part of the period during which this book was researched and written, and I am grateful to them for this. I would also like to thank the staff of the following libraries and record offices, who provided courteous and friendly assistance: Bristol University Library, the British Library, East Sussex County Record Office, Edinburgh University Library, the Institute for Historical Research, the Public Record Office and the Wellcome Institute for the History of Medicine.

Conversations with the following people provided insights which assisted the development of ideas and interpretations in this book: Bill Bynum, Michael Clark, Anne Digby, Nick Hervey, Roy Porter, Huw Richards, Andrew Scull, Michael Shepherd, Nancy Tomes, Trevor Turner and John Harley Warner. The responsibility is my own.

Finally, my greatest debt of thanks is to Neil Morgan, for love and support while this book was written.

Introduction

Despite the rapid and extensive growth in the history of psychiatry and mental health care as a field of scholarship, no full-length study exists of the history of a private asylum in England. Parry-Jones's survey of *The trade in lunacy* provides an informative overview of the development of private madhouses in the eighteenth and nineteenth centuries, but one which leaves some wider historical questions unexplored.[1] The object of this book is not only to provide a more detailed history of one private asylum, but to identify the way in which that story can be used to illuminate aspects of social, as well as medical, history. Through the work of historians like Foucault, Rothman and Doerner, the growth of public and voluntary institutions for the insane from the late eighteenth century has long been associated with the bourgeoisie's desire for social order and social control in a period of rapid economic and political change.[2] In addition, Scull has emphasized the importance of psychiatrists' quest for professional status and security as a motor of institutional proliferation and expansion throughout the nineteenth century.[3] However, neither of these models is easily applicable to the development of the private sector. Private madhouses catered for a predominantly middle- and upper-class clientele, and are known to have existed before the eighteenth century; in addition, they were often owned and managed by lay, rather than medical, proprietors.

In seeking to develop alternative explanations for the development of the trade in lunacy, this study focuses on two relatively neglected aspects of the history of private asylums. Firstly, the role of medical and non-medical lunacy practitioners as entrepreneurs. As Porter has argued, the proliferation of private madhouses in the eighteenth century can be seen as part of the wider growth of service industries in Georgian England.[4] Although this is not a business history in an economic sense, it explores the way in which private asylum proprietors sought to develop, maintain and protect a share of the market in mental health care, attempting to mould, and responding to, changes in consumer demand. Proprietors who were

1

Introduction

medically qualified succeeded in dominating this market; but for lunacy doctors, madhouse-keeping represented only one form of private practice, together with consultancy and keeping single patients. This book therefore examines more broadly the extent to which lunacy doctors in private practice were able to influence the attitude of the medical profession, and successive governments, to proposed lunacy reforms, which were directed at the stricter regulation of private care both in and out of the asylum.

The second relatively neglected area which this study aims to elucidate, is the role of the family in decisions about care and treatment.[5] A working premise is that, in the case of mental health, it is patients' families, as well as or rather than patients, who decide when referral is necessary. However, pauper admissions depended, at the very least, on co-operation from magistrates and hospital subscribers, as well as doctors; and many cases were referred by the police or Poor Law officials. Although the development of charitable and county asylums can tell the historian a great deal about philanthropic, governmental and medical attitudes to mental health, it tells us little about the views of patients and their families.[6] In contrast, the history of private care and treatment was largely determined by consumer choice. Although private admissions required medical certification from 1774, and a minority of middle- and upper-class admissions were made via the courts, in non-criminal cases it was likely to be relatives or friends who made the initial decision to call in certifying doctors. Following certification, patients' families could exert significant influence on where and how the patient was treated. It is therefore possible to reconstruct middle- and upper-class attitudes to mental disorder, certification and confinement, as well as their changing evaluation of different forms of care, both in and out of the asylum. In addition, the response of patients' families to particular modes of treatment, such as mechanical restraint or moral therapy, can be documented. In order to reconstruct more fully the experience of families confronted with the problem of mental disorder, evidence is drawn from published diaries, letters and autobiographies, as well as the records from Ticehurst private asylum.

The experience of patients is more difficult to retrieve, although two former patients at Ticehurst in the nineteenth century, John Perceval and Herman Merivale, published autobiographical accounts of their confinement.[7] From these, as well as case notes and administrative records, it is possible to delineate a relatively full picture of patients' lives in the asylum; and to build up an impression of middle- and upper-class Victorian lunatics' psychiatric careers. The archives from Ticehurst are exceptional, both for the completeness with which they have survived, and for the detail in which some of them were kept. They represent a unique source for historians of nineteenth-century psychiatry. From them, it is possible to develop an understanding of the extent to which the treatment

Introduction

which was prescribed reflected a coherent therapeutic strategy, as well as the wishes and requests of patients' families.[8] Since Ticehurst was owned and managed by four generations of doctors in one family – the Newingtons – from 1792, it also represents a good case study through which to examine changes in the entrepreneurial approach of medically qualified proprietors.

However, Ticehurst has limitations as a case study in certain other respects. By the 1850s, the Newingtons' clientele were exceptionally wealthy; and, by the 1870s, Ticehurst was widely acknowledged in political and medical circles as one of the most successful and highly reputable private asylums. Its story therefore cannot be taken as typical of private madhouses in the mid-Victorian period. In so far as it illuminates a wider social history of medicine and of the family in this period, it is informative only about the social elite. The evident success of Ticehurst does mean, however, that it is possible to be certain that the care and treatment offered there accurately reflected the wishes and expectations of patients' relatives and friends.

The first chapter provides a brief overview of the development of the trade in lunacy in the eighteenth century, examining the extent to which it was changes in family relationships, as well as the consumer revolution, which stimulated the proliferation of madhouses. The early history of Ticehurst, as an asylum and as a family business, is described in Chapter 2. In considering how the Newingtons were able to begin to develop an increasingly wealthy clientele, Chapter 3 explores the way in which they sought to align their practice with fashionable preoccupation with moral reform in the 1830s. Chapter 4 returns to the question of the role of the family in choices of care. What kind of behaviour led middle- and upper-class Victorians to refer patients for treatment? And what were the alternatives to private asylum care? This chapter also explores the impact of the lunacy reform movement on public perceptions of private asylums; and the growing influence of the Lunacy Commissioners and Lord Chancellor's Visitors in Lunacy on decisions about care and treatment.

One of the functions of the Lord Chancellor's Visitors was to ensure that lunatics whose estates were protected by the Court of Chancery did not suffer any detriment to their standard of living. Chapter 5 considers the care and treatment provided at Ticehurst in the prosperous mid-Victorian period, and examines the extent to which this reflected a coherent medical strategy as well as a concern to please their wealthy clientele. Unlike county asylums and registered hospitals, Ticehurst was relatively free of resource constraints. Chapter 6 explores the extent to which, despite this, standards of care and treatment at Ticehurst were influenced by growing therapeutic pessimism in the late-Victorian period, as well as the economic slowdown from the 1870s. In the 1880s, increasingly vocal calls for lunacy reform led to successive bills which proposed the stricter regulation of private lunacy

3

Introduction

practice. Chapter 7 examines the responses of private lunacy practitioners to these proposals, and considers the extent to which they were successful in moulding medical and political opinion. This final chapter also explores the impact of therapeutic pessimism, and the 1890 Lunacy Act, on the choices of care made by late-Victorian and Edwardian families.

Throughout this book, I have adopted contemporary historical usage of terms like 'medical psychology', in preference to the more anachronistic 'psychiatry'. In some cases, however, in the interests of varied style, I have not attempted to sustain historical nuances precisely: for example 'madhouse' and 'asylum' are used fairly interchangeably; as are 'lunatic', 'insane', 'mentally disordered' and so on. In emphasizing the social context of referral and treatment, no implicit judgement is being made on whether or not those people who became patients in private madhouses were 'really' mad. As Michael Shepherd has argued, psychiatry is, necessarily, 'closely embedded in the social matrix in which the subject is practised';[9] and it is that social matrix in earlier times which this book aims to elucidate. I hope it will be of interest to psychiatrists and other mental health workers, as well as to historians.

Finally, a brief explanation of the way in which records from Ticehurst are referred to in the notes. The bulk of this book was completed before the archives deposited at the Wellcome Institute for the History of Medicine had been catalogued. The notes therefore refer to items from this collection by first letters of titles, and volume numbers or dates, rather than accession numbers. For example, 'CB4' refers to Case Book number 4, 'RA1845–81' to the Register of Admissions for 1845–81, and so on. Accession numbers are listed in the bibliography.

NOTES

1. W. Ll. Parry-Jones, *The trade in lunacy. A study of private madhouses in England in the eighteenth and nineteenth centuries*, London, Routledge & Kegan Paul, 1972.

2. M. Foucault, *Madness and civilisation. A history of insanity in the age of reason*, London, Tavistock Publications, 1967; D. Rothman, *The discovery of the asylum*, Boston, Little Brown, 1971; K. Doerner, *Madmen and the bourgeoisie: a social history of insanity and psychiatry*, Oxford, Basil Blackwell, 1981.

3. A. Scull, *Museums of madness. The social organization of insanity in nineteenth-century England*, London, Allen Lane, 1979.

4. R. Porter, *Mind-forg'd manacles. A history of madness in England from the Restoration to the Regency*, London, Penguin Books, 1990, pp. 164–7.

5. These issues are also explored in an American context by N. Tomes, *A generous confidence. Thomas Story Kirkbride and the art of asylum-keeping, 1840–83*, Cambridge, Cambridge University Press, 1985.

6. J.K. Walton, 'Casting out and bringing back in Victorian England: pauper lunatics, 1840–70', in W.F. Bynum, R. Porter and M. Shepherd (eds), *The anatomy of madness*, vol.II, London, Tavistock Publications, 1985, pp. 132–46, is an interesting attempt to explore family attitudes to the certification of pauper lunatics.

4

Introduction

7. [J. Perceval] *Narrative of the treatment experienced by a gentleman during a state of mental derangement . . .*, London, Effingham Wilson, 1838 and *idem, A narrative of the treatment experienced by a gentleman during a state of mental derangement*, London, Effingham Wilson, 1840; [H. C. Merivale], *My experiences in a lunatic asylum, by a sane patient*, London, Chatto & Windus, 1879.

8. Trevor Turner argues that it is possible to identify present-day diagnoses from the case notes from Ticehurst, in 'A diagnostic analysis of the case books of Ticehurst House Asylum, 1845–1890', University of London MD thesis, 1990; see also supplement of *Psychological Medicine* with same title, in press for 1992.

9. M. Shepherd, *The psychosocial matrix of psychiatry. Collected papers*, London, Tavistock publications, 1983, p. ix.

1

The commercialization of care

The making of the asylum

For nearly thirty years, historians and sociologists have been debating the reasons why institutions for the insane developed on an unprecedented scale in eighteenth- and nineteenth-century Europe. Earlier Whiggish evaluations in terms of medical and humanitarian progress – the realization that insanity is an illness, the rise of the welfare state – gave way in the 1960s–70s to more sceptical appraisals linking the birth of the asylum to a repudiation of the irrational in the age of reason (Foucault), or a quest for social control in newly industrialized societies (Doerner).[1] Both Foucault and Doerner included England in their broader European analyses, but it remained for Scull to provide a more detailed study of the genesis of English asylums in terms of social control. Scull linked the rise of the asylum to the demands which an industrial–capitalist labour market placed on family resources, arguing that segregation of the dependent insane freed other family members to participate in the market, as well as endorsing the social order by removing the disruptive or deviant. He also emphasized the self-promotion of the medical profession as experts in insanity as the motor of continuous growth of the asylum system throughout the nineteenth century.[2]

As Scull acknowledged, however, with the exception of Bethlem, the first asylums to develop in England were private madhouses; and it is not so easy to fit these into an explanatory framework based on social control.[3] Since 1714, magistrates had been empowered to confine those who were 'furiously Mad, and dangerous to be permitted to go Abroad' (12 Anne, c.23); but those who were detained under this legislation were most likely to be confined in bridewells and workhouses, rather than specialized institutions for the insane, despite the fact that from 1744 parishes carried a statutory responsibility for 'curing such Person during such Restraint' (17 Geo. II, c.5).[4] In other words, although some of the vagrant and violent

The commercialization of care

insane were initially detained under public order legislation, this did not in itself lead to the development of asylums. Private madhouses accommodated some pauper patients whose fees were paid by the parish, but their inmates were otherwise private fee-paying patients – unlikely targets of a bourgeois offensive against the idleness of the insane poor. In addition, as MacDonald has argued, the development of these asylums antedated industrialization.[5] Although Scull noted that asylums did not necessarily develop first in urban and industrial areas, and was careful therefore to link the growth of the asylum system more broadly to 'the advent of a mature capitalist market economy', he clearly envisaged this economic change as a consequence of industrialization, making it difficult to explain earlier eighteenth- century developments.[6]

In contrast, MacDonald's evaluation of social and cultural attitudes to madness in seventeenth- and eighteenth-century England hints at one possible explanation for the development of private madhouses. He argues that the Anglican ruling classes of eighteenth-century England embraced medical approaches to insanity before the labouring classes because they were eager to repudiate religious enthusiasm and thaumaturgic explanations of recovery from mental disorders. From this perspective, a predisposition amongst the ruling classes to lodge the mentally disordered with medical practitioners would seem self-explanatory, whether or not Georgian mad-doctors were as self-aggrandizing as their nineteenth-century counterparts. Nevertheless, as MacDonald is aware, the link between Anglican advocacy of medical therapy and the eighteenth-century asylum movement is not self-evident.[7] Private madhouses were opened by lay proprietors of varied religious beliefs, as well as by medical men; by medically qualified Dissenters, as well as by Anglican doctors; and wealthy insane were as likely to be lodged with Anglican clergy as with Anglican medical men. For example, the Baptist Joseph Mason (d. 1779), who started an asylum at Fishponds near Bristol, was not medically qualified; but the Quaker Edward Long Fox (1761–1835), who ran Cleeve Hill near Bristol 1794–1806, and subsequently purpose-built the prestigious Brislington House, had an MD from Edinburgh. The Anglican Revd Francis Willis (1718–1807), MD (Oxon.), ran an asylum at Greatford in Lincolnshire from 1776, and is best known as the physician who treated George III's insanity; while Revd John Lord was not medically qualified, but opened a small madhouse at Drayton Parslow in Buckinghamshire, which primarily catered for insane Oxford undergraduates.[8] In other words, it seems unlikely that the growth of private asylums can be explained by a shift towards a medical model for mental disorders, whether this is perceived in terms of scientific progress or ideological retrenchment amongst the Anglican elite.

Most recently, Porter has argued that there may be a simpler explanation for the proliferation of madhouses in eighteenth-century

The commercialization of care

England. He suggests that the expansion of the Georgian trade in lunacy can best be understood as part of the growth of service industries capitalizing on the boom in spending which accompanied the Industrial Revolution but was not confined to consumption of manufactured goods.[9] In Porter's model, the emphasis is not on the buoyancy of demand for the asylum – from scientific rationalists eager to assert their hegemony over crazed and troubled minds, or a new bourgeoisie anxious to discipline a maverick labour force – but on the entrepreneurial creation of new markets by 'captains of confinement', the private-madhouse proprietors.

> Madhouses and mad-doctors arose from the same soil which generated demand for general practitioners, dancing masters, man midwives, face painters, drawing tutors, estate managers, landscape gardeners, architects, journalists and that host of other white-collar, service, and quasi-professional occupations which a society with increased economic surplus and pretensions to civilization first found it could afford, and soon found it could not do without.[10]

In providing an economic rationale for the growth of asylums which depends on an increase in disposable income, rather than fully fledged industrialism, this argument appears to avoid many of the difficulties of timing implicit in Scull's analysis. Equally, it delineates a shared entrepreneurial agenda amongst asylum keepers, who were not necessarily united in their religious and medical beliefs.

Nevertheless, Porter's interpretation poses new questions about the madhouse business. For example, it has been argued that the consumer boom reached 'revolutionary proportions' in the third quarter of the eighteenth century, but is this when the biggest expansion in the trade in lunacy took place? To what extent did madhouse keepers see themselves, first and foremost, as entrepreneurs? Who were the consumers of private asylum services, and was this an area of spending in which upper-class or middle-class spenders led the way? One aspect of the recent emphasis on consumption, particularly domestic consumption, has been a sharpened interest amongst economic historians in the influence of the family on consumer choices.[11] Who took decisions about spending on health care within the family, and what made them interested in the services offered by madhouse proprietors? If the growth of private asylums reflected an increasing upper- and/or middle-class acceptance of, perhaps even a demand for, non-familial, commercialized care for their insane dependants, how does this relate to the contemporaneous restructuring of family relationships?[12] Finally, to what extent did health-care consumers, as well as madhouse entrepreneurs, help to shape the character of the treatment and care provided in private asylums?[13] (Perhaps even encouraging that ugly word 'madhouse' to be dropped in favour of 'asylum'.)

The commercialization of care

The madhouse business

It is in fact difficult to estimate the scale of the eighteenth-century trade in lunacy prior to the introduction of licensing legislation in 1774 (14 Geo. III, *c*.9). There are occasional documentary references to individual madhouses from the seventeenth century, as well as earlier literary evidence that the insane were sometimes lodged with keepers in exchange for money.[14] From the early eighteenth century, increasing evidence of the trade survives, such as handbills and advertisements in newspapers for private asylums, books touting the skills of particular madhouse keepers, protest literature alleging wrongful confinement and references to sequestration of the insane in diaries and letters. In addition, the case of *Rex* v. *Turlington* (1761), in which a successful habeas corpus plea led to the release of Mrs Deborah D'Vebre from Turlington's madhouse in Chelsea, was widely publicized, and helped mount pressure for government regulation of private asylums. However, subsequent investigations into the madhouse business by a Commons select committee in 1763 were perfunctory, and it was a further eleven years before legislation was passed requiring private asylums to be licensed, and introducing annual inspections by two magistrates and a physician in the provinces, and five Commissioners from the Royal College of Physicians in the metropolitan area.[15]

Increasing documentary evidence relating to madhouses, and mounting public concern about malpractices, both suggest impressionistically that the trade in lunacy may have been becoming more noticeable because it was expanding. Nevertheless, prior to registration, the evidence is necessarily only impressionistic, and could be misleading. For example, Daniel Defoe estimated that there were fifteen private madhouses in the metropolitan area in 1724; and in 1774, sixteen metropolitan houses were licensed under the new legislation. By 1807, this number had risen to only seventeen; nor are there strong grounds for believing that non-registration would have been common in the metropolitan district.[16]

The 1774 Act imposed a penalty of £500 for keeping more than one lunatic without a licence; but laid down no circumstances in which a licence could be refused or revoked, except for denial of access to the metropolitan Commissioners or provincial magistrates when they called to inspect. Although concern to maintain discretion on behalf of lunatics' families is often cited as the main reason for opposition to regulation, it was in fact the removal, in response to lobbying by the legal profession, of clauses giving powers to the Commissioners to revoke licences in other circumstances which ultimately enabled the bill to pass the Lords as well as the Commons.[17] Victims of malpractice were required to prove a misdemeanour under common law 'in the same Manner as if this Act had not been made'.[18] Notice of private patients' admission had to be sent

The commercialization of care

within three days in London, and within two weeks in the provinces; but there was no penalty for failure to do this. Madhouse keepers therefore need have had no qualms about holding back notice of admission when relatives were particularly keen that a person's confinement should be kept secret. In short, the most severe penalty was for practising without a licence, and private asylum proprietors had few reasons to fail to register under the 1774 Act.

In the early eighteenth century, Defoe persistently criticized the ease with which people could be confined in madhouses, and lobbied for regulation of the trade in lunacy. His estimate of the number of madhouses in 1724 may have been an exaggeration, but however his comments are interpreted they suggest that the madhouse business was already well established in London in the first quarter of the eighteenth century. At least two of the madhouses known to have been operating in London in the mid-eighteenth century had opened in the seventeenth century (Hoxton House, and Wood's Close, Clerkenwell); while two known to have been open by the 1730s were amongst the largest metropolitan asylums by the early nineteenth century (Hoxton House, and Wright's, later known as the White House, in Bethnal Green). Whitmore House, Hoxton, opened c.1750, also became one of the largest early-nineteenth-century licensed houses.[19] Overall, the impression by mid-century is of increasingly vested interests controlling a limited market, in which it was easier for existing houses to expand, than for newcomers to enter the market. The Monros, who acted as physicians at Bethlem over several generations from 1728, opened Brooke House in Clapton; but, after a brief period operating houses on the Islington Road, William Battie, the physician at St Luke's Hospital from 1751, took over an established madhouse in Wood's Close, Clerkenwell.[20]

The ability of the College of Physicians to resist regulation of private madhouses for twenty years, and then to be authorized as the licensing body, is equally suggestive of powerful vested interests reluctant to forgo their monopoly. Indeed, one way to read Turlington's misfortunes in 1761 and 1763 would be to suspect that he had somehow offended members of the College of Physicians; a similar habeas corpus plea in 1762, on behalf of Mrs Anne Hunt, who was confined in Clarke's madhouse in Clapton, failed when Monro swore an affidavit that she was insane.[21] The College of Physicians lacked powers to refuse licences, but from 1774 all private admissions required medical certification, increasing the powers of medical practitioners to restrict the business of unpopular competitors. One of the few non-medical licensees of a metropolitan asylum, Benjamin Faulkner, who ran a madhouse in Little Chelsea from 1785, criticized the vested financial interests of medical proprietors as likely to jeopardize patients' chances of recovery, because 'the desire of profit . . . will, with too many, have more weight than the reputation of an early cure'. Strikingly,

The commercialization of care

however, two years after the mad-doctor Francis Willis had been called to treat George III in preference to the King's regular physicians, Faulkner recommended that patients should be able to choose a reputable general physician, rather than a specialist mad-doctor.[22]

In the metropolitan area, therefore, the trade in lunacy was to a great extent controlled by the College of Physicians. The biggest growth was through expansion of existing practices, rather than a proliferation of small businesses. Noticeably, those like Hoxton House, the White House and Whitmore House, which grew largest and eventually became the subject of government investigations, expanded by taking patients who were not subject to inspection under the 1774 Act, such as paupers and predominantly lower-grade members of the armed forces.[23] If there was a rapid growth in private asylums catering for upper- or middle-class patients in the second half of the eighteenth century, it was not centred on London.

What was the situation in the provinces? As with London, there are isolated examples of provincial madhouses operating in the early eighteenth century. At Box in Wiltshire since the seventeenth century; at Guildford in Surrey by 1700; at Fonthill Gifford in Wiltshire from 1718; and at Hook Norton in Oxfordshire from c.1725. Little is known about the proprietors of these establishments, although Hook Norton was managed 'for upwards of Half a Century' by Mrs Sarah Minchin (d. 1778), who may have been an apothecary's widow.[24] Some of those who started provincial asylums in the 1740s–60s were physicians. Nathaniel Cotton's Collegium Insanorum was opened c.1745 in St Albans; Anthony Addington managed a small madhouse in Reading, 1749–54; and John Hall ran St Luke's in Newcastle-upon-Tyne from 1766. Nevertheless, there is ample evidence that people who were not medically qualified became madhouse keepers. The Baptist Joseph Mason, for example, opened Fishponds near Bristol in 1760, to which patients were transferred from another private asylum which he had kept since 1738. While William Finch, the non-medical proprietor of Laverstock House in Wiltshire, was practised enough to claim 'great success in curing people disordered in their senses', in the earliest surviving advertisement from 1779.[25]

In contrast to London, many provincial madhouses are known to have opened in the last quarter of the eighteenth century. Establishments like Greatford in Lincolnshire (1776); Droitwich in Worcestershire (1791); and Ticehurst in Sussex (1792). Some of these evolved out of long-standing smaller practices. Francis Willis kept patients at his home in Dunston from the 1760s, before opening Greatford; as Samuel Newington probably did in Ticehurst. However, this evolution does not mean that proprietors did not adopt an entrepreneurial approach. Willis was eager to open a madhouse because he believed 'an accustom'd House for wrongheads' would be a lucrative bequest for his sons; and it is possible that Newington

The commercialization of care

had similar motives.[26] What these examples make clear, however, is that for some proprietors, opening a private asylum was a carefully considered risk, rather than a hasty speculation. Madhouse keepers like these would be likely to have a view to establishing a long-term market, rather than maximizing short-term profit.

Porter emphasizes 'captains of confinement': physicians, mainly, like Addington, Battie and Thomas Arnold (1742–1816), whose ambitions led them to seek status and renown, as well as to manage private asylums. Men who, Porter argues, helped to build a new medical specialism around caring for the insane, through publicizing their work.[27] Equally striking, however, are the number of Georgian provincial madhouse keepers who founded family businesses which were able to survive for several generations. Mrs Minchin at Hook Norton (run by family until 1825, closed 1854); Joseph Mason at Fishponds (run by family until 1852, closed 1859); Francis Willis at Greatford (closed 1838; Shillingthorpe, opened by his son *c.*1816, closed 1859); William Finch at Laverstock House (run by family until 1854, closed 1955); Samuel Newington at Ticehurst (run by family until 1917, still open); Thomas Burman in Henley-in-Arden (opened 1795, run by family until it closed 1859); and Edward Long Fox, who ran an asylum at Cleeve Hill near Bristol before opening Brislington House in Bristol (opened 1806, run by family until it closed 1951). In London, only Brooke House in Clapton, operated by the Monro family, is comparable to these asylums (run by family until late-nineteenth century, closed 1940).[28] Only three of these proprietors were physicians – Monro, Willis and Fox; and one – Newington – was a surgeon-apothecary. None of them published accounts of their practice, other than advertisements; and only Willis and Fox achieved anything like national repute. Willis is the only one who, by being called to treat George III, could be said to have contributed to the recognition of mad-doctoring as a medical specialty.[29] What is most striking about these people, however, is their business acumen and success in creating a long-term market.

What factors influenced the market-confidence of those considering madhouse-keeping as a business venture? In contrast to London, there is substantial evidence to suggest that many provincial keepers found their first clients in the 1760s, and were able to expand their practices on an unprecedented scale in the 1770s–90s. As well as those described above, several other private madhouses flourished in the 1770s–90s. Some of these – like William Perfect's house at West Malling in Kent, and Thomas Arnold's asylum in Leicester – became relatively well known through their proprietors' publications; others, like Mr Stroud's at Bilstone in Staffordshire, and Great Foster House at Egham in Surrey, remained relatively obscure.[30] The timing of this expansion would place the development of private asylums in the provinces in line with national trends in consumer spending; and suggests that, as with other types of

The commercialization of care

expenditure, London established a precedent which the provinces subsequently followed.[31] Enough is known about when and where madhouses developed to be confident that the apparent expansion from the 1770s is not an optical illusion created by the introduction of licensing legislation. Indeed, some counties were slow to assume the responsibilities regulation entailed, and there is evidence of private asylums like the one at Droitwich in Worcestershire operating without a licence; in this case, evidently with the knowledge of local magistrates, who confined pauper lunatics there.[32]

However, the regulation of madhouses may have helped the provincial trade in lunacy to expand. Relatives and friends who at one time might have favoured the anonymity of a private asylum in London had more reason to fear the curiosity of the Commissioners than that of most county visitors. Even allowing for the fact that the admission of paupers did not need to be notified, it is clear from the 'Country Register', in which notified admissions were recorded, that the admission of many private patients went unreported.[33] From 1788, public discussion of George III's illness may have helped to reduce the stigma of insanity in the family, particularly amongst the upper classes; and Willis's apparently successful treatment of the King increased public confidence in those who specialized in treating the insane. All of these factors helped to improve business expectations amongst potential licensees, making them prepared to risk the initial outlay of £200 (including two £50 sureties that they would be of good behaviour).[34]

The viability of provincial private asylums obviously depended on the ability of proprietors to secure a clientele in their locality. Madhouses mainly developed, or were able to prosper, in the rural hinterland of burgeoning commercial centres like Bristol and Birmingham (at Henley-in-Arden); in smaller developing towns like Newcastle-upon-Tyne and Leicester; and in or near gentrified spas like Tunbridge Wells (at West Malling and Ticehurst) and Bath (at Box, and at Brislington, on the Bath road from Bristol). By 1807, there were twenty-eight provincial madhouses, most of which were located in the southern counties. The prosperity of private asylums depended on their ability to build up a reasonably affluent clientele, but they also supported other local businesses, purchasing food, clothes, and services such as hair-cutting and wig-making for their patients. In addition, madhouses provided direct employment for local people as attendants and domestic staff. From 1774, medical certification meant that private asylums also generated business for other local doctors; and, since the 1774 Act did not prohibit such arrangements, physicians who certified patients and acted as their consultant physicians, could also act as visiting physician with the local magistrates.

Despite the costs they incurred, madhouses could be lucrative, depending on the class of patients they accommodated. In the 1760s,

13

The commercialization of care

Cotton charged 3–5 guineas a week at the Collegium Insanorum.[35] Battie's estate was estimated to be worth over £100,000 in 1776, and most of this is believed to have been acquired through the private practice he ran alongside his appointment as physician at St Luke's.[36] George III's equerry claimed that the King had offered Revd Dr Francis Willis the preferment of his choice if he would give up mad-doctoring, and Willis refused.[37] By 1815, Thomas Warburton was said to be paid £1,500 a year for accommodating the Duke of Atholl's son in Hoxton House.[38] Obviously, this represents an extreme upper end of the market. Nevertheless, lunatic-keeping was profitable enough for Colquhoun to list it in 1803 as one of the more lucrative middle-class occupations: he estimated 40 families derived an average income of £500 a year in this way, making it comparable to some of the church's more generous livings, or the income derived from teaching at one of the better schools.[39]

Typically, parishes would be charged 10 shillings a week for pauper patients; and private patients might be charged a guinea a week for board and lodging, with additional charges for extras such as larger accommodation, a personal attendant, or foodstuffs which were regarded as luxuries, such as oranges or gingerbread. Medicines, wine and laundry were sometimes included in standard charges, and sometimes charged for separately.[40] Fees like these brought private asylum care within the reach of anyone who had a private income of £50 a year or more; and short stays within the reach of those with family incomes which were not much higher.

This figure is significant, since it represents the level above which income tax was levied from 1802. The proportion of the population whose family income fell between £50 and £400 a year (the level at which full-rate taxation began), is estimated to have risen from 15 per cent to about 25 per cent of the population between 1750 and 1780; and it is their purchasing power in particular which has been seen as sustaining the consumer boom in the latter decades of the eighteenth century. As late as 1834, the author of an advice manual on household economy, gave one guinea a week as the minimum income needed to support a genteel life-style.[41] From the 1750s, an increasing proportion of the population could afford to pay for private asylum care; and families who paid madhouse fees of £50 a year or more could be confident that their relatives would receive genteel treatment.

As in other areas of consumer growth, gentrifying clergy and farmers – beneficiaries of the agricultural revolution – may have been amongst the first to purchase treatment in eighteenth-century madhouses. As the century progressed, however, this clientele was increasingly joined by parvenu commercialists, who also swelled the crowds at spas like Bath and Cheltenham.[42] Many provincial private asylums accommodated some pauper lunatics; but even the largest, like Laverstock House, did not necessarily take predominantly pauper patients, as the large metropolitan

The commercialization of care

houses did.[43] The rapid expansion in provincial madhouses from the 1770s continued into the early nineteenth century; and, from the 1800s, was accompanied by a comparable expansion in metropolitan licensed houses. Between 1807 and 1819, the total number of licensed houses almost doubled, from 45 to 89. By 1819, 2,585 people are known to have been confined in private asylums. This figure includes pauper lunatics, but is almost certainly incomplete. About 400 private admissions a year were notified between 1775 and 1815; and for some establishments this is known to be an undercalculation by 50 per cent or more.[44]

A very rough estimate based on national returns would suggest that up to one in a thousand of those with sufficient means to pay for private care were confined in licensed houses by 1819; with about one in three thousand being admitted each year. However, a study of admissions to Ticehurst between 1792 and 1817 suggests an annual admissions rate approaching one in a thousand of the local population; and only about one in ten of these are known to have been pauper admissions.[45] Whatever the exact figures were, it seems reasonable to estimate that, by 1819, amongst those with middle-incomes, at least one family in two hundred had a relative confined in a private asylum. Obviously, the overall proportion of middle-class families who had, at some stage, had one of their relatives admitted, or considered private care, would have been far higher than this. The next section considers what made private care an attractive option; enabling the trade in lunacy to continue to expand until the mid-nineteenth century.[46]

Servicing the family

In the late eighteenth century, madhouse fees were coming within the reach of an increasing proportion of the population. Nevertheless, private asylums represented a relatively expensive option, particularly for long-term care. Employing a domestic servant to act as an attendant in the home, for example, would have been cheaper, with wages starting at a few pounds a year, plus board and lodging. Factors other than economy evidently influenced the decision to confine an insane relative in a madhouse. Equally, although holidays at spas were fashionable for health, treatment away from home was not the norm for physical illness in middle- and upper-class families. Hospitals were charitable initiatives to treat the 'deserving' poor, which also provided surgeons and physicians with experience which they could then use in treating private patients at home.[47] Thus, even if it is assumed that medical approaches to mental disorders were becoming more widely accepted by the economic elite, this does not by itself explain the choice of asylum care.

On the other hand, medicalization did mean that the advice of doctors could be influential in determining treatment. There is ample evidence

15

The commercialization of care

that medical men with an interest in insanity were consulted by patients and their families at home, placing them in a strong position to advocate certification. Some asylum keepers, like William Perfect, placed a strong emphasis on the allegedly therapeutic value of separating the patient from their ordinary surroundings, even recommending in certain cases that friends and relatives should not be allowed to visit patients in asylums. Other medical men, however, like William Pargeter, who is not known to have had any direct interest in a madhouse, sometimes prescribed a simple change of scene, in preference to certification.[48] Nevertheless, most mad-doctors were agreed that early treatment was vital to maximize chances of recovery; and publications by both medical and lay proprietors lamented the reluctance of families to refer relatives until their mental disorders were far advanced.[49]

Despite differences in opinion, therefore, specialists in insanity encouraged families to seek help, rather than conceal mental disorder. As the proprietors' advocacy of early treatment made clear, a common gambit to win the confidence of potential clients was the promise to cure, as well as care for, the insane. Few advertised brazenly, as David Irish did in 1700, that 'those *Lunaticks* which are not Curable, he will take . . . for the term of Life, if paid Quarterly'.[50] The claim to be able to cure insanity was not a product of medicalization. Since the late seventeenth century, madhouse keepers had touted their therapeutic expertise, as well as the comforts of their houses. Thus, in 1740, the Baptist Joseph Mason promised 'to cure Hypochondriacs, Mad and Distracted People, with great success. . . . No Cure, No Pay. Boarding excepted'.[51] In the 1770s–90s, both medical and non-medical proprietors, like William Finch and Samuel Newington, based their therapeutic claims on years of experience, rather than training.[52] Nevertheless, it is questionable whether promises of cure were taken seriously by potential clients.

In 1792, Pargeter summarized the public image of licensed houses in this way:

> The idea of a *mad-house* is apt to excite, in the breasts of most people, the strongest emotions of horror and alarm; upon a supposition, not altogether ill-founded, that when once a patient is doomed to take up his abode in those places, he will not only be exposed to very great cruelty; but it is a great chance, whether he recovers or not, if he ever more sees the outside of the walls.[53]

For Pargeter, the solution lay in the restriction of licences to medical proprietors; while Benjamin Faulkner, who was a non-medical licensee, believed confidence could only be restored by a complete separation of medical and proprietorial functions.[54] Public differences of opinion like this can only have fuelled scepticism about the motives of mad-doctors and other keepers. The insistence of some proprietors, like Battie and Perfect,

The commercialization of care

that relatives and friends must not visit inmates, was also viewed with cynicism by critics of private asylums.[55] Given such mistrust, it is easy to understand that families might view certification as a last resort, referring relatives only when their behaviour became unmanageable. On the other hand, such an interpretation makes it difficult to explain the progressive expansion of the madhouse business.

While asylum proprietors cavilled at public reluctance to refer the mentally disordered, critics of the trade in lunacy throughout the eighteenth century alleged, on the contrary, that some families were only too eager to confine their relatives. In 1740, the author of an anonymous pamphlet suggested that:

> several are put into Mad-houses . . . without being mad, Wives put their Husbands in them that they may enjoy their Gallants . . .; and Husbands put their Wives in them, that they may enjoy their Whores . . .; Children put their Parents in them, that they may enjoy their Estates before their time; Relations put their Kindred in them for wicked Purposes.[56]

Medical certification and annual inspection notwithstanding, Pargeter quoted a newspaper article dated December 1791, which alleged:

> Private mad-houses are become so general at present, and their prostitution of justice so openly carried on, that any man may have his wife, his father, or his brother confined for life, at a certain stipulated price! The wretched victims are concealed from the inspecting doctors.[57]

There is extensive evidence that, as Pargeter complained, 'the strict letter of [the 1774 Act was] not adhered to'.[58] However, the sheer scale of non-compliance with the regulations governing licensing and notification of confinement, suggests administrative inertia and dogged localism, rather than individual corruption; although, of course, as the newspaper article implied, such negligence left the way open for abuses to develop.

Recently, MacDonald has drawn attention to the inefficiency and corruption of the Georgian Court of Chancery, which was charged with supervising the estates of those found lunatic by inquisition. These cases were heard before a jury, making corruption and miscarriages of justice unlikely at the point of certification. However, MacDonald argues that escalating costs, and routine procrastination, made the Court of Chancery increasingly inaccessible, particularly to families seeking to protect smaller estates.[59] This would almost certainly have included those on middle-incomes of £50–£400 a year; and families with newly established wealth may have been particularly anxious to protect their assets. For these families, medical certification and confinement in a private asylum offered more immediate protection against irrational spending; and might enable

The commercialization of care

them to secure temporary powers of attorney. The importance of property issues in determining private confinement could explain the preponderance of male patients in licensed houses, despite the fact that there were more female than male lunatics in other types of asylum, and amongst pauper patients confined to private madhouses.[60] Despite the preponderance of male private patients, more men than women authorized certification, suggesting that this was seen as a decision about family finances as much as health; obviously, proprietors would have required a reasonable guarantee of payment.[61]

The Vagrancy Acts of 1714 and 1744 stipulated clear criteria which justified confinement by magistrates: a lunatic must be considered 'dangerous to be permitted to go Abroad'. Juries at lunacy inquisitions were primarily called to assess whether or not the person against whom a writ had been issued was capable of managing their financial affairs.[62] In either case, wrongful confinement was relatively unlikely. Magistrates would presumably want to keep the number of parish dependants to a minimum; and, so long as they were not corrupted, juries had no investment in the outcome of lunacy trials. In contrast, medical certification relied on doctors' claims to specialist expertise in diagnosing insanity, rather than common-sense criteria of dangerousness or financial incompetence; and doctors had a direct interest in certification fees and, in some cases, vested interests as visiting physicians and consultants to licensed houses. There is, therefore, more reason to suspect some corrupt practice.

Medical corruption and wrongful confinement were among the problems addressed by the Madhouse Act of 1828, which introduced independent certification by two medical men for private patients; made it illegal for doctors to certify admissions to an asylum in which they had a vested interest; and gave the Home Secretary powers to appoint fifteen Metropolitan Commissioners, including only five physicians.[63] As appears to have been the case after 1774, from 1828 provincial licensed houses proliferated more rapidly than metropolitan asylums. By 1849, there were 99 provincial madhouses (over 40 more than in the late 1820s); and only 47 in the metropolitan district (one less than in 1828). However, this contraction was primarily due to the removal of pauper lunatics to Middlesex County Asylum, which had accommodation for 1,000 inmates, rather than tighter regulation of licensed houses. The overall continuing growth in the number of madhouses, and in the number of private patients confined in them, suggests that relatively lax regulations and corrupt practice had not been the most significant motor of expansion prior to 1828.[64]

What factors influenced the willingness of families to refer their mentally disordered relatives to private asylums? Obv ously, for some families, financial considerations would have been decisive. Those with private incomes could best afford to pay for long-term care. In the late eighteenth century, a single, incurable lunatic needed an annuity of £50 or more to

18

The commercialization of care

live in a private asylum. By the late 1820s, this figure had approximately doubled.[65] For those dependent on earned income, the cost had to be weighed against the expectations they had of treatment. Families who were dependent on the earned income of a male breadwinner who became insane, may have been willing to spend a high proportion of any savings they had in the hope of recovery or cure; and this could also help to account for the preponderance of male over female patients in private asylums.

In general, it is only possible to make rough estimates of the proportion of income families would have been prepared to spend on private asylum care. Burnett estimated that, in the early nineteenth century, about half of a typical middle-class income would be spent on food and servants, with rent and rates accounting for between one-eighth and one-fifth more.[66] This would leave at least 30 per cent of the family income to be spent on variable items such as clothing, school fees, holidays and health, making a family income of about £150 a year the level above which private asylum fees could be afforded. On the other hand, Branca has drawn attention to the fact that, from the 1820s, advice manuals on domestic economy recommended spending up to one-eighth of the family income on 'illness and amusement'.[67] By this calculation, only those with incomes of £800 a year or more in the late 1820s would have been willing to spend £100 a year on private asylum fees, placing this kind of care beyond the reach of all but the wealthiest of families. However, other items of expenditure included in these model budgets, such as the keeping of a financial 'reserve', might easily have been transferred to pay madhouse fees. Others, such as 'Education', were obviously only relevant at some stages of the life cycle.[68] Certainly, some patients at Ticehurst paid their fees in kind – for example, in faggots, flour or groceries – in a way which suggests that some families on lower incomes were prepared to use any reserves they had in the hope of securing the patient's recovery.[69]

It is worth noting that, despite Pargeter's gloomy representation of madhouses as destinations with no return, up to two-thirds of private admissions to licensed houses stayed less than six months.[70] Assuming that many of these were removed by their relatives, rather than discharged recovered, this suggests a degree of pragmatism on the part of referring families. Patients may have been removed because promises or hopes of cure had not been fulfilled, or for financial reasons. Families who suffered a serious long-term drop in income would have been forced to consider cheaper options, such as public asylums or attendance at home, as the patient's insanity began to appear incurable. It is also possible that some financially secure families referred long-term insane to private asylums intending a short confinement, to give themselves, or the patient's other long-term carers, a break. Patients are known to have been discharged to public asylums, to single care and to other licensed houses, as well as to their homes.[71]

Up to one in five private admissions to licensed houses stayed two years

19

The commercialization of care

or more; and about the same proportion died in confinement.[72] Evidently, some families viewed private asylum care as a long-term option, or became dependent on the service offered by proprietors. Those who were able to pay madhouse fees for many years would have needed an income at the upper end of the scales described earlier, so that the decision to remove a patient from a private asylum cannot be taken as evidence of dissatisfaction with the service provided. Despite the relatively high removal rate, the trade in lunacy continued to expand. Nevertheless, the perception of Pargeter and other mad-doctors, that families were reluctant to refer their relatives to private asylums, is significant; since a relatively high removal rate might suggest that, in the absence of recovery, madhouse proprietors were only partially successful in convincing their clientele that the services they offered were worth continuing to pay for.

One factor influencing the initial willingness of families to refer the mentally disordered may have been the fact that insanity was seen as a hereditary disorder.[73] Those with newly acquired wealth had particular reason to fear their relatives' insanity becoming public knowledge, since it might jeopardize their chances of forming advantageous alliances through marriage. However, the way in which this would have influenced family decision-making is not clear. Certification could lead to embarrassing gossip; but the long-term removal of an insane relative might be one of the best ways of maximizing secrecy. Nevertheless, it is arguable that, if this concern had been decisive, single confinement would have been a more discreet option than private asylum care, particularly after the introduction of certification and inspection. Despite the fact that madhouse proprietors only partially complied with legal requirements regarding licensing and notification of confinement, and most kept no patient records, the extent to which they could guarantee confidentiality was limited.

More broadly, the trend towards confinement away from home can be seen as part of the aspirations to gentility which accompanied increased spending power. Social emulation was expressed in changes in manners and standards of acceptable behaviour, as well as through acquisition. Gentrifying clergy and farmers who remodelled their houses, so that they could eat and sleep in rooms which were segregated from those used by servants and labourers, may also have chosen to distance themselves from the uncontrolled behaviour of their disturbed relations. In the late eighteenth century, licensed houses developed most rapidly in the southern regions which were also the first to be affected by rural gentrification.[74] However, the link between gentrification and the expansion of the trade in lunacy is in some ways a paradoxical one. The domestic segregation of employees from their employers is said to have been associated with an increasingly high evaluation of privacy within the family; and a shift towards family relationships based on love and affection,

The commercialization of care

as well as financial or business interests.[75] It is perhaps surprising that an increasing emphasis on emotional bonds between family members should have been associated with a trend towards confinement of the insane away from home. On the other hand, both Stone and Shorter suggest that the new quest for emotional fulfilment within the family was characterized by growing individualism.[76] Arguably, this could have led to decreased tolerance within the family of bizarre or violent behaviour, making certification an attractive option.

It would be wrong to exaggerate the degree of segregation of the insane achieved by the development of private asylums. In addition to the relatively high removal rate, there is other evidence that some families tried to keep the separation caused by certification to a minimum. At Ticehurst, at least one patient was admitted accompanied by his mother.[77] Several licensed houses allowed patients to bring their own servants with them, which provided continuity between the patient's home and asylum environments. Indeed, since attendants on the insane were sometimes described as 'servants', it is difficult to know whether these were specialist attendants for single cases, who had cared for the patients at home, or ordinary domestic servants. In 1807, Finch concluded an advertisement for Laverstock House with a 'P.S – Patients are attended by Mr F. at their own houses; and careful and experienced servants sent in cases which will not admit of a removal'.[78] Despite the fact that some mad-doctors advocated a ban on family visits, many proprietors allowed frequent visits and correspondence; and others, like Pargeter, established practices which appear to have been exclusively based on treating the insane at home.[79]

Edward Long Fox's publicity for Brislington House, c.1806, stressed the benefits of separating: 'the insane from their own houses and friends . . . they submit more patiently to discipline from strangers . . . than from relations and dependants, who are timid, unskilled and frequently the objects of irritation'.[80] Fox imagined that dependants would find it difficult to override the conventional authority of a head of household, just as the King's illness had raised issues of constitutional authority. Confinement away from home allowed families to avoid this dilemma. However, the increasingly high evaluation of close and more egalitarian family relationships made it more difficult for families to agree to separation when it was advised. By 1836, Fox's sons were boasting that, at Brislington, 'many of the houses and cottages in the neighbouring parishes are . . . adapted for those patients whose cases do not require . . . a separation from their own family circle', suggesting that these were let to whole families, rather than used to accommodate single patients.[81] Thus, for those who could afford them, a range of options became available, from attendance at home by a mad-doctor, to certification and confinement in a madhouse; and many private patients experienced different kinds of care, from holidaying as a single patient with an attendant, to being placed in a private asylum.

The commercialization of care

In marketing their services, mad-doctors and lay-keepers strove to accommodate a range of family wishes. Overall, however, in the first half of the nineteenth century the trend was towards increased segregation of the insane, and the average length of stay for private patients gradually rose.[82]

Despite the overall trend towards segregation, the fact that a range of options were provided confirms that some families were reluctant to agree to certification or long-term confinement in an asylum. Admission to an asylum might be justified by the hope of a cure; but chronic care was different. Traditionally, some families had coped with long-term disability by lodging relatives locally, freeing themselves from the responsibility of any necessary nursing or restraint, but maintaining some social contact. George Austen (1766–1838), for example, one of Jane Austen's brothers, was subject to fits, and possibly deaf and dumb; from childhood, he was lodged with the Culham family in Monk Sherbourne, together with one of his maternal uncles, Thomas Leigh, who appears to have been mentally handicapped.[83] The efforts of madhouse proprietors like the Foxes to provide family accommodation supported by specialist help, suggest that cost and confidentiality were not the only factors at stake for families of the mentally disordered when deciding on care. Despite growing individualism, some families were loath to exile the insane from their family circle.

However, family relationships and domestic comfort were valued partly because it was believed that they could offer a cosy retreat from an increasingly impersonal and commercial world outside.[84] If business relationships were based on financial interests, family relationships sprang from affection. If commercial relationships were cut-throat, family relationships were solicitous. If work was tiring and hectic, family life was leisurely and refreshing. If (as time went on) industrial workplaces were noisy and dirty, home was tranquil and comfortable; and preferably situated in a rural setting, at some distance from the workplace. Insanity in the family could place a strain on cherished ideals of domestic harmony. The mentally disturbed might be emotionally distant, mistrustful, sleepless, noisy, obscene, neglectful of their appearance and surroundings, and violent. Although families might be reluctant to seek outside help, or remove the insane, the difficulty of coping with an insane relative within the family can only have been exacerbated by raised expectations of family life.

Apart from the impact of economic growth in widening the availability of home comforts, domesticity was popularized in novels and poetry which portrayed contented family life as a vital source of happiness and virtue.[85] The mad-doctor Nathaniel Cotton was amongst those who published poetry celebrating the pleasures to be gained from home and family, in a volume which was more popular when it was reissued in 1791, after his death, than it had been when it was first published in 1751.[86] One of the

The commercialization of care

most widely read celebrants of domesticity, William Cowper, had himself been a patient in Cotton's Collegium Insanorum in the 1760s, where he recovered after a conversion experience which led him to become an Evangelical Christian.[87] Cowper never married or had children. His own domestic circle was formed by the clergyman's family with whom he lodged after leaving Cotton's madhouse. Nevertheless, for Cowper, 'Domestic life in rural pleasures pass'd' formed the cornerstone of living in knowledge of God. Simple contentment ('Fireside enjoyments, homeborn happiness'), honest toil ('Absence of occupation is not rest,/A mind quite vacant is a mind distress'd'), and appreciation of the countryside ('not a flower, but shows some touch . . . of His unrivall'd pencil'), were wholesome paths to God, and mental equilibrium.[88] Cowper's certainty that God could be experienced directly in ways which were mentally stabilizing rather than enthusiastic partly accounts for his popularity. More importantly, he appealed to those who felt overwhelmed by modern life, counselling the virtue and benefits of a cosy and contemplative life, free from 'anxious thoughts how wealth may be increased'.[89] The voguish admiration for writers like Cowper from the 1790s, suggests that many families found the demands of a more commercialized existence highly stressful. Certifying an insane relative, or allowing them to receive chronic care in a private asylum might provoke guilt; but it could also relieve families of additional pressure, enabling them to enjoy a more peaceful domestic life which accorded with their expectations. In time, mad-doctors began to argue that the removal of the insane was advisable because it protected the family from the patient's anger and resentment at being restrained, rather than because it was therapeutic for the patient.[90]

Madhouse proprietors also sought to gain the confidence of potential clients by stressing the home-like atmosphere of private asylums. As Porter argues, early-eighteenth-century keepers had promised to provide comfortable surroundings and generous diets for asylum inmates; and this style of advertising continued in the late eighteenth and early nineteenth centuries.[91] However, advertisements for licensed houses also increasingly emphasized the privacy, domesticity and rural surroundings available at their establishments. Thus, in 1807, Finch boasted that Laverstock House offered 'every requisite for domestic comfort (the house on a healthy eminence with many acres of garden and pleasure ground . . .)'. Individual rooms, and whole apartments, were provided for high-fee-paying patients.[92] By 1816, Droitwich Lunatic Asylum was advertising a range of accommodation, at four guineas a week for 'Separate apartments', two guineas a week for 'convenient rooms', and between one and one and a half guineas for beds on the wards, depending on diet – 'one guinea per week; not allowed tea'. Patients who paid two guineas a week or more were invited to dine with the proprietor's family 'when their cases will admit of it'.[93] Obviously, private apartments might help to preserve patient

The commercialization of care

confidentiality; but the emphasis on dining with the proprietor (their substitute family), and, in Finch's advertisement, on opportunities for outdoor exercise, suggest that this was not their main attraction. Rather, opportunities for privacy and the creation of a domestic environment within licensed houses, enabled families to be reassured that private patients would continue to enjoy the comforts of a genteel home despite their separation from the family. It was this above all which encouraged those families who could afford it to allow their insane relatives to become long-term patients in private asylums.

Treatment

> And now, with nerves new braced, and spirits cheer'd,
> We tread the wilderness, whose well-roll'd walks,
> With curvature of slow and easy sweep –
> Deception innocent – give ample space
> To narrow bounds. The grove receives us next;
> Between the upright shafts of whose tall elms
> We may discern the thresher at his task . . .
> Come hither, ye that press your beds of down
> And sleep not; see him sweating o'er his bread
> Before he eats it. – 'Tis the primal curse,
> But soften'd into mercy; made the pledge
> Of cheerful days, and nights without a groan.
> (William Cowper, *The Task*, 1784, Book 1, 'The Sofa')

The nature of treatment in eighteenth-century asylums has been a subject of extensive debate amongst historians. Until relatively recently, historians of psychiatry largely accepted the retrospective condemnation of nineteenth-century lunacy reformers, who portrayed the eighteenth century as a dark age in which the insane had been subjected to physical cruelty and neglect – chained, whipped, bled, purged and underfed.[94] In critically analysing early-nineteenth-century developments, Scull aimed to morally neutralize this humanitarian critique of Georgian methods, by arguing that the restraint and beatings which seem inhumane from a modern perspective, appeared appropriate to an eighteenth-century world view which saw insanity as a loss of the only capacity which distinguished human beings from animals – that is, reason.[95] Most recently, Porter has questioned the received view of Georgian treatment, marshalling evidence which suggests that, at least in private madhouses, adequate diets and physical comfort were not unusual.[96]

On the face of it, Porter's supposition that 'It would be surprising if the kind of clientele that was seeking . . . "health-farm" conditions for its mad relations would have tolerated maltreatment', appears plausible.[97]

24

The commercialization of care

Nevertheless, when Willis was treating George III, he was able to gain the consent of other members of the royal family to beat and starve the King.[98] The crux of the issue may have been the extent to which treatment was perceived as therapeutic. Harsh methods might be tolerated if it was believed that they would lead to recovery; but not if they were seen as simply being used for the proprietor's convenience in managing patients. Bleeding, purging and reduced diets were (however reluctantly) accepted as modes of treatment for physical disorders, which might logically be applied in cases of insanity, if it was perceived as an illness. Physical restraint could be portrayed as a practical way to prevent violence and injury. However, although convicts and slaves were subject to chaining, it is difficult to imagine that this would have been readily tolerated by families of private patients. The earliest recorded use of strait waistcoats was in a private madhouse in the 1730s; and some later commentators, such as Thomas Arnold and S. G. Bakewell stressed that the use of physical restraint should, if possible, be confined to lower-class patients.[99] Beating and whipping were accepted in private schools and in the armed forces, as well as in the treatment of criminals; nevertheless, the 1714 Act expressly exempted lunatics from the whippings which could be meted out to other vagrants. Practitioners like Willis might reserve the right to physically coerce private patients, but it was the instillation of fear which was seen as producing beneficial docility, and actual beatings were probably rare.[100] In the late eighteenth century, keepers like Joanna Harris reassured potential clients that, in managing patients, they would use 'the utmost Tenderness ... that such unhappy Cases will admit of';[101] and, judging by their proliferation, such promises helped proprietors to secure patients.

The emphasis on management in treating the insane originated from Battie's *Treatise on madness* (1758). Battie criticized the routine use of bleeding, vomits and purges which was common in established practice (most notoriously, at Bethlem); and advocated management in preference to medicine.[102] Management was a broad term, which did not preclude physical treatment. In medical literature, it was used to refer to the physician's instructions to the patient on how to regulate the non-naturals (air, diet, excretion, emotions, exercise and sleep); and to distinguish advice on regimen from the prescription of drugs.[103] In relation to the insane, however, it carried additional connotations of establishing control over patients who were, by definition, irrational and subject to extreme emotions. Georgian commentators emphasized the importance of gaining psychological ascendancy over the patient. This could be achieved by the use of force; but some mad-doctors, including Willis and Pargeter, also stressed their ability to dominate patients with an intimidating look. As Porter emphasizes, those treating the insane increasingly relied on such interpersonal skills, with which they sought to influence the patient's mind, rather than their body.[104]

The commercialization of care

In an article on 'The domestication of madness', Scull has argued that, in the late eighteenth century, there was a shift in the cultural consensus on insanity, which informed changes in treatment. The mad had been seen as wild beasts and objects of terror, but increasingly they came to be seen as people who, despite their disorders, could be assimiliated into an ersatz family (the asylum).[105] In many ways, this echoed Foucault's earlier description of a transition from a world in which 'Madness . . . partook of animal ferocity', to a world in which 'the asylum would keep the insane in the imperative fiction of the family'. From the point of view of management, the significance of this is that it led to a transition from a situation in which 'Unchained animality could be mastered only by discipline and brutalizing', to strategies of control based on the idea that the insane could be coaxed and cajoled, or (as Foucault believed) manipulated by guilt.[106] Neatly enough, the linguistic use of 'manage' and 'management' changed in the eighteenth century in ways which complement such a shift. Whereas, in the early eighteenth century, 'manage' retained some of the meaning of its original French derivation, and could be used to refer to the training of horses, by the late eighteenth century 'management' had acquired a new meaning – to handle people skilfully, or show them consideration.[107]

As Bynum has argued, what was distinctive about what came to be known as moral therapy was not its direct appeal to the patient's mind, which had equally been the object of more intimidating methods, but rather its emphasis on 'kindness, reason and tactful manipulation' – on persuasion, rather than coercion.[108] In practice, some proprietors, like Nathaniel Cotton, treated the mentally disturbed with gentleness and compassion, as well as medicine, as early as the 1740s. As already noted, from the 1770s keepers' advertisements laid increasing emphasis on tenderness and consideration. In the 1780s–90s, books on insanity explicitly evaluated the relative merits of coercive and mild treatment; with both lay and medical proprietors, like Faulkner and Perfect, concluding that gentle methods were preferable to physical coercion.[109]

Promises of predominantly moral management, and minimal use of restraint, enabled the new private asylums which opened from the 1770s onwards to prosper. The system of moral therapy outlined by Samuel Tuke in 1813, in his *Description of the Retreat*, found a ready audience partly because it articulated a growing consensus on what constituted good moral- therapeutic practice.[110] By 1816, when a select committee investigated conditions in licensed houses, it was mainly older madhouses which received predominantly pauper patients, like those at Box and Fonthill Gifford in Wiltshire, or Hoxton House, the White House and Whitmore House in London, which were criticized for brutality and excessive use of mechanical restraint.[111] In contrast, a witness who had visited Finch's asylum in Wiltshire, enthused that 'In this establishment I

The commercialization of care

saw all that Tuke has written realized; and no words . . . can characterize it in too high terms.'[112]

It would be wrong to see the growing emphasis on moral therapy as tantamount to a rejection of medical therapy, or a policy of non-restraint. Tuke's repudiation of medical therapy was too strongly worded for most eclectic mad-doctors, who were anxious to defend the value of their medical expertise. Bleeding, blistering, vomitives, purges and narcotics, were recommended on an individual basis, to supplement control of the patient's condition which could be achieved by regimen.[113] Even Tuke advised that limited use of gentle means of mechanical restraint could be beneficial.[114] As late as the 1830s, a former prime minister's son, John Perceval, was removed to an outhouse and chained at night at the purpose-built and relatively prestigious Brislington House.[115] Well-regarded madhouses thus continued to use some medicines and mechanical restraint, but physical regimen and psychological management formed the cornerstones of treatment. Proprietors boasted of the airiness and elevation of their locations and accommodation.[116] Mad-doctors regulated lunatics' diets, and monitored their excretions, prescribing purgatives and diuretics if necessary. Inmates were encouraged to take regular exercise, in grounds which were carefully cultivated to provide variety and interest. In rural locations, sports like fishing and hunting were permitted. Exercise helped patients to sleep well, but if they were restless mild sedatives might also be prescribed. Care was taken to keep the insane mentally amused with books, music, drawing, sewing and conversation; and, where possible, inmates were encouraged to work, for example, at gardening or writing.[117] In short, keepers strove to restore a healthful equilibrium in patients' lives, which would minimize their vulnerability to mental imbalance.

Medical management counselled that displays and extremes of emotion should be avoided; but the strategies to achieve influence over patients recommended by physicians like Willis and Pargeter required bluff self-confidence, if not charisma. Tuke noted that the Retreat's superintendent could deter patients from violence with a look, but moral therapy was innovative because it mostly removed such elements of mystique from psychological management, developing techniques which could be described in a more instrumental way.[118] Violence might lead to the patient being placed in a strait waistcoat; but threats were more likely to be met with a practical demonstration of superior force, such as calling five or six attendants into the room. Seclusion was sometimes used in preference to restraint; and, when patients showed self-control, they were praised.[119] Environmental influences were considered important. Furniture and decorations were arranged to resemble those in an ordinary home, and some inmates brought their own clothes, possessions and pets into the asylum.[120] Lunatics who were dirty or neglectful of their

The commercialization of care

appearance were kept clean and tidy, in the hope that they would begin to take an interest in caring for themselves. Patients were encouraged to form friendly attachments with the attendants and proprietor who were caring for them, so that they would covet their esteem.[121] Fear of a loss of affection thus to some extent replaced physical threats. As is well known, Tuke explicitly compared the insane to children, and the Retreat's keepers to judicious parents.[122] Foucault saw inmates as having been passively enmeshed in the new, mock-familial ethos of the asylum;[123] however, in contrast to the frank domination of earlier methods, the success of moral therapy ultimately depended on the patient's co-operation and developing initiative. Lunatics whose behaviour improved might be invited to dine with the proprietor's family as a reward, and a step towards preparing to return home. The asylum provided a substitute family, but the painfulness of exclusion from their own home was also expected to act as an incentive to inmates to recover.[124]

This belief in the ability of the insane to co-operate with treatment was important, because it suggested that they retained free will. Madness was no longer seen as tantamount to animality. Despite emphasizing the benefits of management, many practitioners also believed it was vital for the patient to achieve a spiritual equilibrium. Religious enthusiasm, like any other extreme emotion, was seen as detrimental to mental health.[125] Some mad-doctors might have been sceptical of Cowper's conversion experience, but many would have understood Cotton's dual role as medical and spiritual adviser.[126] Amongst lay keepers, Tuke regarded moral treatment as part of 'the divine art of healing'; and even Thomas Bakewell, who believed madness had physical origins requiring physical treatment, saw the clergy, as well as the families of sufferers, as the most likely audience for his *Domestic guide in cases of insanity* (1809).[127] Many patients, like Cowper and Perceval, experienced and articulated their mental distress in religious terms.[128] Whatever the beliefs of individual proprietors, attention to inmates' spiritual needs, and opportunities to worship, were expected by the clientele of private asylums. Prayer meetings formed a communal focus in many licensed houses, and a few had private chapels; like dining with the proprietor's family, attendance at parish church was used as a reward for good behaviour, and seen as a sign of progress towards recovery.[129] Obviously, only Anglican proprietors were particularly concerned with attendance at parish church, but the attack on religious enthusiasm, and concern for inmates' spiritual wellbeing, cut across denominations.

Some believed that, even with medical and moral therapy, recovery was only possible through the grace of God. This is not to suggest that keepers saw themselves as spiritual healers; although, as Anne Digby has stressed, this possibility cannot be ruled out for some, non-conformist practitioners.[130] But many mad-doctors and their clients, including some

The commercialization of care

Anglicans, had a providential, rather than a mechanistic, understanding of madness, and the effectiveness of therapy. When Cowper experienced a recurrence of deep depression in 1773–4, he visited Cotton to ask for advice, but did not enter an asylum. Cotton bled him and prescribed medicine. Cowper then returned home, and resolutely gardened every day. Eventually, he felt better. One long section of his extended poem, *The Task* (1784), is a celebration of gardening, in which he suggests that it is possible to come close to God through cultivating and appreciating nature, but only with God's grace.[131] In the 1790s, Pargeter sternly reminded his readers that, although madness was distressing, 'the severest dispensations which Providence vouchsafes to mankind, are for some good and wise intention'.[132] Such attitudes helped madhouse proprietors and their clientele to accept that recovery might not always be possible. A willingness, nevertheless, to treat the insane with kindness and consideration, or, as Pargeter expressed it, 'alleviate what we cannot remove', was a practical way of demonstrating acceptance of God's will.[133]

More broadly, the writings of Cowper and Pargeter can be seen as part of an increasingly popular Evangelical critique of modern luxury, and the commercialization of existence. In the wake of the French Revolution, there was widespread concern that growing commercialism and the perceived loosening of moral bonds of social obligation threatened the social order. Moral regeneration seemed imperative; and Evangelicals argued that this could only be achieved through the spiritual rebirth and 'real religion' of individual Christians, who would provide the moral leadership needed in society. Many of the newly affluent, who felt their financial and social position were relatively precarious, welcomed Evangelical criticism of the profligacy and extravagance of the aristocracy and gentry. Cowper articulated the anxieties and guilt of a newly prosperous middle class when he warned that, 'human life/Is but a loan to be repaid with use [i.e., interest]/When [God] shall call His debtors to account'.[134] Although Evangelicals emphasized conversion and direct religious experience, they perceived 'real religion' as characterized by moral seriousness and sobriety, rather than enthusiasm. Devotion to family life, and a commitment to the moral improvement of society, were the hallmarks of a serious Christian.[135] In the early nineteenth century, Evangelical values gained a wide currency amongst the middle classes; and, from 1828, their direct and continuing influence on asylum management was ensured by the appointment of the young Evangelical Lord Ashley, as one of the metropolitan commissioners.[136]

Attitudes to madness, and the treatment of the insane, were informed by moral and social contradictions. Pargeter viewed luxury as a possible cause of insanity, closely seconded by 'enthusiasm'.[137] From this perspective, madness could result from being one of God's bad debtors; but might be cured by a dose of plain living. On the other hand, insanity

The commercialization of care

was not always caused by profligacy. It could be the product of heredity, misfortune, or an unintelligible providence; and it was not always curable. Mad-doctors argued that families needed to be protected from the violence and irrationality of the insane. Nevertheless, proprietors of licensed houses increasingly described their establishments as 'asylums', rather than madhouses, as though to emphasize that the insane also needed shelter from the outside world, of the kind which home provided for the family circle. Moreover, the most therapeutic environment for the insane was the one which best approximated to home. Domestic comforts, and predominantly moral management, were reassuring to a clientele who highly valued gentility and refinement. An emphasis on the similarities between home and the asylum also helped to assuage any guilt caused by the family's unwillingness or inability to cope with an insane member.[138] Despite limited therapeutic success, the madhouse business expanded in the late-eighteenth and early-nineteenth centuries. The viability of individual asylums depended, above all, on their ability to fulfil the social expectations of consumers of asylum care – that is, inmates' families, rather than the patients themselves.

Notes

1. For evaluations in terms of medical and social progress, see for example, G. Zilboorg, *A history of medical psychology*, New York, W.W. Norton, 1941; K. Jones, *Lunacy, law and conscience, 1744–1845*, London, Routledge & Kegan Paul, 1955. M. Foucault's *Folie et déraison: histoire de la folie à l'age classique*, Paris, Librarie Plon, 1961, argued that the institutionalization of the insane arose out of the fear of the irrational in the age of reason; whilst K. Doerner, *Burger und irre: zur sozialgeschüchte u. wissenshaftssoziologie d. psychiatrie*, Frankfurt, Fischer, 1975, sees the development of asylums as a bourgeois strategy to maintain social order during industrialization. Both of these have been translated: Foucault as *Madness and civilisation. A history of insanity in the age of reason*, London, Tavistock Publications, 1967; and Doerner as *Madmen and the bourgeoisie: a social history of insanity and psychiatry*, Oxford, Basil Blackwell, 1981.

2. A. Scull, *Museums of madness*, London, Allen Lane, 1979.

3. Digby and Tomes both also make the point that it is difficult to apply arguments based on social control to institutions with a bourgeois clientele. See A. Digby, *Madness, morality and medicine. A study of the York Retreat, 1796–1914*, Cambridge, Cambridge University Press, 1985, p. 8; N. Tomes, *A generous confidence*, Cambridge, Cambridge University Press, 1985, p. xi.

4. 12 Anne, *c.*23, *Act for reducing the laws relating to rogues, vagabonds, sturdy beggars and vagrants . . .* ; and 17 Geo. II, *c.*5, *Vagrancy Act*; for discussion see R. Porter, *Mind-forg'd manacles*, London, Penguin Books, 1990, pp. 117–19.

5. M. MacDonald, 'Insanity and the realities of history in early modern England', *Psychological Medicine*, 1981, 11: 23.

6. Scull, op. cit., note 2 above, p. 30.

7. MacDonald, op. cit., note 5 above, pp. 22–3 raises the question of how eighteenth-century medicalization relates to institutionalization; for the importance of Anglican anti-enthusiasm to the development of a medical

The commercialization of care

psychology, see also 'Religion, social change and psychological healing in England, 1600–1800', in W. Shiels (ed.), *The church and healing*, Oxford, Basil Blackwell, 1982, pp. 101–26; and M. MacDonald, *Mystical Bedlam. Madness, anxiety and healing in seventeenth-century England*, Cambridge, Cambridge University Press, 1981, pp. 11, 229–30.

8. See W. Ll. Parry-Jones, *The trade in lunacy*, London, Routledge & Kegan Paul, 1972, Chapter 2; and Porter, op. cit., note 4 above, p. 140.

9. For the consumer revolution see N. McKendrick, J. Brewer and J.H. Plumb, *The birth of a consumer society: the commercialization of eighteenth-century England*, London, Europa, 1982.

10. Porter, op. cit., note 4 above, pp. 164–7.

11. McKendrick *et al.*, op. cit., note 9 above, p. 9. On family spending see, for example, article by N. McKendrick, 'Home demand and economic growth. A new view of the role of women and children in the industrial revolution', in N. McKendrick (ed.), *Historical perspectives. Studies in English thought and society*, London, Europa, 1974; and R.J. Morris, 'The middle class and the property cycle during the industrial revolution', in T.C. Smout (ed.), *The search for wealth and stability*, London, Macmillan, 1979.

12. For a useful synopsis of literature on the history of the family, see M. Anderson, *Approaches to the history of the western family, 1500–1914*, Studies in Economic and Social History for the Economic History Society, Houndmills, Hants and London, Macmillan Education, 1980; also L. Stone, *The family, sex and marriage in England, 1500–1800*, London, Weidenfeld & Nicolson, 1977; and R. Trumbach, *The rise of the egalitarian family; aristocratic kinship and domestic relations in eighteenth-century England*, New York, Academic Press, 1978.

13. Porter argues patients' families were able to influence care and treatment in 'Was there a moral therapy in the eighteenth century?', *Lychnos*, 1981–2, pp. 12–26.

14. See Parry-Jones, op. cit., note 8 above, pp. 7–8; and Porter, op. cit., note 4 above, p. 137.

15. Ibid., Porter, pp. 148–52.

16. Ibid., p. 138; Parry-Jones, op. cit., note 8 above, p. 30.

17. 14 Geo. III, *c.*9, *An act for regulating madhouses*, 1774; Jones, op. cit., note 1 above, p. 37.

18. R. Hunter and I. Macalpine, *Three hundred years of psychiatry, 1535–1860*, London, Oxford University Press, 1963, p. 453.

19. Ibid., pp. 200–1, 265; Parry-Jones, op. cit., note 8 above, pp. 39, 223.

20. Parry-Jones, op. cit., note 8 above, p. 77.

21. Ibid., pp. 9, 224.

22. See Porter, op. cit., note 4 above, pp. 144–5.

23. Parry-Jones, op. cit., note 8 above, pp. 43, 67–8.

24. Ibid., pp. 8–9, 38, 132.

25. Ibid., pp. 38, 61, 76–7, 116.

26. Ibid., pp. 75–6, 121; also see Chapter 2, this volume.

27. Porter, op. cit., note 4 above, p. 167.

28. Parry-Jones, op. cit., note 8 above, pp. 36, 76–7, 112–13, 116, 131–3, 276–7.

29. Porter, op. cit., note 4 above, p. 175.

30. Ibid., p. 147; Parry-Jones, op. cit., note 8 above, pp. 124, 261.

31. McKendrick *et al.*, op. cit., note 9 above, p. 21.

32. Parry-Jones, op. cit., note 8 above, p. 122.

33. Ibid., p. 46; and see Chapter 2, this volume.

34. Hunter and Macalpine, op. cit., note 18 above, p. 452.

35. Parry-Jones, op. cit., note 8 above, p. 124.

The commercialization of care

36. *Munk's roll*, entry on William Battie.

37. Jones, op. cit., note 1 above, p. 41.

38. Porter, op. cit., note 4 above, pp. 141–2.

39. Cited in P. Branca, *Silent sisterhood. Middle-class women in the Victorian home*, London, Croom Helm, 1975, p. 42; see also Roy Porter, *English society in the eighteenth century*, London, Penguin, 1982, pp. 388–9.

40. Parry-Jones, op. cit., note 8 above, pp. 124–5.

41. McKendrick *et al.*, op. cit., note 9 above, p. 24.

42. J. Luckcock's *Hints for practical economy in the management of household affairs*, Birmingham, 1834, cited in L. Davidoff and C. Hall, *Family fortunes. Men and women of the English middle class, 1780–1850*, London, Hutchinson, 1987.

43. See Parry-Jones, op. cit., note 8 above, p. 116.

44. Ibid., pp. 46, 54.

45. See Chapter 2, this volume.

46. Parry-Jones, op. cit., note 8 above, pp. 30–1, 55.

47. See R. Porter, *Disease, medicine and society in England 1550–1860*, Studies in Economic and Social History for the Economic History Society, Houndmills, Hants, and London, Macmillan Education, 1987, pp. 35–9; and J. Woodward, *To do the sick no harm. A study of the British voluntary hospital system to 1875*, London and Boston, Routledge & Kegan Paul, 1974, p. 37.

48. For Perfect, see Porter, op. cit., note 4 above, p. 220. W. Pargeter, *Observations on maniacal disorders*, Reading, for the author, 1792, p. 52.

49. Parry-Jones, op. cit., note 8 above, p. 198.

50. Quoted in Hunter and Macalpine, op. cit., note 18 above, p. 279.

51. Quoted in Parry-Jones, op. cit., note 8 above, p. 103.

52. See note 25 above; for Newington, see Chapter 2, this volume.

53. Pargeter, op. cit., note 48 above, p. 123.

54. Ibid., pp. 124–5; Porter, op. cit., note 4 above, p. 145.

55. W. Battie, *A treatise on madness*, London, Whiston & White, 1758, pp. 68–9.

56. Hunter and Macalpine, op. cit., note 18 above, p. 366.

57. Pargeter, op. cit., note 48 above, p. 127.

58. Ibid., p. 129.

59. M. MacDonald, 'Lunatics and the state in Georgian England', *Social History of Medicine*, 1989, 2: 311.

60. Parry-Jones, op. cit., note 8 above, pp. 48–50.

61. See Chapter 2, this volume.

62. Hunter and Macalpine, op. cit., note 18 above, pp. 373–5.

63. Jones, op. cit., note 1 above, pp. 142–3.

64. Parry-Jones, op. cit., note 8 above, pp. 18, 30–1, 54–5.

65. See Chapter 3, this volume.

66. J. Burnett, *A history of the cost of living*, London, Penguin, 1969, cited in Davidoff and Hall, op. cit., note 42 above, p. 361.

67. Branca, op. cit., note 39 above, pp. 26–8.

68. Ibid., p. 27.

69. See for example, BB1819–26, pp. 46, 47.

70. For Hook Norton and Witney, see Parry-Jones, op. cit., note 8 above, pp. 210–11; for Ticehurst, see Chapters 2 and 3, this volume.

71. Ibid., p. 211; and Chapters 2 and 3, this volume.

72. Ibid., pp. 208–9, 211, 327; and Chapters 2 and 3, this volume.

73. Pargeter, op. cit., note 48 above, p. 37.

74. J.C.D. Clark, *English society, 1688–1832*, Cambridge and New York, Cambridge University Press, 1985, p. 68.

The commercialization of care

75. These changes are discussed at length in Stone, op. cit., note 12 above; and in E. Shorter, *The making of the modern family*, London, Collins, 1976.

76. Ibid., Shorter, p. 21; and Stone, op.cit., note 12 above, p. 4.

77. BB1802–11, p. 22.

78. Quoted in Parry-Jones, op.cit., note 8 above, p. 117.

79. See Chapter 2, this volume; Pargeter describes treating patients at home in Pargeter, op. cit., note 48 above, pp. 32–4, 50–2, 78–9.

80. Parry-Jones, op. cit., note 8 above, p. 233.

81. Ibid., p. 114.

82. See ibid., p. 209; and Chapters 2 and 3, this volume.

83. P. Honan, *Jane Austen. Her life*, London, Weidenfeld & Nicolson, 1987, p. 24.

84. Davidoff and Hall provide a detailed exploration of these beliefs in op. cit., note 42 above, *passim*.

85. For examples of this literature, and discussion, see ibid., pp. 155–80.

86. Ibid., p. 166.

87. Cowper's breakdown, and his treatment at Cotton's, are described in Porter, op. cit., note 4 above, pp. 146, 265–7; and R. Porter, *A social history of madness. Stories of the insane*, London, Weidenfeld & Nicolson, 1987, pp. 93–102.

88. Quoted in Davidoff and Hall, op. cit., note 42 above, pp. 164, 165, 26.

89. Ibid., p. 164.

90. See, for example, T. Mayo, *Elements of the pathology of the human mind*, London, J. Murray, 1838, p. 99.

91. Porter, op. cit., note 4 above, p. 139.

92. Quoted in Parry-Jones, op. cit., note 8 above, pp. 116–17.

93. Ibid., p. 123.

94. Porter, op. cit., note 4 above, pp. 4–5.

95. A. Scull, 'Moral treatment reconsidered: some sociological comments on an episode in the history of British psychiatry', *Psychological Medicine*, 1979, 9: 421–8.

96. Porter, op. cit., note 4 above, pp. 146–7; and *idem*, op. cit., note 13 above, *passim*.

97. Ibid., p. 15.

98. R. Hunter and I. Macalpine, *George III and the mad business*, London, Allen Lane, 1969, contains a detailed account of Willis's treatment and the royal family.

99. Hunter and Macalpine, op. cit., note 18 above, p. 469 quote Arnold; for Bakewell, see Parry-Jones, op. cit., note 14 above, p. 175.

100. Porter, op. cit., note 4 above, pp. 117, 216.

101. Quoted in Parry-Jones, op. cit., note 8 above, p. 132.

102. Battie, op. cit., note 55 above, p. 68.

103. See S.W. Jackson, introduction to Revd W. Pargeter, *Observations on maniacal disorders*, London, Routledge, 1988 reprint, p. xxx.

104. Porter, op. cit., note 4 above, pp. 209–12.

105. A. Scull, 'The domestication of madness', *Medical History*, 1983, 27: 233–48.

106. Foucault, 1967 translation cited in note 1 above, pp. 75, 254.

107. *Oxford English Dictionary*, entries on 'manage' and 'management'.

108. W. F. Bynum, 'Rationales for therapy in British psychiatry, 1780–1835', *Medical History*, 1974, 18: 318–19.

109. Porter, op. cit., note 4 above, p. 146; B. Faulkner, *Observations on the general and improper treatment of insanity*, London, H. Reynell for the author, 1789, p. 23; and W. Perfect, *Select cases in the different species of insanity*, Rochester, Gillman, 1787, p. 131.

110. S. Tuke, *Description of the Retreat*, York, W. Alexander, 1813; and see Porter, op. cit., note 13 above, p. 18.

111. Parry-Jones, op. cit., note 8 above, pp. 250, 252.

The commercialization of care

112. Ibid., p. 117.

113. Porter, op. cit., note 4 above, pp. 220–1; and see Chapters 2 and 3, this volume.

114. Tuke, op. cit., note 110 above, p. 173.

115. [J. Perceval], *Narrative*, London, Effingham Wilson, 1838, p. 137.

116. See, for example, Parry-Jones, op. cit., note 8 above, pp. 116–17.

117. Digby, op. cit., note 3 above, pp. 33–56; Porter, op. cit. note 4 above, pp. 146–7; and Chapters 2 and 3, this volume.

118. Tuke, op. cit., note 110 above, pp. 172–3.

119. Digby, op. cit., note 3 above, pp. 73–4; Parry-Jones, op. cit., note 8 above, p. 136; and Chapters 2 and 3, this volume.

120. Digby, op. cit., note 3 above, pp. 37–42.

121. Tuke, op.cit., note 110 above, p. 157.

122. Ibid., p. 178.

123. Foucault, 1967 translation cited in note 1 above, pp. 253–4.

124. Tuke, loc.cit., note 121 above.

125. MacDonald, op. cit., note 5 above, p. 14.

126. Porter, op. cit., note 4 above, p. 146.

127. Parry-Jones, op. cit., note 8 above, p. 93.

128. Porter, op. cit., note 87 above, pp. 93–102, 167–88.

129. See Chapters 3 and 4, this volume.

130. Digby, op. cit., note 3 above, p. 27; and p. 35.

131. J. King, *William Cowper. A biography*, Durham, Duke University Press, 1986, pp. 88–9.

132. Pargeter, op. cit., note 48 above, pp. 139–40 and see also pp. 14–15.

133. Ibid., p. 139.

134. *The Task*, Book 3, quoted in Davidoff and Hall, op. cit., note 42 above, p. 92.

135. For Evangelicalism see ibid., pp. 81–95; and I. Bradley, *The call to seriousness: the Evangelical impact on the Victorians*, London, Cape, 1976.

136. Jones, op. cit., note 1 above, p. 143.

137. Pargeter, op. cit., note 48 above, pp. 29–31.

138. Tomes discusses the feelings of families and friends about commital, in nineteenth-century America, in op. cit., note 3 above, pp. ix, 13–14, 90–128.

2

Starting a family business

No documentary evidence exists of the reasons a private madhouse was opened at Ticehurst in Sussex in 1792. However, it is possible to reconstruct some of the reasons why opening a licensed house would have seemed like a viable commercial proposition to Samuel Newington and to identify some of the factors which enabled this family business to prosper. Nationally, Francis Willis's apparently successful treatment of George III had raised public confidence in mad-doctors' claims to expertise in treating the insane. Like Willis, Samuel Newington probably had experience of caring for patients in his own home before he opened Ticehurst. Locally, the well-established and benign practice of William Perfect (1737–1809) at his private madhouse in West Malling in Kent, only seventeen miles from Ticehurst, created a grounding of public opinion on which the new asylum could build.

A county historian and Canterbury school teacher, Charles Seymour, described Perfect in 1776 as treating his patients:

> with the affection of a parent and the abilities of a man, who has, from study and observation, reduced into a practical science, the method of restoring the most wild and fixed madness, to cool sense and rational judgement.[1]

The author of several medical texts promoting his methods of treatment, William Perfect favoured using only a minimum of restraint, with attention to diet and some medicine.[2] Perhaps fearing the competition from Ticehurst (which had opened in August), William Perfect placed an advertisement for West Malling next to one for Ticehurst in the *Sussex Weekly Advertiser* for 26 November 1792.

The Newingtons may also have hoped to benefit from their proximity to the spa-town of Tunbridge Wells, only ten miles from Ticehurst. The chalybeate springs of Tunbridge Wells had become renowned in the seventeenth century for their reputed medicinal properties, notably in the treatment of infertility and (of particular interest in this context) of

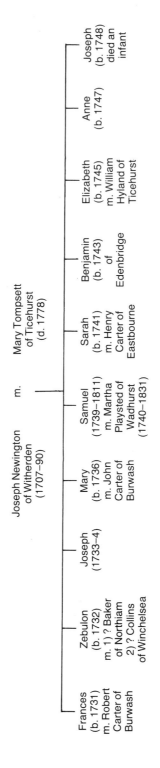

Figure 2.1 Newington family tree: Joseph Newington and Mary Tompsett.

Starting a family business

melancholia.[3] Aided by its proximity to London, Tunbridge Wells became a fashionable health resort of the aristocracy in the late-seventeenth and early-eighteenth centuries. Throughout the second half of the eighteenth century, however, Tunbridge Wells declined in popularity. In his writings, William Perfect touted the benefits nervous patients could derive from drinking the waters of chalybeate springs.[4] However, by the 1790s, Tunbridge Wells faced severe competition from the increasingly fashionable sea-bathing resort of Brighton, and more distant spa-towns like Cheltenham, which was patronized by King George III during his illness of 1788. In 1793, the Pantiles – the cobbled streets of Tunbridge Wells – were relaid with paving stones and, in emulation of Brighton, renamed the Parade. Although local interest in restoring Tunbridge Wells to its former prosperity as a spa-town ultimately proved unsuccessful, its eventual reshaping as a gentrified, residential new town of the Regency period ensured an affluent local clientele.[5]

It is therefore possible to reconstruct some of the grounds for Samuel Newington's market confidence when Ticehurst was opened. The personal reasons underlying his decision to become a madhouse keeper are more difficult to ascertain. Unlike some of his contemporaries who decided to open madhouses at this time, such as Edward Long Fox (1761–1835) in Bristol, and William Tuke (1732–1822) in York, Samuel Newington had no non-conformist religious affiliations.[6] Nor was he an ordained Anglican, like Francis Willis or John Lord. The Newington family had lived in Ticehurst since the fifteenth century.[7] Little is known of Samuel Newington's parental family, except that he was the fifth of ten children (see Figure 2.1). Like William Perfect, Samuel Newington was a village surgeon and apothecary.[8]

Advertisements for the new asylum suggest that Samuel Newington was licensed as a madhouse keeper for the first time at the Lewes Quarter Sessions in October 1792. However, he may have treated mentally disturbed patients in his own home – the Vineyards – since the 1760s. An advertisement in the *Morning Chronicle* for 26 January 1793 noted that he had: 'for thirty years past had patients under his care afflicted with this melancholy disorder, most of whom have been sent home to their friends in a sound state of mind'.[9] In the absence of alternative information, it seems plausible to suggest that Samuel Newington may have decided to extend his practice as a mad-doctor in order to provide employ- ment and income for his children as they entered adulthood. Samuel and Martha Playsted had ten sons and five daughters, only one of whom died in infancy (see Figure 2.2). As noted in the previous chapter, Francis Willis certainly believed 'an accustom'd house for wrongheads' would be a lucrative bequest for his sons; while John Lord opened his small private madhouse in Buckinghamshire to improve his financial situation, having twelve children and encumbered estates.[10] The death of Samuel Newington's own father in

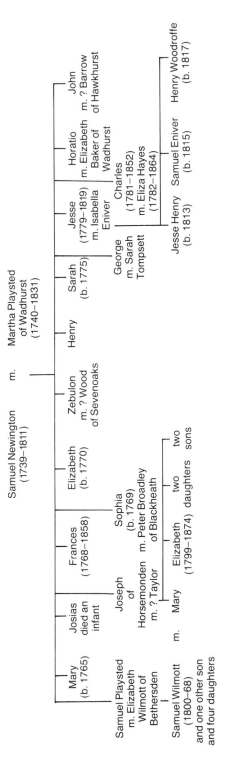

Figure 2.2 Newington family tree: Samuel Newington and Martha Playsted.

Starting a family business

1790 may have provided him with the necessary capital to open a new house, rather than simply caring for patients in his own home.

Early account books show that payments were sometimes made to Joseph, Zebulon, George and John Newington, as well as to Samuel. When Samuel Newington went to collect patients to bring them to the asylum, he was sometimes accompanied by one of his sons, or in the case of female patients, by one of his daughters.[11] Four of Samuel and Martha's sons eventually qualified as surgeons. The eldest, Samuel Playsted, practised in nearby Goudhurst in Kent. Zebulon moved to Spitalfields in London. Jesse and Charles assisted their father until his death in 1811, when they took over the running of Ticehurst.[12]

The building which housed the new asylum was not purpose-built. Early advertisements refer simply to the house having been 'fitted up and neatly furnished'.[13] Ground plans of the asylum which appeared in a prospectus in 1828 suggest the layout of a country mansion, with no system of classification, or special provision for the most violent and refractory patients, such as was found in the purpose-built private asylum of Brislington House, which was opened in 1806.[14]

Throughout June and July in 1792, regular advertisements appeared in the *Sussex Weekly Advertiser* for the new asylum, which (it was announced in mid-July) would be ready on 1 August. In fact the first patient, a Mr James Bigg, was admitted on 23 July. Despite continuing advertisements, however, admissions came slowly at first. By Christmas, only six patients had been admitted, and only four were resident in the asylum.[15]

Fees fell within the middle range of those charged by private madhouse proprietors. The first patients at Ticehurst paid one guinea a week, inclusive of washing and medicines.[16] This was significantly more than, say, the £30 a year plus a two-guinea admission fee, charged in 1787 by a Mr Stroud in Staffordshire, but considerably less than the four guineas a week which Francis Willis boasted he charged patients at Greatford in 1788.[17] It would make Ticehurst comparable to the Islington madhouse where Charles Lamb's sister Mary was confined in 1796 after stabbing her mother, where fees started at around £50 a year; or to the private madhouse run by Thomas Burman in Henley-in-Arden, who explained in 1795: 'My general terms are one guinea/week for board and medicines, the patient finding their own linen and washing. If any person chuses a servant constantly to attend on them, board and wages are separately considered'.[18]

Similarly at Ticehurst, the first patient to pay more than one guinea a week, a Mr Daniel Lintall, who was admitted on 5 November 1792, paid board and wages for a servant, in addition to two guineas a week, exclusive of washing and medicines.[19] Presumably, like Mary Lamb, who paid more than £50 a year, but had a room as well as a servant to herself, Daniel Lintall enjoyed a higher standard of accommodation than could be obtained at

Starting a family business

Ticehurst for one guinea a week.[20]

As well as offering competitive prices, Samuel Newington needed to generate confidence in the quality of care he was offering at Ticehurst. Despite sluggish admissions, advertisements suggest he favoured a selective admissions policy. In January 1793 he wrote:

> The house has an attic storey, and contains many neat apartments; is rendered perfectly safe and so contrived as to admit of every convenience requisite for the reception of patients who do not require strict confinement.
>
> Mr Newington begs leave to inform his friends that he does not wish to receive into his house any patients but such as are of a quiet and tractable disposition, as the comfort and convenience of all his Patients are what he means particularly to attend to, and, therefore, if any offer of a more violent turn, that such will be suitably provided for in his neighbourhood until by his management they become more tractable and proper to be received among those of the above description.[21]

Simultaneously, Ticehurst was represented here as exclusive, and protected from the worst extremes of madness; while Samuel Newington's capabilities in dealing with the insane were promoted.

In the first half of 1793 the admissions rate doubled, so that twelve more patients had been admitted by the end of June. After that, it remained at a similar level (twenty to twenty-eight admissions per year, including readmissions) for the next four years. The number of patients in the asylum rose by July 1795 to around sixteen, with more men than women generally resident in the asylum (see Table 2.1).[22]

At first, the policy of excluding violent and intractable patients was put into practice. In July 1793, the first patient to be charged in the accounts for the repair of broken windows was temporarily removed to a Mr Badcock's. With the onset of winter in October 1794, Samuel Sands 'Was carried to St Luke's having been here 22 weeks, about three months out of the House'. In March 1795, a patient called Thomas Avan was also

Table 2.1 Number of patients resident, 1795–1815

Figures are for 31 July of each year				
Year	*Men*	*Women*	*Sex unknown*	*Total*
1795	8	8		16
1800	8	3		11
1805	16	7		23
1810	17	13		30
1815	18	14	1	33

Sources: BB1792–1802, BB1802–11, BB1811–19

Starting a family business

transferred to St Luke's Hospital in London after breaking windows.[23]

At the same time another, higher-class patient, Revd Richard Podmore, the vicar of nearby Cranbrook in Kent, remained in the asylum after breaking windows. Thereafter, other patients who behaved in a similar way were allowed to stay. Only one other patient appears to have been boarded out: in July 1801 a Mrs Shrivell was boarded for four months with a Widow Skinner, having already spent four months in the asylum. The reasons for her seclusion are not known, although since for the last three weeks of her confinement she paid for the upkeep of a child as well as herself, it seems possible that this was a case of insanity during pregnancy.[24]

Details of treatment which can be gleaned from the account books are necessarily fragmented. However, even the solitary example of Samuel Sands being kept outside for three months – perhaps in an outhouse or barn, since the accounts show clearly when patients were boarded out with local people – suggests that some of the thinking which informed what were by 1815 to be regarded as the worst abuses of the private asylum system, also informed practices at Ticehurst in the early years.[25] However, there is no evidence to suggest that patients at Ticehurst were subjected to the kind of systematic neglect reported to the Commons select committee of 1815–16; nor that the harshest treatment was reserved for pauper patients.[26] (A small, but slightly increasing percentage of admissions to Ticehurst before 1817 were paupers: see Table 2.2).

The extent to which mechanical restraint was used at Ticehurst is unclear. For the first few years, the boarding-out of violent and refractory patients may have made the restraint of patients in the asylum uncommon. In 1801, a patient was billed 7s.7d. for a 'straight waistcoat', but this could have been because he or his family wanted him to have one of his own, or to replace one which he had damaged, rather than meaning that this was the only occasion on which mechanical restraint was used. Certainly Mary

Table 2.2 Pauper admissions, 1792–1817

Numbers in brackets represent known readmissions
Years run from 1 August to 31 July

Years	Men	Women	Sex unknown	Total
1792–7	0	0	0	0
1797–1802	3	2	0	5
1802–7	5	5	1	11
1807–12	*9 (1)	*4	1	14 (1)
1812–17	7 (3)	11 (4)	1	19 (7)
Subtotal	24 (4)	22 (4)	3	49 (8)
Total	28	26	3	57

* Including one patient who only had part of their bill paid by the parish
Sources: See Table 2.1

Starting a family business

Lamb took her own strait waistcoat in and out of her asylum with her; while John Perceval, who later became a patient at Ticehurst, described how when he was first confined in Dublin he tore his way out of one.[27] Although a selective admissions policy may have kept the number of violent patients to a minimum, the frequent charges for the repair of broken windows, and in one case for the replacement of a broken chamber-pot, suggest both that there were patients whose behaviour needed restraining, and that such restraint was not habitual.[28]

Equally, the nature and frequency of medical treatment is unclear. That 'medicines' were at first included in a fixed charge along with board and washing suggests that their routine use was anticipated. However, later entries only rarely specify whether washing and 'wine', rather than 'medicines', were included or excluded, and patients were sometimes charged separately for both. Wine may have been prescribed as part of a stimulating diet in cases of melancholia; unfortunately where 'medicines' were charged for separately, they were not itemized.[29] The normal use of depleting medicines and methods of treatment, such as bleeding, to control states of mania might indirectly explain why a pregnant patient like Mrs Shrivell was, unusually, boarded out: late-eighteenth and early-nineteenth-century texts on midwifery advise against using severe depleting medicines on pregnant women, even in states of acute mania.[30]

On the other hand, Samuel Newington's emphasis on 'management' in advertisements for Ticehurst suggests that he did not rely exclusively on medical treatment. Indeed, his concern with the 'comfort and convenience' of his patients would place him within the tradition of eighteenth-century asylum proprietors whose desire to create a 'civilised and calming environment' has been taken by Roy Porter as evidence of moral therapeutic objectives in practice before the influence of Pinel and Samuel Tuke.[31] There is ample evidence that care was taken at Ticehurst to foster patients' feelings of self-esteem: regular payments for shaving, hair-dressing, and new items of clothing record the attention paid to patients' dress and appearance. In addition, some patients were allowed extras – like pipes, tobacco and snuff, as well as cheese, gingerbread, liquorice, oranges, sugar-candy and wine – which suggest a liberal regimen.[32]

Extensive freedoms were enjoyed by some patients, particularly those paying higher fees. Thus the extras Daniel Lintall paid for in 1794–5 included fishing-tackle, gun-cleaning and the keep of his horse and dog.[33] The image this conjures up of patients who, despite their insanity, pursued the normal leisure activities of the English squirearchy is a leitmotif of Ticehurst's history. Yet even if these activities were encouraged because they were believed to have therapeutic effects, it is unclear how far this might be because the principles which informed treatment at Ticehurst were 'moral'. Eighteenth-century madhouse keepers frequently recommended exercise as part of physical regimens for the insane, and even Samuel Tuke

Starting a family business

lists exercise as part of both medical and moral treatment.[34]

In many respects, the treatment offered at Ticehurst is reminiscent of what is known of Francis Willis's methods of treatment, both of King George III and in his private madhouse in Lincolnshire. The desire to test a patient's returning self-control with increased freedom and exposure to risk was evident in Willis's treatment of King George III when he allowed the King access to a razor and penknife to shave and cut his nails.[35] If Daniel Lintall was permitted to ride and to use his gun while he was at Ticehurst, similar thinking may have informed the decision. Exercise formed a central part of the regime at Greatford. A visitor to Willis's asylum in 1796 commented that:

> As the unprepared traveller approached the town, he was astonished to find almost all the surrounding ploughmen, gardeners, threshers, thatchers and other labourers attired in blackcoats, white waistcoats, black silk breeches and stockings, and the head of each 'bien poudré, frisé et arrangé'. These were the doctor's patients, and dress, neatness of person, and exercise being the principal features of his admirable system, health and cheerfulness conjoined to aid recovery of every person attached to that most valuable asylum.[36]

Although there is no evidence that patients at Ticehurst were employed, the regular attention paid to patients' appearance, as well as payments for shoe-mending, fishing-tackle and horse-keep, suggest the same kind of priorities. In addition, rational mental recreations were permitted: thus Daniel Lintall's other purchases included the 'Beauties of Stern', 'Speaker Endfield's' and 'Magazines'.[37] In a similar spirit, during King George III's lucid intervals, Francis Willis conversed and played backgammon with him.[38] Other activities patients at Ticehurst engaged in included spinning and sewing, playing the harpsichord and violin, drawing and writing.[39]

In other respects, the account books suggest differences between the asylum and the outside world were kept to a minimum. Apart from the musical instruments above, some patients bought items of furniture, such as a sofa or writing desk, which suggest the Newingtons tried to establish as domestic and everyday an environment as possible. One patient bought a birdcage, and presumably kept pet birds in his room. More importantly, another patient came accompanied by his mother, who stayed with him in the asylum; and two female patients brought their own maidservants with them. Regular charges for writing paper and postage imply that patients were not discouraged from communicating with their friends and relations.[40]

From all of these activities it is possible to infer that attempts were made at Ticehurst to solicit patients' 'rationality, self-restraint and self-esteem' – the qualities which Roy Porter has emphasized as central goals of moral therapy. The advocacy of this kind of treatment can certainly be taken as evidence of a tradition of moral therapeutic ideas before the publication

Starting a family business

of Samuel Tuke's *Description of the Retreat* (1813). Fragmented as the evidence of therapeutic practice at Ticehurst is for this early period, it clearly included non-medical and non-mechanical elements. However, there is insufficient evidence to assess how readily mechanical restraint was resorted to; whether medical treatment was directed at mental disorders as well as intercurrent physical derangement; and how far psychological management was effected through fear rather than through kindness. The close parallels between what is known of treatment at Ticehurst and some of the more genial practices of Francis Willis – whose less sympathetic treatment of King George III has been taken as the archetype of what William Bynum has described ironically as 'immoral therapy' – suggest how continuous the spectrum between moral and medical/mechanical therapy may have been in practice, especially in middle- and upper-class asylums.[41]

It seems important to stress the value which high standards of physical care and attention to patients' appearance could have in reassuring a prospective clientele. Excluding violent and destructive patients from Ticehurst, and maintaining an appearance of normalcy by engaging patients in ordinary activities could serve a similar function. Claims that Francis Willis and others could calm patients with an authoritative look reflect how crucial it was for asylum proprietors to assume an almost magical competence in dealing with patients whose behaviour caused friends and relations to feel helpless.[42] In this context it is worth noting that, while it is striking that treatment at Ticehurst bears closest comparison to the practice of another Anglican mad-doctor, the mix of medical and moral therapy, and reliance on assertions of psychological authority, suggest that MacDonald may have exaggerated the eighteenth-century Anglican repudiation of psychological healing.[43]

From the patient's perspective, the benefits of madhouse proprietors' concern with appearances could be less self-evident. Rather than enhancing his self-esteem, John Perceval experienced routine shaving and nail-cutting at Brislington House in the early 1830s as an indignity and assault on his individuality; although he also complained that he was shaved only three times a week, and not every day. In contrast, although retrospectively humiliated to have been put in such a situation, he recalled the two weeks he spent chained up in an outhouse on a bed of straw as a comparatively happy period:

> Here there was comparative peace, seclusion, freedom from intrusion. Here I had no servant sleeping in the room with me. Here I might hollo or sing as my spirits commanded . . . and although my right arm was fastened by a short chain to the wall and the strap pressed rather tightly across my chest, it was still something to have one arm free even in the straight waistcoat, and not to be galled by the fastening on the other.[44]

Starting a family business

Table 2.3 Admissions, 1792–1817

Numbers in brackets represent known readmissions
Years run from 1 August to 31 July

Years	Men	Women	Sex unknown	Total
1792–7	51 (11)	48 (6)	2	101 (17)
1797–1802	50 (9)	33 (8)		83 (17)
1802–7	54 (5)	47 (5)	3	104 (10)
1807–12	66 (4)	52 (12)	2	120 (16)
1812–17	62 (11)	67 (22)	1	130 (33)
Subtotal	283 (40)	247 (53)	8	538 (93)
Total	323	300	8	631

Sources: See Table 2.1

Whatever the exact nature of the treatment at Ticehurst, the formula was a successful one, and during the first twenty-five years admissions rose steadily (see Table 2.3). By 1815, the asylum had more than doubled its population of 1795 (see Table 2.1). The connections between Ticehurst and the kind of therapy offered by the Willises are underpinned by the fact that three patients came to Ticehurst via the Willis family. In February 1797, a Revd Chambers was referred to Ticehurst by Dr Robert Darling Willis in London. Another patient, a Revd Lofty from Canterbury was accompanied from Dr Willis's in Lincolnshire to Ticehurst in December 1799, although it is unclear whether he had been a patient at Greatford, or travelled all the way to Lincolnshire – a return journey of six days – to consult Francis Willis. Equally, since attendance was charged only to and from Barton, it is not certain whether whoever accompanied Revd Lofty to Ticehurst actually visited Greatford themselves. In 1808, a Mr Darnay was transferred to Ticehurst from Greatford.[45]

However, it is worth stressing that patients such as these, who paid above-average fees of two or three guineas a week, and enjoyed the kind of extra privileges described, represent the upper end of Ticehurst's market. Despite wartime inflation, and a gradual increase in the percentage of patients paying higher fees, most patients continued to be accepted at one guinea per week until the late 1820s.[46] The former occupations, or social class, of patients is known for only nineteen male and three female admissions before 1815, apart from those described as paupers. Of these, all three women, and two men, were described as 'independent'. There were eleven clergymen, one admiral, one captain, one merchant, one surgeon–apothecary, one druggist and one clerk from India House.[47] Since all except two of these (the captain and one of the female patients) paid more than one guinea a week, it seems reasonable to assume that the majority of Ticehurst's inmates during this period came from the lower-professional and commercial middle class, and the families

45

Starting a family business

Figure 2.3 Place of origin of first admissions to Ticehurst, 1792–1817.

Starting a family business

of moderately prosperous tenant farmers, rather than the higher bourgeoisie and gentry who formed the Willises' clientele at Greatford.[48]

The vast majority of first admissions to Ticehurst during the the first twenty-five years the asylum was open came from Sussex or Kent (see Figure 2.3). An analysis of these admissions over time suggests a gradually expanding and consolidating reputation throughout South-East England, but with admissions heavily concentrated in Sussex and Kent (see Figure 2.4). Indeed, the country parishes which sent most patients to Ticehurst clustered within a thirteen-mile radius of the asylum. Patients travelled further from the commercial (and except Rye, larger) centres of Brighton, Hastings, Lewes and Rye (see Figure 2.5). However, no close correlation exists between the size of the towns and villages sending most patients to Ticehurst, and the number of patients they sent. The percentage of the population these admissions represented was far greater for rural parishes than in towns. To take two extremes, the proportion of the population of Frant admitted to Ticehurst (1 : 24) was ten times the same proportion for Brighton (1 : 240). Nor can this be explained by greater distance alone. The proportion of admissions from Tonbridge, twelve miles from Ticehurst (1 : 99), was far lower than admissions from Tenterden (1 : 46) or Yalding (1 : 37), both thirteen miles away. The evidence from Ticehurst would therefore lend no support to the hypothesis that there was a simple correlation between living in larger centres of population, and a preference for institutional solutions.[49]

How unusual it was for lunatics to be cared for in asylums in Kent and Sussex during this period remains obscure. Pauper lunatics may more frequently have been cared for in poorhouses, or boarded out individually, than admitted to private asylums; but there is also later evidence that paupers from Kent and Sussex were sometimes sent to licensed houses in London. An 1819 return of the number of lunatics confined in licensed houses in England lists only two small private asylums in Kent, at West Malling and Blackheath, containing eleven and seven patients, respectively. The accuracy of early returns is questionable, however, since this one also claims that there was 'No Licensed House within the County of Sussex', listing Ticehurst in error as a county asylum.[50] Error aside, it is difficult to assess the scale of unlicensed practice and private single care, since although the 1774 Act for Regulating Private Madhouses (14, Geo. III, *c*.49) policed with a light touch, it did breach the guarantee of confidentiality which may have been the prime concern of private patients and their families.

What factors made it likely that a patient would be referred to Ticehurst? There is evidence to suggest that resort to institutional confinement may sometimes have been linked to social stress. Thus a higher proportion of the population of Hastings (1 : 45), which was expanding exceptionally rapidly during this period, were admitted to Ticehurst than from other

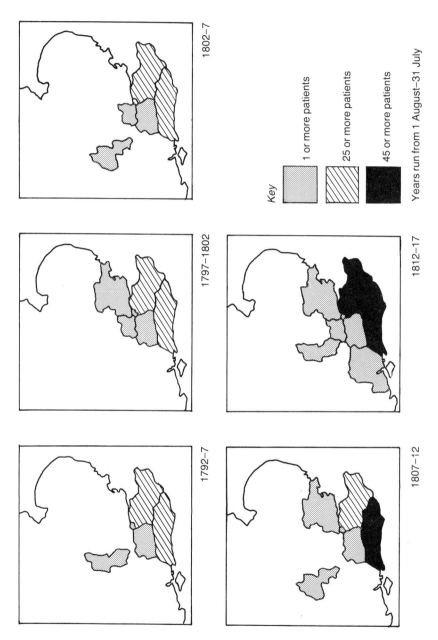

Figure 2.4 Place of origin of first admissions to Ticehurst in five-year periods, 1792–1817.

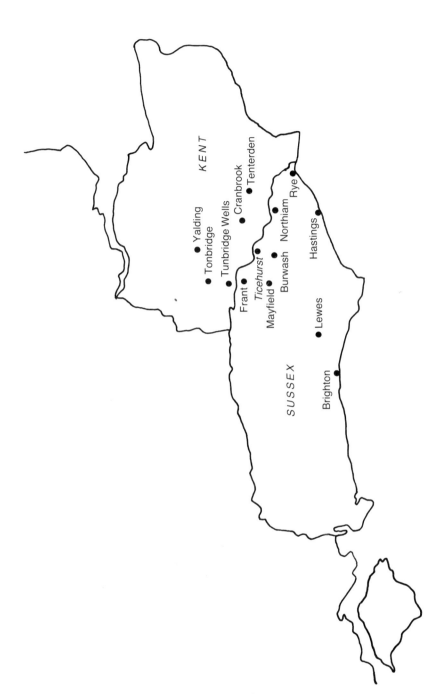

Figure 2.5 Towns and villages from which nine or more patients were admitted to Ticehurst, 1792–1817.

Starting a family business

towns. The 1811 census showed the population of Yalding to have larger than average families – of six or seven members rather than four or five – and a disproportionate number of patients admitted to Ticehurst from Yalding were paupers (five out of eleven, compared to two from Burwash and one each from Lewes, Mayfield and Rye).[51] Overcrowded housing and overstretched family incomes may have made it more difficult for families to care for an insane member themselves, or pay for their upkeep. However, in these cases it seems unlikely that asylum care was a preferred choice; and, like Ticehurst's highest fee-payers, they represent a minority of admissions.

Another factor which could have influenced the referral of patients to Ticehurst was the presence of local doctors sympathetic to asylum treatment, or personally and/or professionally supportive of the Newingtons. Evidence of who the referring doctors were survives for those patients admitted between 6 April 1802 and 23 December 1812, whose admission was recorded in the Country Register. These represent only slightly over one-third of admissions recorded in the account books of the asylum (including readmissions). A further seven patients who were still resident in 1828 had the names of their certifying doctor recorded in a register of patients which was opened then.[52] Five doctors certified three or more of these 104 patients. Thomas Bishop, a surgeon from Tenterden (3); Charles Crouch, a surgeon from Hastings (3); Samuel Newington from Goudhurst (4); Robert Watts, MD from Cranbrook (9); and Robert Montague Wilmot, MD from Hawkhurst in Kent (3). Of these, only Samuel Newington is known to have had a close connection with Ticehurst, although after 1812 Robert Watts sometimes acted as a consultant physician to the asylum.[53]

There is no evidence (apart from the breaking of windows at Ticehurst) of the kind of behaviour which may have led to certification. One patient is known to have been epileptic. Of those patients who were still resident in the asylum in 1842 when a register of patients listed diagnoses, seven were by then described as suffering from 'imbecility' or 'amentia', and one woman as subject to 'delusions'.[54] The Country Register listed the name of the family member or friend by whose direction the patient was confined, although the exact relationship was only rarely listed; in addition, there is information on who authorized the confinement of eight other patients who were still resident in 1828. As might be expected, most patients were admitted on the authority of one or more relation. More men than women authorized confinement, although more male than female patients had their certification authorized by women. This would suggest that women generally only signed certificates when a close male relative who would normally undertake such legal responsibilities, like a husband or son, was being certified.[55]

The length of time new admissions spent in the asylum increased gradually during the first twenty-five years, from a median of between one

50

Starting a family business

Table 2.4   Length of stay of first admissions, 1792–1817

Years run from 1 August to 31 July

Length of stay	1792–7	1797–1802	1802–7	1807–12	1812–17	Total
Up to 7 days	4	3	2	2		11
8 days–4 wks	17	15	15	8	5	60
4+–13 wks	31*	39*	37*	47	42	196
13+–26 wks	25	13	24	31*	38*	131
26+ wks–1 yr	9	4	12	17	23	65
1+–2 yrs	4	2	4	2	9	21
2+–5 yrs	3	2	4	6	8	23
5+–10 yrs	1	2	1	4		8
10+–20 yrs		2	2	2	2	8
20+–35 yrs	2		2			4
35+–55 yrs	1			1	3	5
55+ yrs	1	1				2
Unknown	3		1			4
Total	101	83	104	120	130	538

*Median length of stay
Sources: BB1792–1802 to BB1840–6; RDD1845–90

and three months to between three and six months (see Table 2.4). Less than 15 per cent of new admissions spent more than one year in the asylum. While this suggests a rapid turnover of patients, some of the earliest admissions became very long-stay. Thus John Daniel Lucadon, admitted within the first twelve months after opening, was resident in the asylum for almost sixty-one years, until his death in 1854; and Revd Chambers, referred by Dr Robert Darling Willis in 1797, was a patient for over thirty-seven years before his discharge in 1834.[56] Long-stay patients gradually accumulated, so that by 31 July 1815 almost one-third of the patients resident in Ticehurst had a total length of stay of more than twenty years. When patients are looked at in profile, the median length of stay increased from between one and two years on 31 July 1795 to between five and ten years on 31 July 1815 (see Table 2.5).

Male patients stayed in the asylum slightly longer than female patients. Over half the men admitted for the first time between August 1792 and July 1817 remained in the asylum for more than three months, while most women admitted for the first time in the same period were discharged in less than three months. Although a slightly higher proportion of female than male patients were readmitted, some of whose admissions extended over a total period of more than five years, more than two-thirds of new admissions who stayed more than five years continuously in the asylum were men. By 31 July 1815, more than half the male patients resident in the asylum could expect a total length of stay of 10–20 years, compared with 2–5 years for female patients.[57]

Seventy-six per cent of first admissions to Ticehurst during this period

Starting a family business

Table 2.5 Length of stay of patients resident, 1795–1815

Figures are for 31 July of each year					
Length of stay	1795	1800	1805	1810	1815
Up to 4 wks	1				
4+–13 wks	3		1	2	1
13+–26 wks	1		1	2	6
26+ wks–1 yr	2		2	2	2
1+–2 yrs	3*	2	2	1	1
2+–5 yrs	2	1	4	5	4
5+–10 yrs	1	3*	4*	4*	4*
10+–20 yrs		1	4	6	6
20+ yrs	3	4	5	8	9
Total	16	11	23	30	33

*Median length of stay
Sources: See Table 2.4

are known to have been discharged (409 patients), and 13 per cent to have died in the asylum (70 patients). The outcome of treatment for the remaining eleven per cent is unknown (59 patients). The death rate for male patients was slightly higher than for female patients (see Table 2.6). The condition of those who were discharged was rarely recorded, although occasionally a patient was listed as having gone home 'well' or 'cured'. Fourteen patients are known to have been transferred to other asylums when they left Ticehurst: ten to St Luke's, two to Bedlam, one to Fisher House and one to Holly House in Hoxton.[58] Not surprisingly, the pattern of discharge and death is significantly different when the patient population is looked at in profile. By 31 July 1800, almost two-thirds of the patients who were resident in Ticehurst would eventually die in the asylum. The ratio of deaths to discharge remained around 2: 1 until 31 July 1815, when it dropped to 1: 1 (see Table 2.6). If a majority of relatives removed patients when they lost hope of a cure, others were evidently prepared to continue to pay for care when there was little prospect of recovery.

Table 2.6 Outcome of stay for patients resident, 1795–1815

Figures are for 31 July of each year									
Year	Died			Discharged			Unknown outcome		
	Men	Women	Both	Men	Women	Both	Men	Women	Both
1795	3	1	4	4	5	9	1	2	3
1800	6	1	7	1	2	3	1		1
1805	7	5	12	5	1	6	5		5
1810	10	7	17	5	6	11	2		2
1815	8	6	14	7	8	15	3		4*

*One patient's sex is unknown
Sources: See Table 2.4

Starting a family business

Although only one patient in eight was described as having been 'well' when they left Ticehurst, there is other evidence which suggests satisfaction on the part of the Newingtons' clients, and the full recovery of some patients. Thus when a Miss Baker left the asylum in May 1794, in addition to paying her bill she spent eleven guineas on 'Presents to our [the Newington] family', presumably in gratitude for the treatment she had received. Revd William Courthope (1768–1847), who was a patient from November 1798 to January 1799, went on to become chaplain to the Earl of Chichester, vicar of Brenchley in Kent (1802–47) and rector of St John's Southover in Lewes (1805–21). This case in particular may have contributed to (or reflected existing) local confidence in the asylum, since Revd Courthope's elder brother George (1767–1835) was one of the local magistrates with responsibility for licensing and inspecting madhouses under the 1774 Act.[59]

Financially, the asylum was successful. Although most new admissions continued to be charged one guinea a week, by 31 July 1810 most patients resident in the asylum were paying two guineas per week or more. Since the number of patients in the asylum also doubled, the Newingtons' business income quadrupled between 1795 and 1815. Even allowing for the increase in expenditure necessitated by wartime inflation, this would suggest an increase in income in real terms of around 100 per cent.[60] If Samuel Newington had originally hoped that the asylum would provide long-term financial security for his family, he had no reason to fear that this would not be the case when he died in 1811.

The two sons who succeeded him, Charles and Jesse, were both qualified as surgeons; and from 1812 the accounts show that outside medical advice was also consulted from local physicians like Dr Robert Watts in Cranbrook, and Dr John Mayo (1761–1818) in Tunbridge Wells.[61] In 1812, Charles married Eliza Hayes, the daughter of a former canon of St Pauls, and built a new house for his future family, the Highlands (see Figure 2.6). Perhaps emulating the varied walks advocated as therapeutic in Samuel Tuke's *Description of the Retreat* (1813), Charles and Jesse employed men who had been demobilized after the battle of Waterloo to landscape and ornament over forty acres of grounds in 1816.[62] Over two miles of footpaths led through the plantations, orchard and gardens, past summer houses (one of which was fashionably gothic), a pheasantry, an aviary of singing birds, a moss-house, a pagoda, a hermitage and a bowling green. The accounts from this period of post-war deflation suggest a new financial confidence. Thus in February 1816, when a Mr Pilgrim was 'too poor to pay as he ought for every kindness shewn to his daughter', £11.12s. was deducted from the bill; in April 1817, when a Mrs Whitehead could not afford to pay her bill, the Newingtons 'gave the poor woman' two guineas.[63]

It is unclear how far the accumulation of high-fee-paying, long-stay, mostly male patients represented an intentional policy to maximize profit.

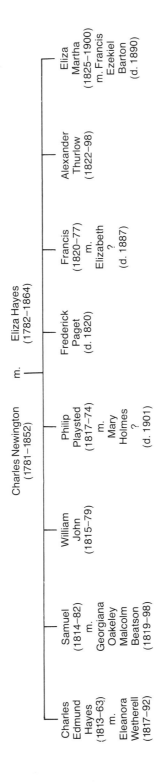

Figure 2.6 Newington family tree: Charles Newington and Eliza Hayes.

Starting a family business

The Newingtons' increasing charity to poorer patients could be said to count against this interpretation. It seems equally likely that relatives who could afford it might have offered higher fees for long-stay patients, hoping that this would guarantee a continuing adequate degree of care. Some long-stay patients paid increased fees which kept step with inflation to maintain standards of treatment. Only one admitted during this period eventually decreased his fees, presumably because his family was unable to support the continuing financial burden.[64] In December 1821, another patient who had been admitted in February 1817 left the asylum when her husband became bankrupt, and her last bill was not paid until 1826.[65]

On the whole, long-stay patients guaranteed a core income for the Newingtons; while their relationships with local, and in the case of John Mayo, prestigious physicians ensured the patronage which would bring higher-class patients to the asylum. The newly landscaped grounds revealed the younger Newingtons' social aspirations as well as a fashionable adherence to contemporary modes of treatment. High standards of physical accommodation underpinned their reputation, encouraging more families to continue to opt for asylum care despite limited hopes of recovery. During Ticehurst's first twenty-five years, the foundations of its future success had been securely laid.

Nevertheless, by 1817 the Newingtons had some cause to be concerned that public opinion might turn against private asylums. Although the worst abuses reported to the parliamentary inquiries of 1815–16 involved pauper patients, they included cases of neglect and maltreatment in licensed houses, exposing the lack of effective protection provided by the 1774 Act. Proposed legislation in 1816–19 would have introduced a central board of Commissioners with responsibility for the inspection of the insane. These bills failed partly because of opposition in the House of Lords to increased visitation of private patients, but the debate can have done little to enhance public confidence in licensed houses, particularly amongst those who could afford fees only at the lower end of the range.[66] Magistrates were slow to assume the initiative and erect county asylums, but by 1844 more pauper lunatics were confined in these new institutions than in licensed houses.

Despite this, by 1844 the number of patients confined in private madhouses (5,173) was more than twice that estimated in 1819 (2,585). In 1844, nearly 54 per cent of these were paupers;[67] but some licensed houses catered exclusively or almost exclusively for private fee-paying patients. Well- established family businesses, like Brislington House and Laverstock House, had been amongst the private asylums which were most highly praised in the 1815–16 select committee reports; and houses licensed to the Foxes, Newingtons and Willises (Brislington House, Ticehurst and Shillingthorpe) were able to take mainly higher-class patients by 1844. These institutions led the market in creating and responding to the clientele of private asylums in such a way that their reputations were

55

Starting a family business

consolidated and enhanced, despite the poor public image of licensed houses. To do this, they needed to maintain high standards of physical care in a genteel environment. They also needed to achieve a compromise between families' concern for privacy, and the demands of increased regulation after 1828; and to demonstrate that asylum care was consistent with a high valuation of family life. By 1817, the Newingtons were sufficiently affluent to provide a comfortable and cultivated environment for upper- and middle-class patients. The next chapter explores how they consolidated their reputation, and assuaged families' doubts, by aligning the role of the asylum in cases of insanity to fashionable preoccupation with the moral reform of society.

Notes

1. C. Seymour, *A topographical, historical and commercial survey of the cities, towns and villages of the county of Kent* . . ., Canterbury, for the author, 1776, p. 552.

2. W. Perfect's *Methods of cure, in some particular cases of insanity, the epilepsy, hypochondriacal affections, hysteric passions and nervous disorders*, Rochester, T. Fisher for the author, 1778, went through seven editions under various titles; the final edition appeared in the year of his death as *Annals of insanity*, London, for the author, 1809. In addition he published *A remarkable case of madness, with the diet and medicines used in the cure*, Rochester, for the author, 1791. See R. Hunter and I. Macalpine, *Three hundred years of psychiatry, 1535–1860*, London, Oxford University Press, 1963, pp. 500–1.

3. P.J.N. Havins, *The spas of England*, London, Hale, 1976, pp. 22–4; see also N.G. Coley (1979) ' "Cures without care", "chymical physicians" and mineral waters in seventeenth-century English medicine', *Medical History*, 1979, 23, 2: 191–214.

4. Perfect, op cit., pp. 64–5.

5. Havins, op. cit., note 3 above, pp. 25, 124–5; R. Hunter and I. Macalpine *George III and the mad business*, London, Allen Lane, 1969, pp. 3–13; M. Barton *Tunbridge Wells*, London, Faber & Faber, 1937, p. 310.

6. For Edward Long Fox, proprietor of Cleeve Hill (1794–1806) and Brislington House (from 1806) near Bristol, see W.Ll. Parry-Jones, *The trade in lunacy*, London, Routledge & Kegan Paul, 1972, pp. 112–15; William Tuke founded the Retreat in York, see A. Digby, *Madness, morality and medicine*, Cambridge and New York, Cambridge University Press, 1985, pp. 14–16.

7. For a family tree, see W. Berry, *Pedigrees of the families in the county of Sussex*, London, Sherwood, Gilbert & Piper, 1830, pp. 158–60.

8. *Medical Register*, 1779, pp. 93–4, 136.

9. QO/EW30, 4 October 1792; advertisement quoted in L.J. Hodson and J. Odell, *Ticehurst: the story of a Sussex parish*, Tunbridge Wells, 'Courier' Co., 1925, p. 148.

10. Parry-Jones, op. cit., note 6 above, p. 75; and R. Porter, *Mind-forg'd manacles*, London, Penguin Books, 1990, p. 140.

11. See, for example, BB1792–1802, pp. 10, 52, 78–9, 88, 97.

12. Samuel Playsted is described as a surgeon in the Country Register, and signed certificates for four admissions to Ticehurst in 1809–12 (MH51/735 79595, pp. 63, 64, 121). However, unlike his three brothers he is not listed as a member of the Royal College of Surgeons in its *List of members* . . ., London, J. Adlard, 1805,

Starting a family business

pp. 15, 54.

13. Hodson and Odell, op. cit., note 9 above, p. 148.

14. *Ticehurst private asylum for insane persons*, place of publication unknown, *c.* 1828, last three unnumbered pages.

15. *Sussex Weekly Advertiser*, 18 June–24 December 1792, 46 no. 2391–418; BB1792–1802, pp. 1–6.

16. Ibid., *passim.*

17. Parry-Jones, op. cit., note 6 above, p. 124; Hunter and Macalpine, op. cit., note 5 above, p. 71.

18. Parry-Jones, op. cit., note 6 above, pp. 124–5.

19. BB1792–1802, p. 5

20. Letter from Charles Lamb to Samuel Taylor Coleridge, 3 October 1796, in 'E.R.' (ed.), *The letters of Charles Lamb*, London, Everyman, 1909, p. 38.

21. Quoted in Hodson and Odell, op. cit., note 9 above, p. 148.

22. C. MacKenzie, 'A family asylum: a history of the private madhouse at Ticehurst in Sussex, 1792–1917', London University PhD thesis, 1987, p. 476.

23. BB1792–1802, pp. 4, 19, 21.

24. Ibid., pp. 26, 35, 49, 83.

25. *Report from the committee on madhouses in England*, PP1814–15(296.)IV.801–, pp. 4, 6.

26. The worst private asylum conditions reported in the 1815–16 select committee report were in those which took large numbers of pauper lunatics, most notably Thomas Warburton's Red and White Houses in Bethnal Green, *Report from the select committee appointed to consider of provision being made for the better regulation of madhouses in England*, PP1816(227)VI.249–, pp. 37–8.

27. BB1792–1802, p. 87. Bryan Proctor, one of the Commissioners in Lunacy, described Charles and Mary Lamb with her strait waistcoat in a memoir of Charles. Quoted in A. Birrell's introduction to Charles Lamb, *The essays of Elia*, London, Everyman, 1901, p. xx. [J. Perceval] *Narrative*, London, Effingham Wilson, 1838, p. 56.

28. See, for example, BB1792–1802, pp. 19, 32, 35, 49, 63, 65, 76, 82; BB1802–11, pp. 4, 16, 35, 44, 49, 62; BB1811–19, pp. 17, 21, 52, 62, 72.

29. Separate payments for washing and/or medicines can be found in BB1792–1802, pp. 18, 22, 28, 35, 36, 40; entries on pp. 66 and 67 specify that the basic charge includes wine and washing; entries on pp. 72, 74, 78 specify that the basic charge excludes these. Only two patients' accounts specify the medicine given: 'A Draught', 'Mixture' and 'Drops' for Mr Acton, and 'Drops' for Mr Holmwood (pp. 37, 43. Samuel Tuke recommended the use of alcohol in diets for melancholia in *Description of the Retreat*, York, W. Alexander, 1813, p. 128.

30. C. White, *A treatise on the management of pregnant and lying-in women . . .*, London, for E. & C. Dilly, 1773, p. 67 recommends only minimal bleeding during pregnancy for physical disorders; T. Denman, *An introduction to the practice of midwifery*, London, J. Johnson, 1801, advises against the use of 'powerful medicines, and very severe treatment' in cases of puerperal mania (see Hunter and Macalpine, op. cit., note 2 above, p. 797).

31. R. Porter 'Was there a moral therapy in the eighteenth?' *Lychnos*, 1981–2, p. 18.

32. Payments were made to the barber, glover, hairdresser, mantua-maker, shoemaker and tailor; and for items such as bonnets, hair-ribbon, stockings, suits, wigs and worsted, BB1792–1802, pp. 1, 4, 24, 26, 49, 55, 63, 67, 68, 73, 78, 86. For purchases of foodstuffs see, for example, BB1792–1802 pp. 11, 17, 29, 40, 45, 74, 88; BB1802–11, pp. 34, 40; BB1811–19, pp. 7 & 68.

33. BB1792–1802, pp. 29, 34.

Starting a family business

34. For example, Benjamin Faulkner, the lay owner of a private madhouse at Little Chelsea in London, recommended exercise in *Observations on the general and improper treatment of insanity* . . ., London, H. Reynell for the author, 1789, p. 23; Tuke, op. cit., note 29 above, pp. 130, 154–5.

35. Hunter and Macalpine, op. cit., note 5 above, pp. 282–4.

36. Parry-Jones, op. cit., note 6 above, pp. 183–4.

37. See, for example, BB1792–1802, pp. 10, 19, 32, 34, 42, 82; BB1802–11, pp. 2, 41, 57, 83; BB1811–19, pp. 22, 72, 131. Daniel Lintall was the only patient to pay for horse-keep (BB1792–1802, pp. 29, 34), but other patients later paid for horse-hire (BB1802–11, p. 40 and BB1811–19, pp. 33, 45, 48, 54); L. Sterne, *The beauties of Sterne*, London, 1783; and W. Endfield, *The speaker* . . ., London, 1774. Benjamin Faulkner was also amongst those who advocated 'presenting objects of amusement, directing the attention, and humouring the imagination in those little sallies which sometimes indicate a desire of mental exertion' in the insane, op. cit., note 34 above, p. 23.

38. Hunter and Macalpine, op. cit., note 5 above, pp. 66, 71.

39. BB1802–11, p. 35 and BB1811–19, pp. 25, 45, 61, 99.

40. For items of furniture see, for example, BB1802–11, p. 99; BB1811–19, p. 45; Mr Green came with his mother in 1802 (BB1802–11, p. 22); Mrs Hayes and Mrs Chatfield with their servants (BB1792–1802, p. 61 and BB1802–11, p. 13). For writing paper/postage see, for example, BB1792–1802, pp. 10, 31, 72; BB1802–11, pp. 28, 57, 92; BB1811–19, pp. 45, 66.

41. Porter, op. cit., note 31 above, p. 20; and W.F. Bynum 'Rationales for therapy in British psychiatry, 1780–1835', *Medical History*, 1974, 18: 319.

42. William Pargeter also claimed to be able to control patients with an authoritative look; see Hunter and Macalpine, op. cit., note 2 above, pp. 538–9.

43. Michael MacDonald discusses Anglican advocacy of a medical approach to insanity, and the links between moral therapy and a dissenting tradition of psychological healing in 'Insanity and the realities of history in early modern England', *Psychological Medicine*, 1981, 11: 11–25; and 'Religion, social change and psychological healing in England 1600–1800', in W. Shiels (ed.), *The church and healing*, 1982, Oxford, Basil Blackwell, pp. 101–26.

44. [J. Perceval], op. cit., note 27 above, pp. 137, 142, 147–8, 149.

45. APA1828; BB1792–1802, p. 72; BB1802–11, index.

46. Revd Chambers paid three guineas a week, Revd Lofty and Mr Darnay two guineas a week (BB1792–1802, pp. 49, 72; BB1802–11, p. 68). For full details of the initial range of fees see MacKenzie, op. cit., note 22 above, p. 43.

47. BB1792–1802, pp. 26, 31, 46, 49, 61, 72, 86; BB1802–11, pp. 5, 27, 87; BB1811–19, pp. 61, 90, 110, 111; APA, 1828; *Medical Register*, 1783, p. 112.

48. BB1792–1802, pp. 10, 26, 31, 46, 49, 61, 72, 87; BB1802–11, pp. 5, 27, 87; BB1811–19, pp. 41, 61, 64, 78, 90, 103, 110, 111. Parry-Jones describes the Willises' clientele as 'fashionable and noble', op. cit., note 6 above, p. 76, note 1.

49. See MacKenzie, op. cit., note 22 above, p. 479.

50. *A return of the number of houses in each county or division of the county licensed for the reception of lunatics*, PP1819 (271.) XVII.131., pp. 2, 4.

51. The population of Hastings rose from 3,848 in 1811 to 6,085 in 1821 – an increase of about 60 per cent, in contrast to an overall growth in the county of around 20 per cent. Most Sussex towns expanded only slowly, for example, the population of Lewes rose from 6,221 to 7,083, and that of Rye from 2,681 to 3,599. *Abstracts of population returns for 1811*, PP1812(316.)(317.)XI.1–, pp. 336–8, 341; and *Population . . . according to the census of 1821*, 1822(502.) XV.1–, pp. 336–7, 341. Compare 1811 figures for Yalding, 312 families in a population of 2,059; and

58

Starting a family business

Mayfield, 415 families in a population of 2,079, *Abstracts . . . for 1811* pp. 141, 336, 339.

52. Country register, MH51/735 79595, pp. 62–4, 121; APA1828. The number of admissions to Ticehurst between 6 April 1802 and 23 December 1812, the period covered by the country register, was 254 (excluding paupers), compared to 97 admissions listed in the country register. Parry-Jones, op. cit., note 6 above, p. 46, note 1, cites the example of Droitwich Asylum, where only 2 of 619 admissions were listed in the country register.

53. See note 12 above; BB1811–19, p. 22.

54. A.S.L. Newington and H.F.H. Newington, 'Some incidents in the history and practice of Ticehurst asylum', *Journal of Mental Science*, 1901, 47: 64, transcribe a certificate dated 5 April 1803:

> To Mr Newington, Surgeon Ticehurst. By the direction of Mr Johnson, of Tenterden, I advise you to receive into your house Mr S. Johnson, jun., his son, who from epileptic fits is rendered incapable of conducting himself in society.

Other patients are listed in AP, 1843–5.

55. See MacKenzie, op. cit., note 22 above, p. 480.

56. APA, 1828; and RA, 1845–81.

57. Thirty-two male and thirty-one female patients were eventually readmitted. Of these, only four had a total length of stay of more than five years – two men and two women. For length-of-stay analysed by sex, see MacKenzie, op. cit., note 22 above, pp. 68 (note 83), 481–2.

58. Seven men and three women were transferred to St Lukes; two men to Bedlam; one man to Fisher House; and one woman to Holly House in Hoxton. BB1792–1802, pp. 17, 19, 21, 25, 37, 44; BB1802–11, pp. 9, 26, 32, 54, 55; BB1811–19, pp. 62, 95, 104.

59. BB1792–1802, p. 18; for Revd Courthope see *Alumni Cantab.*

60. For the effect of the Napoleonic wars on the British economy see, for example, G.D.H. Cole and R. Postgate, *The common people, 1746–1946*, London, Methuen & Co., 1971, p. 191. For fees see MacKenzie, op. cit., note 22 above, pp. 43 and 478.

61. BB1811–19, pp. 3, 22, 42, 110, 112. John Mayo (1761–1818) was a prominent FRCP – BA (Oxon) 1782; MD 1788; Censor of the Royal College of Physicians 1790, 1795, 1797, 1804, 1808; Harveian orator 1797; physician to the London Foundling Hospital 1787–1809, and Middlesex Hospital 1788–1803; Physician in Ordinary to the Princess of Wales. He lived in Tunbridge Wells during the summer months, where he '. . . took the undisputed lead in the medical business and emoluments of that town and neighbourhood' (*Munk's roll* II, p. 396) and settled there in 1817. See *Dictionary of national biography*.

62. M.A. Lower, *The worthies of Sussex . . .*, Lewes, printed for subscribers only by G.P. Bacon, 1865, p. 254. Newington and Newington, op. cit., note 54 above, p. 63.

63. BB1811–19, pp. 69, 98.

64. Of those patients admitted before 31 July 1817 who eventually stayed more than twenty – years, six paid the same on 31 July 1817 as they had paid on admission, meaning a decrease in real terms, and six had increased their fees. Despite post-war deflation, nine eventually increased their fees, two stayed the same, and one decreased his fees. BB1792–1802 – BB1851–61.

65. Mrs Owen, who came at £250 a year, BB1811–19, p. 95.

66. For conditions in licensed houses in 1815–16, see Parry-Jones, op. cit., note

Starting a family business

6 above, pp. 249–52; K. Jones, *Lunacy, law and conscience, 1744–1845*, London, Routledge & Kegan Paul, 1955, pp. 102–7; and A. Scull, *Museums of madness*, London, Allen Lane, 1979, pp. 79–81. For proposed legislation, see Jones, ibid., pp. 108–11 and Scull, ibid., pp. 82–6.

67. Scull, ibid., p. 190.

3

The asylum and moral reform

Vociferous public criticism of private madhouses in the late-Regency period was not a new phenomenon. Allegations of wrongful confinement, physical neglect and cruelty had accompanied the growth of the madhouse business. In the absence of new legislation, the 1815–16 select committee reports had few direct implications for institutions like Ticehurst. Indeed, in so far as the inquiries found little evidence of improper detention, and praised the treatment of private patients in some licensed houses, they helped to shift the focus of concern onto the absence of appropriate provision for pauper lunatics. However, in criticizing existing treatment of pauper patients, lunacy reformers reasserted the asylum's potential to cure, as well as care for, the insane. Claims like this helped to promote the case for spending public money on new county asylums, but could equally provide grounds for removing a patient who failed to recover from a private madhouse. In addition, prominent witnesses like the Quaker Edward Wakefield questioned the value of medical treatment in cases of insanity, and the vested interests of medical men in public and private asylums.[1] Given this, it is pertinent to consider how medical proprietors of respected licensed houses responded to the issues raised by the inquiries; and how they sought to justify continuing asylum care in the absence of recovery.

For licensees of established private asylums, decreasing the number of pauper admissions and low-fee-paying patients minimized the risk that abuses would develop through neglect and understaffing; but increased the importance of recruiting, and arguably keeping, high-fee-paying patients. Creating a genteel domestic environment could reassure prospective purchasers of asylum care, but it did little to further claims that asylum proprietors had developed special expertise in curing insanity. It is partly for this reason that Andrew Scull has argued that moral treatment formed a weaker professional ideology than medical models of insanity.[2] However, successful medical licensees like the second William Finch and Samuel Newington had always been eclectic in approach, stressing the

The asylum and moral reform

importance of management as well as medicine. In advertisements for Ticehurst, Samuel Newington had emphasized his ability to cure, as well as to manage, patients; but the asylum built its reputation on high standards of physical care rather than rates of recovery. Between the select-committee investigations of 1815 and 1816 Edward Wakefield visited Laverstock House, and was so impressed by Finch's regime that he became persuaded that madness 'in its incipient state is capable of relief from medicine'.[3] Nevertheless, the evidence from Ticehurst suggests that in the 1820s–30s the principles of moral therapy became increasingly dominant in treatment. Although the simplicity of moral treatment provided a weak basis for claims to professional expertise, its lack of pretension meant its principles were readily understood by the families of private patients. In the absence of recovery, moral management promised to moderate the extremes of mental disorder through persuasion rather than coercion; and continued confinement protected the family from irrational or bizarre behaviour. In the increasingly constrained moral climate of the 1830s, this had widespread middle- class appeal. The Newingtons were also able to capitalize more directly on the growing preoccupation with moral probity because, from the 1830s, doctors at Ticehurst made increasing use of the new diagnosis of 'moral insanity', and emphasised that this disorder might be amenable to moral treatment. Nevertheless, they never repudiated the value of medical therapy. It is worth exploring in more detail the kind of treatment which made Ticehurst highly marketable.

Doctors, patients and the asylum

Two sources make it possible to delineate a fuller picture of the kind of treatment which was offered to patients at Ticehurst in the 1820s and 1830s than when the asylum first opened. Firstly, the medical texts of Thomas Mayo (1790–1871), who became visiting physician to the asylum after the death of his father, John Mayo, in 1818. In addition to performing the routine inspections this appointment required him to carry out, Thomas Mayo acted as a consulting physician to patients in the asylum, and therefore shared decisions concerning treatment with Charles and Jesse Newington.[4] His writings make clear the influence of Evangelical moral values on treatment at Ticehurst. Secondly, a patient's perspective on treatment is provided by John Perceval's account of his stay at the asylum in the early 1830s. As a son of the former British prime minister, Spencer Perceval, John Perceval represented one of the higher-class patients the Newingtons increasingly sought to attract. Nevertheless, his writings are critical of the way in which he was treated by Mayo and Charles Newington.[5]

What was Thomas Mayo's evaluation of medical and moral treatment?

The asylum and moral reform

As the son of a high-class physician, he had received a classical education with private tutors and at Oriel College, Oxford, where he graduated with a first-class degree in 1811. In 1813, Mayo was elected a fellow of Oriel College, and went on to take a BM (1815) and DM (1818). Amongst those to whom he could have talked over dinner and in the common room, were two men who were to help shape the religious and educational character of Victorian England, John Keble (1792–1866) and Thomas Arnold (1795–1842). In 1817, Mayo published his first book, *Remarks on insanity, founded on the practice of John Mayo, M.D.*, in which he outlined his philosophy of mental disorders. The book revealed his commitment both to medicine and to Christianity.

In the wake of criticism of medical treatment in the select committee reports, Mayo argued strongly that insanity was a physical disease. Although he suggested that mental diseases could have mental causes, it was implicit from the rest of his argument that these could never be sufficient. Insanity was always accompanied by physical changes requiring physical treatment, and although courteous attention should be paid to patients' feelings, Mayo assessed the relative value of medical and moral therapies in this way:

> We will suppose a patient left negatively, if we may use the expression, in respect of moral regimen. He is continued in the same comfortable state which he was in before he became insane; – he is treated, when violent, with humanity, but he is repressed by the strait waistcoat. No precaution is taken to break morbid associations – no care to furnish him with others that are agreeable – no attempt to make an impression by well-chosen appeals upon his wavering intellect. . . . Allow us the medical regimen which we have sketched, and we shall indulge fair hopes of curing the patient. But, reverse the means of cure; let the degree of medical regimen be no more than analogous to the moral in the first case which we have supposed, – we shall no longer answer for the event: though we are very far from denying, that even here nature may cure the patient in spite of the physician.[6]

From this perspective, the extensive new 'pleasure grounds' at Ticehurst, and attempts to rouse patients' interest in rational recreations, would be seen as having negligible therapeutic value.

As Bynum has argued, Mayo's repudiation of moral therapy was partly inspired by the threat which lay therapists might pose to the medical profession if insanity were seen as a psychological rather than a physical disorder – he wrote 'To vindicate the rights of [his] profession over Insanity, and to elucidate its medical treatment.'[7] Yet a deeper fear which was implicit in his attacks on 'metaphysical views of insanity' was the challenge which psychogenetic theories of mental disorder posed to the Christian theological doctrine of free will. For the same reason he attacked

63

The asylum and moral reform

the vitalism of Cullen for seductively and almost imperceptibly opening the door to a materialist philosophy of mind.[8]

Since Mayo saw insanity as being due to vascular congestion of the brain, the therapy he recommended was primarily depletive: bleeding and cupping; the almost daily use of purges and nauseants; and the application of caustic issues and setons as counter-irritants. Sweat-promoting and cooling agents were also, although less strongly, recommended.[9] Mayo criticized the Chester surgeon George Nesse Hill (1766–1831) for attempting to introduce a distinction between sthenic and asthenic cases, and prescribing tonic medicines for asthenic patients. Mayo believed that even in cases of extreme physical weakness, tonic medicines were inadvisable, although a tonic regimen of regular exercise and a supportive diet was recommended. He advised against the use of sedative drugs, rather than depletion, to quell excitement.[10]

What little evidence there is in the accounts reflecting treatment at Ticehurst during these years does not contradict this profile, although it is impossible to estimate whether depletive therapies were as prominent as Mayo advised. In July 1818, a patient called John Chatfield 'began with three glasses of port per day', presumably as part of a tonic diet. Other patients also made routine payments for port and other wines.[11] However, payments made to Dr Mayo do not specify what treatment was given, nor whether medicines were prescribed. Only one patient was listed as being charged for 'medicines', and her bill does not specify what these were.[12] A belief in the importance of nutrition was evident in the fact that Charles Newington's only published article described an instrument which he had devised to force-feed patients. 'An instrument invented for administering food and medicine to maniacs by the mouth, during a closed state of the teeth' (1826) vividly conveys the face-to-face confrontation between patient and doctor that force-feeding involved. 'I can truly aver', wrote Charles Newington, 'that no part of actual and personal superintendence can be more disagreeable or revolting than the task of forcing food upon a contumacious patient by the methods usually pursued'. He claimed that his own method – of passing a piece of curved metal piping through the gap behind the patient's molar teeth, into which food could be injected from a syringe – resulted in fewer cut lips and broken teeth than feeding with a feeding-cup or 'boat'.[13] This apparatus was in fact a modification of the stomach-pump which had been invented by a local manufacturer of hydraulic syringes, John Read (1760–1847).[14]

Charges made to two patients in 1827 and 1828 for 'Waistcoats (strait)' suggest that mechanical restraint continued to be used at Ticehurst.[15] This impression is confirmed by John Perceval's account of his confinement at Ticehurst in 1832. Following an escape attempt in April, Perceval had his hands confined at night.[16] However, as for the earlier period, it is difficult to assess how routinely mechanical restraint was used. Although after

Charles Newington's death in 1852 the Commissioners in Lunacy claimed that he had: 'gradually but steadily discard[ed] the use of instrumental restraint to an extent which of late almost amounted to its abolition,'[17] it seems likely that, if this was more than a rhetorical tribute to a mid-nineteenth-century psychiatrist, it was a policy which Charles Newington pursued most vigorously after the non-restraint movement gained popularity in the late 1830s and early 1840s. Commissioners' reports in the early 1840s commented regularly on how few patients were restrained at Ticehurst.[18] It is however clear that by the early 1830s, seclusion was used as well as restraint. One of John Perceval's fellow patients, John Allsopp, showed Perceval a room 'in which he was confined when violent', although Perceval does not make it clear whether or not this room contained instruments of restraint.[19] In 1838, Mayo wrote of the value of 'coercion gently applied' in protecting patients against themselves, as well as the importance of 'perfect quiet and a darkened room'.[20]

These were prosperous years for the Newington family. Although admissions began to decline, by 31 July 1820 the number of patients resident in the asylum had risen to fifty (see Tables 3.1 and 3.2). Despite post-war deflation which returned most prices to pre-war levels, the median charge

Table 3.1   Admissions to the asylum, 1817–42

Figures do not include admissions to the Highlands
Numbers in brackets represent known readmissions
Years run from 1 August to 31 July

Years	Men	Women	Sex unknown	Total
1817–22	59 (4)	57 (7)	1	117 (11)
1822–7	40 (4)	46 (7)	1 (1)	87 (12)
1827–32	34 (3)	38 (3)		72 (6)
1832–7	28 (6)	21 (2)		49 (8)
1837–42	24 (1)	10 (1)		34 (2)
Subtotal	185 (18)	172 (20)	2 (1)	359 (39)
Total	203	192	3	398

Sources: BB1811–19 to BB1840–6

Table 3.2   Number of patients resident in the asylum, 1820–40

Figures are for 31 July of each year and do not include the Highlands

Year	Men	Women	Total
1820	27	23	50
1825	29	18	47
1830	30	18	48
1835	30	25	55
1840	34	27	61

Sources: See Table 3.1

The asylum and moral reform

Table 3.3 Pauper admissions to the asylum, 1817–42

Numbers in brackets represent known readmissions
Years run from 1 August to 31 July

Years	Men	Women	Both
1817–22	1	3 (1)	4 (1)
1822–7		3*	3
1827–32			
1832–7			
1837–42			
Subtotal	1	6 (1)	7 (1)
Total	1	7	8

*Including one patient who only had part of their bill paid by the parish
Sources: See Table 3.1

for first admissions remained one guinea per week until the late 1820s, and that for patients resident in the asylum dropped by only one quarter, to one and a half guineas per week.[21] In May 1819 the first recorded admission had been made to Charles Newington's own home, the Highlands, certified by Thomas Mayo and Samuel Playsted Newington; but the house was not licensed to take more than one patient until 1830.[22]

The increase of pauperism in Sussex and Kent in the 1820s–30s did not lead to more pauper admissions to Ticehurst. On the contrary, the proportion of pauper patients admitted declined, and the last pauper admission was made in 1825 (see Table 3.3). While Charles Newington may have wanted to decrease the number of pauper admissions, it is also likely that, burdened by increasing numbers of dependants, parish overseers were unwilling to pay fees as high as one guinea a week. In 1825, a second private asylum had been opened in Sussex at Balsdean in Rottingdean. This asylum, which took mainly pauper patients, transferred to a former army barracks at Ringmer in 1829. Up to twenty pauper patients were maintained there, at a cost of 15s. per week each. Nevertheless, magistrates who visited the asylum in 1830 complained that even this charge was too high.[23] Although a return for 1830 lists more pauper lunatics than were maintained at Ringmer as being cared for in private madhouses, it is also known that some pauper lunatics from Sussex were sent to metropolitan asylums.[24] In 1833, Kent became one of the few counties in England to build a county asylum for pauper lunatics under the permissive legislation of 1808 (48 Geo. III, *c.*96).

However, the economic depression of these years is reflected in the continuing occasional instances of patients who were unable to settle their bills. For example, in May 1819, a Mr Robinson paid only £10 of a £21 bill because 'he could not pay any more' (*sic*); in 1823, a Miss Bertrand was given four weeks' treatment free of charge; and in 1827, a Mrs Cosham

The asylum and moral reform

from Laughton and a Mr Boorman from Cranbrook were given £5.13s.0d. and £3.19s.8d., respectively. Other patients were permitted to settle their bills in kind: by flour, by timber, by faggots and by groceries.[25] One of Charles Newington's obituarists recalled his generosity towards patients:

> there were at the Asylum, for years, many inmates who had seen better days, who had been admitted upon a nominal payment, and who in the course of time had become almost friendless: these, however, were fed, clothed, and cared for, on a pittance which scarcely renumerated him for their daily bread.[26]

However, at least until 31 July 1830, most patients who would eventually stay more than twenty years in the asylum paid either the same fees or more than when they were admitted. Only five patients had reduced their fees, by a total of £165 a year; while the increase of six guineas a week paid by one patient alone from December 1827 onwards amounted to over £300 a year. The only patient who actually became bankrupt was removed from the asylum.[27] The waiving of fees in cases like those illustrated above enhanced Charles Newington's reputation for disinterested kindness without in any way damaging the increasing profitability of Ticehurst.

Profits were ploughed back to improve the attributes of the asylum. As the obituarist above rather laconically expressed it: 'There was always some new conservatory or aviary, some pagoda or flower garden, some ever-green alley or artificial fountain, to construct, in order to make the place more attractive and comfortable.'[28] In 1826, a gallery for patients was built in Ticehurst parish church; and in the early 1830s work was begun on a chapel in the asylum. The 1828 Madhouses Act had stated that divine service should be performed in asylums on Sundays; and Ticehurst was slower in fulfilling this than both Brislington House and Laverstock House, where Anglican services were available from 1828–9.[29] Nevertheless, the decision to build a gallery for patients in the parish church in 1826, suggests Charles Newington had some spontaneous interest in providing opportunities for worship. Similarly, his generosity towards poorer patients may reveal a preoccupation with probationary acts of benevolence, which was characteristic of Evangelicals who painted on the narrow canvas of private business, rather than a broad canvas of political and social reform.

A prospectus drawn up in 1827–8 reflected the lavish scale of Ticehurst.[30] The ground plan included in the prospectus illustrated the availability of private, as well as shared, facilities; but all the pictorial engravings are of the asylum's exterior and grounds rather than the interior. The presence of children – perhaps representing Charles and Eliza Newington's youngest son and daughter, Alexander and Eliza – and of men riding out on horseback and in a gig suggest the desired impression was of an ordinary, if substantial, country house (see Plates 1 and 2). It is not clear, for example, that windows to the patients' bedrooms and sitting

A South-East View of the Asylum at Ticehurst, Sussex.

Plate 1

A View of the Pleasure Grounds and Aviary.

Plate 2

The asylum and moral reform

rooms were barred.[31] The grounds' total appearance, with sheep and cattle grazing, and gardeners at work, suggests an ordered and well-tended country estate. It is difficult to imagine struggles to force-feed patients, or get them into strait waistcoats, going on inside here. Only the presence of attendants walking several paces behind their charges in some of the smaller illustrations reflected the supervisory role of the asylum (see Plate 3).

John Perceval's account of his confinement at Ticehurst from February–December 1832 provides more details of what the interior of the asylum was like.[32] At £360 per annum, or six and a half guineas per week, John Perceval was one of Ticehurst's highest-paying patients, and the quality of care which he received must represent the upper end of Ticehurst's range.[33] However, it seems likely that the basic style of decoration and furnishings would have been the same throughout the asylum. The ethos which John Perceval described was one which approximated as closely as possible to a fairly prosperous middle-class domestic environment.

As a high-fee-paying patient, John Perceval had both a single bedroom and a single sitting room. This is how he described his sitting room:

> [It] had the walls papered, the floor carpeted, a sofa in it, a small book-case, mahogany table and chairs, a marble chimney-piece, a large sash-window; a cheerful fire in the grate without a wire guard; and although there was an appearance of shabbiness and hardness, there was nothing unnecessarily coarse to remind me of my situation, excepting a wooden stake for stirring the fire; which, however, was meant to supply the place of the fire-irons. The absence of these, and of any lock to the door, and the heavy perpendicular iron bars at the window, alone recalled to me in my room that I was a prisoner.[34]

Wooden pokers were probably introduced at Ticehurst after an incident in which Charles Newington was hit over the head with an iron poker by a patient.[35] In addition to the items described above, Perceval was given a writing desk and a piano.[36] His bedroom, too, was:

> cheerful, airy and respectable; the walls were papered . . . a chest of drawers stood in it, with a looking-glass, a washhand-stand and basins etc., etc., only the beds were without curtains or hangings of any description . . . the window, like the fellow to it in my room below stairs, had perpendicular iron bars to it.[37]

At night, his clothes were taken from the room. An attendant slept in the room with him, but even so the door, like the door to his sitting room during the day, was bolted from outside.[38]

The criticisms which John Perceval made of Ticehurst may be divided into two groups: firstly, his objections to being closely supervised, and the object of what he experienced as individually undiscriminating, what

70

The asylum and moral reform

might at a later date be called institutionalized, methods of treatment; and secondly, complaints of bad management. Perceval objected to the lack of privacy caused by the nearly constant presence of attendants, and a spy-hole in the door of his sitting room through which he could be watched even when unattended; he also complained that there were no fastenings on the lavatory doors, so that other people burst in while he was using the toilet.[39] He resented the lack of trust with which he was treated, for example, in not being allowed to travel to London to see a physician, whom he wanted to testify to the deterioration in his health which he claimed had occurred at Brislington House.[40] More surprising than these precautions were Perceval's complaints of poor management: that the food was bad; that the asylum was cold; that pans of excrement were left to be examined in poorly ventilated corridors; and that attendants and patients were frequently 'whistling, singing, fluting, fifing, fiddling, laughing, talking, running, and even occasionally dancing in the passages and wrestling.'[41] For Perceval, the tedium of 'pale and sodden' meat, 'mouldy' bread and pastry, and 'bad' beer (which was brewed on the premises) was relieved only by the occasional glass of sherry.[42]

One striking feature of the treatment Perceval received at Ticehurst was the small part played by medical therapy. He described Charles Newington as reluctant to prescribe medicines, refusing even to let Perceval drink the local chalybeate water. However, Charles Newington's reluctance to give Perceval a tonic was in keeping with their proscription by Thomas Mayo, and cannot be taken as indicating an absence of medical therapy in general. It is possible, for example, that attacks of diarrhoea of which Perceval also complained were the result of the administration of purgatives.[43] The only other medical advice which Charles Newington gave John Perceval was when Perceval began running as well as walking during his daily exercise, and Newington warned him that running might 'overheat' his brain. This caution was clearly coloured by a recent escape attempt which Perceval had made. The centrality of at least moderate exercise to the regimen practised at Ticehurst may be inferred from the fact that the day after his escape attempt, Perceval was allowed to go out for a walk, although accompanied by two attendants rather than one.[44]

How much is it possible to generalize from John Perceval's account of his experiences about treatment at Ticehurst? In the absence of further evidence, it is impossible to say how true Perceval's complaints of bad food, inadequate heating and poor ventilation may have been. Certainly early visitors' reports were univocal in their praise for conditions at Ticehurst.[45] It is easier to substantiate the ways in which patients were encouraged to pursue rational mental activities like making music, writing and reading. Other patients were charged for tuning or repairing a musical instrument, buying writing paper or books; and there was a music room and reading room in the asylum. The encouragement of exercise is documented by

The Moss-house and part of the Pleasure Grounds.

Plate 3

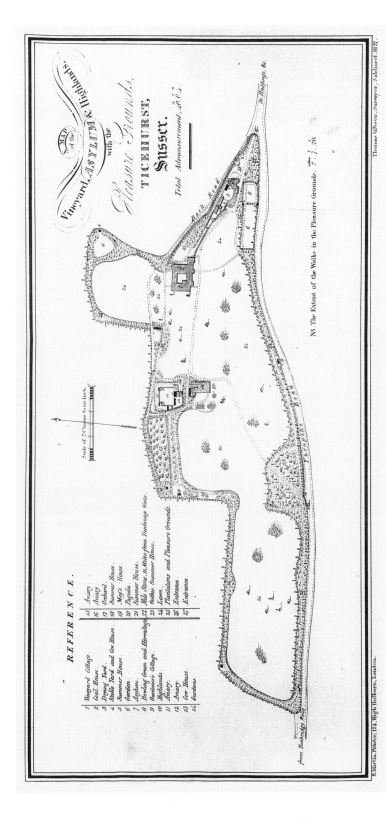

Plate 4

The asylum and moral reform

occasional entries in the accounts for horse-hire and horse-keep, as well as the walks mapped out in the 'pleasure grounds', and the presence of a bowling green in the grounds (see Plate 4).[46]

Perceval was also encouraged to mix with other patients. From the accounts, it is possible to identify who these patients were: Henry Charles Blincowe (who Perceval described as Mr B——, pseudonymed Blake, whose voices called him 'Harry'); Charles Nunn (Mr Nunn, since he was dead by the time of publication); Alexander Goldsmid (Mr G——th, an elderly Jewish gentleman); and John Allsopp (Mr A——p, a medical student). All of these patients paid above-average fees of four guineas a week or more, suggesting that social divisions were maintained within the asylum.[47] Although Perceval described Henry Blincowe as 'imbecile', he was listed in 1845 as suffering from 'delusions'. Other high-fee-paying patients in this period with whom Perceval was not encouraged to mix – such as the the only titled patient in Ticehurst at this time, Sir William Walter Yea (1784–1862); one of Harriet Martineau's cousins, David Martineau (1798–1856), whose sister Emily was also in the asylum; and a patient called Page Keble (1779–1848) – were all described in 1842 as 'incurable', and diagnosed in 1845 as suffering from 'imbecility' or 'amentia'. Although John Allsopp was described by 1842 as 'incurable', Henry Blincowe and Alexander Goldsmid were described simply as 'not cured'.[48] This would suggest that, apart from social considerations, association with other patients who were believed to be curable was encouraged because it was thought to be morally therapeutic. Perceval and Goldsmid struck up a friendship: walking, playing the piano and discussing religion together.[49]

Perceval described Charles Newington as rather snobbish, claiming that he 'seemed to think it a feather in his cap to have one of my name in his asylum'.[50] Whatever Newington's religious convictions were, he was willing to exercise a pragmatic religious tolerance in accepting dissenters and Jews as patients – like the Unitarian Martineaus, the Methodist Stephen Dickenson and Alexander Goldsmid – some of whom also paid high fees.[51] The continuous improvements to the grounds and main building can also be taken as evidence that Charles Newington was eager to better his social standing. In the early 1830s, apart from the chapel, two new wings were built on to the asylum, and a covered walkway – the 'Chinese Gallery' – in which patients could exercise on wet days, was constructed and decorated with black oak which had been excavated at Burwash. By 1835, the buildings and grounds were sufficiently lavish to fill more than six pages of Thomas Horsfield's coffee-table county history of Sussex, including two full-page engravings of the Highlands and the Chinese Gallery.[52]

This was class, but it was also advertising. Horsfield wrote that: 'At Highlands in this parish there is an establishment for the reception of insane persons, the inmates of which are of the highest class.'[53] Admissions

The asylum and moral reform

to the Highlands – which was only licensed to take four patients in 1830 – were indeed almost exclusively upper-class.[54] However, an analysis of the former occupations of first admissions to the Asylum between 1 August 1817 and 31 July 1845 shows a wide social range – from baronets to domestic servants – but suggests about two-thirds of first admissions were middle-class. Unfortunately, these statistics represent only about one-third of male first admissions, and one-fifth of female first admissions. In addition, many female patients' marital status is listed as their 'former occupation', with no indication of their social class.[55] A closer focus on first admissions between 1 August 1827 and 31 July 1832, for which information is available for more than three-quarters of male first admissions, and over half of female first admissions, suggests the professional and commercial middle-class, and tenant farmers, continued to form the majority of new admissions to Ticehurst up until the early 1830s (see Table 3.4). It would make sense for the proprietor of an asylum like this to feel that his reputation might be enhanced by the admission of a former prime-minister's son.

However, after 31 July 1832, the median length of stay for first admissions increased from under six months to over one year (see Table 3.6). The median length of stay for patients resident in the asylum had been rising steadily since 1815, but plateaued from 1830 onwards at 20–35 years (see Table 3.7). Despite the increased accommodation provided by the new wings, and a rise in the number of patients resident in the asylum, the admission rate continued to fall steadily (see Tables 3.1 and 3.2). A sharp increase in fees charged to first admissions after 31 July 1832, to about three guineas, suggests Charles Newington was able to be increasingly selective in his choice of patients.[56] Although details of former occupations of first admissions are available for less than half first male admissions, and less than one-third of first female admissions between 1 August 1832 and 31 July 1845, those which are known reflect an increasing proportion of upper-class admissions (see Table 3.5). The increased protection provided by the 1828 Madhouses Act, and new methods of publicizing the asylum, had worked to Charles Newington's benefit in raising Ticehurst's status.

Most first admissions throughout this period continued to come from Sussex and Kent, but the change in the social composition of first admissions to the asylum was paralleled by an expansion of the geographical area from which they were drawn (see Figure 3.1). Despite the decline in the admissions rate, this suggests a widening reputation which would have further enhanced Charles Newington's freedom to be selective in the patients he admitted. People travelled from as far away as Yorkshire, Wales, Ireland and France to become patients at Ticehurst.[57]

With the ending of pauper admissions, and the expansion of the geographical area from which private patients were drawn, any correlation

The asylum and moral reform

Table 3.4 Former occupations of first admissions to the asylum, 1 August 1827 to 31 July 1832

Figures do not include admissions to the Highlands

	Men	Women	Both
Independent:	3	3	6
No occupation/none		4	4
Church: Clergyman	2		2
Army: Officer	1		1
Captain	2		2
Cornet	1		1
Medicine: Surgeon	2		2
Law: Solicitor	2		2
Agriculture: Farmer	5		5
Commerce/trade: Merchant	2		2
Auctioneer	1		1
Miller	2		2
Grocer's son	1		1
Clerk: Bank of England	1		1
Other: Assistant teacher		1	1
Painter	1		1
Domestic Service: Butler	1		1
Servant		1	1
Wife/Widow		9	9
Spinster		2	2
Unknown	7	18	25
Total	34	38	72

Sources: See Table 3.1; also APA1828 and AP1842–5

Table 3.5 Former occupations of first admissions to the asylum, 1 August 1832 to 31 July 1845

Figures do not include admissions to the Highlands

	Men	Women	Both
Independent:	11*	13	24
No occupation/none	1		1
Church:	9		9
Army: Colonel	1		1
Captain	3		3
Medicine: Surgeon	1		1
Law: Law student	1		1
Agriculture: Farmer	5		5
Commerce/trade: Silk manufacturer	1		1
Other: Sailor	1		1
Unknown	32	30	62
Total	66	43	109

*Including two baronets
Sources: See Table 3.4

The asylum and moral reform

Table 3.6 Length of stay of first admissions to the asylum, 1817–42

Figures do not include admissions to the Highlands
Years run from 1 August to 31 July

Length of stay	1817–22	1822–7	1827–32	1832–7	1837–42	Total
Up to 7 days	1					1
8 days–4 wks	7	2	5		1	15
4+–13 wks	35	20	19	2	3	79
13+–26 wks	34*	27*	17*	10	6	94
26+ wks–1 yr	14	14	12	10	6	56
1+–2 yrs	7	4	2	8*	4*	25
2+–5 yrs	6	11	4	7	4	32
5+–10 yrs	3	5	2	3	1	14
10+–20 yrs	3	1	5	3	3	15
20+–35 yrs	2	2	4	5	5	18
35+–55 yrs	5	1	1	1		8
55+ yrs			1			1
Unknown					1	1
Total	117	87	72	49	34	359

*Median length of stay
Sources: See Table 3.1; also RDD1845–90

Table 3.7 Length of stay of patients resident in the asylum, 1820–40

The figures are for 31 July of each year and do not include the Highlands

Length of stay	1820	1825	1830	1835	1840
4+–13 wks	2	2			
13+–26 wks	5	3	1	2	
26+ wks–1 yr	6	1	1	1	1
1+–2 yrs	4	1	1	4	2
2+–5 yrs	7	5	6	3	4
5+–10 yrs	4*	6	8	4	3
10+–20 yrs	7	7*	6	12	12
20+–35 yrs	4	8	10*	13*	21*
35+–55 yrs	9	11	12	12	13
55+ yrs	2	3	3	4	5
Total	50	47	48	55	61

*Median length of stay
Sources: See Table 3.6

between the asylum's admissions rate and an estimation of existing need or demand within the counties of Kent and Sussex becomes increasingly tenuous. As before, no simple correlation existed between the size of towns and parishes in Sussex and Kent and the number of patients they sent to Ticehurst.[58] However, there was a striking decline in the proportion of first admissions who came from small villages in the immediate vicinity of Ticehurst in favour of more distant and commercial centres, most notably Dover (see Figure 3.2). The growth and gentrification of Tunbridge Wells

The asylum and moral reform

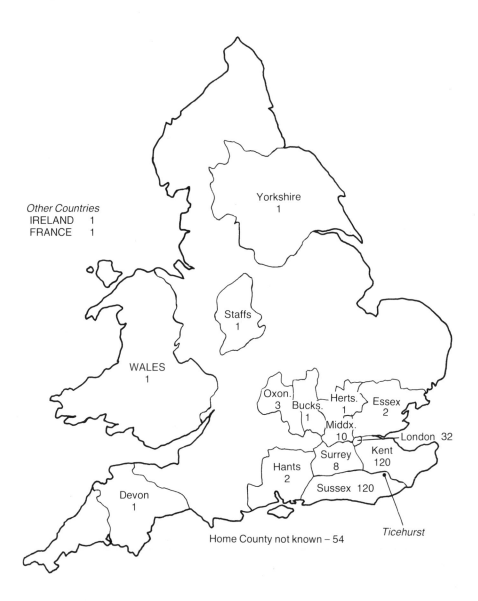

Figure 3.1 Place of origin of first admissions to the asylum, 1817–42.

The asylum and moral reform

in this period is reflected in an increase in the proportion of first admissions who came from there. Towards the end of the period covered by this chapter, in April 1840, Samuel Wilmott Newington, Samuel Playsted's son, opened a small private asylum at Goudhurst in Kent called Tattlebury House, which henceforward shared the Kentish private asylum clientele.[59]

Throughout the 1820s, the only doctor who is known to have referred more than one or two patients was Thomas Mayo. Most of the ten patients whose certificates he signed between 1819 and 1833 were high-class, and high-fee-paying. They included David Martineau, and Sir William Walter Yea. In addition, these patients stayed longer than was average for first admissions: eight of them stayed for more than ten years, and four of these for more than thirty years.[60] Thomas Mayo's involvement in the certification of patients was clearly contrary to the spirit, although not the letter, of the 1828 Madhouses Act, which sought to make it illegal for doctors with an interest in a private asylum to certify admissions to that asylum. Despite this Mayo certified four more admissions to Ticehurst after the passing of the Act, and before he left his appointment as visiting physician in 1835.[61]

The nature of Thomas Mayo's involvement in the treatment of patients at Ticehurst needs to be elaborated. From what has been said so far, it might be possible to infer that some tension existed between Thomas Mayo's advocacy of a strongly medically based therapy, and Charles Newington's pursuit of moral–therapeutic fashionability through the elaborate ornamentation of Ticehurst's grounds. However, later medical writings by Thomas Mayo suggest that his experience in practice at Ticehurst and elsewhere substantially modified the extreme heroicism of his first publication, and persuaded him that moral therapy could be both effective and desirable.

The title of Mayo's *Elements of the pathology of the human mind* (1838) made clear this change of position. In terms of medical treatment there were two striking changes in Mayo's argument: firstly, a new caution about chronic depletion; and secondly, in the absence of depletion, a new reliance on sedatives. Although Mayo still argued that the plethoric inflammation of the brain found in insanity indicated that blood-letting could be beneficial, he now cautioned that the expected advantages from depletion should be weighed against how exhausted the patient was by the disease. Telling a cautionary tale of a patient in 'an establishment' whose condition dramatically worsened after leeches were applied to her temples, Mayo argued that patients of a sanguine or bilious temperament could generally withstand more blood-letting than patients of a nervous or serous temperament. While patients of a serous temperament required moderate depletion through the application of counter-irritants, patients of a nervous temperament required tonics.[62] In practice, this distinction reads as remarkably close to Nesse Hill's distinction between sthenic and asthenic patients which Mayo had repudiated in 1817.

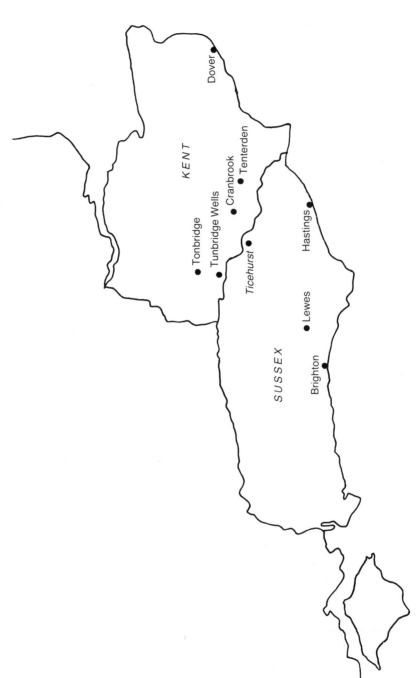

Figure 3.2 Towns and villages from which seven or more patients were admitted to the asylum, 1817–42.

The asylum and moral reform

In 1838, Mayo still strongly recommended the routine use of purgatives and nauseants to decongest the system, although he now advised greater moderation in the use of purgatives on patients of a nervous temperament. The specific drugs he mentioned were different from those which he had formerly recommended: in 1838 he praised colocynth rather than aloes and calomel as a purgative; and ipecacuanha as well as tartrate of antimony as a nauseant. In place of the strong narcotic stramonium, and belladonna, which John Mayo had found counter-productive, Thomas Mayo recommended the use of a more mild mixture of digitalis, camphor and potassium nitrate, as well as a mixture of extract of lettuce, camphor and colocynth – the purgative in the latter instance being included to counteract the depressive effect of sedation. Only extract of henbane (hyoscyamus) was recommended for its sedative properties in both texts; while opium was proscribed in both.[63]

There is insufficient evidence to document the extent to which these various remedies were employed in practice at Ticehurst. One plausible argument might be that increased sedation was associated with a substitution of chemical for mechanical restraint, as well as more moderate depletion. However, Anne Digby has also documented an increased use of sedation at the Retreat during the second quarter of the nineteenth century, the beginnings of which preceded a decrease in the Retreat's already very limited use of mechanical restraint, in the wake of the non-restraint movement in the 1840s and 1850s. In particular, in the 1830s Thomas Allis introduced a combined sedative and nauseating pill (of morphine and tartrate of antimony) which was used in place of more aggressive vomitives.[64] Although by the 1850s there was widespread concern that nauseants like tartrate of antimony were used primarily as a method of chemical restraint, Thomas Mayo's preference for milder sedatives than opium, and concern to counteract the depressive effects of sedation, suggest a desire to leave tranquillized patients mentally alert enough to co-operate actively with moral therapy, whether or not they were physically restrained.[65]

Moral therapy, moral insanity and moral reform

Central to Mayo's understanding of how moral therapy worked, and vital to the preservation of a concept of free will within a psychogenetic theory of mental disorder, was the belief that the patient could play an active role in their recovery.[66] Mayo's first published discussion of the psychology of mental disorders was in an article on 'Insanity and its moral preventive' in the first edition of the *London Review* in February 1829. This appeared alongside Edwin Chadwick's article 'On a preventive police', which became a blueprint for the new police force then being introduced into London by Sir Robert Peel.[67] Mayo's article argued for a strong enforcement of the

81

The asylum and moral reform

law in cases of crimes committed by lunatics, since he believed that the insane could know what was illegal and fear punishment even when they were incapable of making a moral distinction between right and wrong.[68]

Although Mayo's penal philosophy was utilitarian, his psychology was so only in a limited sense, since for Mayo a mental state in which the will was so weakened or absent that the mind was governed by the pursuit of pleasure and avoidance of pain was symptomatic of moral depravity and insanity.[69] In 1829, Mayo called this 'insanity of the heart' rather than 'moral insanity', but it was clear that the organic location was intended metaphorically. What his choice of phrase made clear was the influence of Evangelical writings on his ideas: Mayo's sense that emotional disorders were caused by 'vicious motives' which ought ideally to be restrained through self-control was close to the Evangelical emphasis on the need for a constantly vigilant 'religion of the heart' to prevent moral collapse into a naturally sinful condition.[70]

Like Mayo's metaphorical use of 'heart' in this context, the classical humoral tradition of temperaments provided a language in which to express a common-sense bridging of Cartesian metaphysics. However, in an 1831 *Essay on the influence of temperament in modifying dyspepsia or indigestion*, Mayo felt that it was advisable to spell out that in describing the interdependence of mental and physical states, he was being only softly determinist, since if 'a given bodily state is followed by a corresponding mental state . . . the arranging and ordering of our body, so that it may best assist our moral and intellectual energies involves a part of our probationary duties.'[71] In a later essay, Mayo argued that it was also the duty of parents and educators to 'counteract or modify' temperament. Using Aristotle's argument that people were accountable for actions which spring from deeply seated habits, even when these affected their freedom of will, he suggested that the morally insane were culpable, and should be sent to the penitentiary 'in the way of education'.[72] Mayo was thus unwilling to allow the concept of emotional disorder to become grounds for a blame-free status before the law, as Prichard was prepared to let it become in his now classic description of 'moral insanity' in 1835.[73]

Like his plea in 1817 for heroic medical treatment in cases of insanity, the thrust of Mayo's 1834 *Essay on the relation of the theory of morals to insanity* was towards a more active and interventionist role for medicine. However, the emphasis was now on prevention rather than cure. Seeking to marry the medical profession's responsibility for insanity to widespread middle-class concern with moral reform, Mayo advocated the incarceration of the morally insane who had not committed crimes in new, reforming institutions, 'between a well-regulated school and a madhouse'.[74] Although one of Mayo's descriptions of the morally insane was of two middle-class men – one of whom could not be certified under existing legislation because he was simply 'profusely extravagant . . . stern

The asylum and moral reform

. . . violent . . . [and] utterly unjust', but the other of whom was certifiable because he also heard voices – most of Mayo's examples were drawn from the upper classes and aristocracy.[75] Indeed, his writings on moral insanity can best be understood when viewed as part of the growing middle-class critique of the extravagance, injustice and irreligion of the aristocracy.

A suggestive historical comparison might be the reform of Rugby school carried out by Mayo's college contemporary, Thomas Arnold. Indeed, it was partly to mop up those who had been expelled from the newly reformed public schools that Mayo believed new institutions were needed.[76] As at Ticehurst, fees at Rugby were increased in the early 1830s to exclude the children of local families, and attract a more affluent, upper-class clientele. Just as John Chandos has argued some pupils at Rugby responded to Arnold's moral surveillance of his social superiors as 'dishonourable prying', John Perceval bitterly resented his letters being opened and read at Ticehurst and Brislington House: 'For by what right can a doctor presume to pry into the secrets of a patient's conscience, who is not only a perfect stranger to him, but also a gentleman.'[77] Yet clearly the ethos of moral improvement generated at Rugby School, and purveyed in the writings of Thomas Mayo, was one which resonated with the perceived needs of families who sent their children to Rugby, or referred their mentally disturbed relatives to Thomas Mayo.

Despite broad similarities in the social needs they appealed to, there were significant differences in the philosophies and practice of Mayo and Arnold. While Arnold found it 'very startling to see so much of sin combined with so little sorrow' in the behaviour of his pupils, Mayo argued more naturalistically that individuals who were lacking in moral sense experienced less conflict over their immoral actions than those with larger consciences. Indeed, Mayo explicitly criticized theories of education which were based on a belief in a universal moral sense. However, this was not because he accepted utilitarian arguments for the post-natal formation of conscience through association. For Mayo, the belief that some people who had been given opportunities for moral learning nevertheless failed to acquire a moral sense was evidence that they lacked an innate moral potential; and he argued that to accept such a lack in some instances compromised 'our belief in the general law' of free will less than the idea that the morally insane were weak-willed.[78] In 1838, he drew an analogy between the 'destitution of principle' found in such individuals, and the absence of intellectual capabilities found in idiocy, and suggested, contrary to his earlier opinion, that what he now called 'Brutality' could not properly be regarded as a form of insanity, which implied only 'perversion of tendencies and want of self-control'.[79]

In the absence of moral sense, a rigorous and vigilant authority could only hope to instil morally undiscriminating habits of good behaviour. Thus although Mayo described 'A high and enlightened religious feeling' as the prime moral preventive of insanity, he believed 'the motives and sanctions of revealed religion' to be beyond the comprehension of those who had no conscience, and therefore that religious instruction would be wasted on 'Brutal' patients.[80] This disdain for an empty pursuit of the forms of religion in the absence of moral understanding also confirms the influence of Evangelicalism on Mayo, with its distinction between 'real' and 'nominal' Christianity. The only case Mayo described in detail from Ticehurst where an absence of religious observance was made explicit was of a 'Brutal' boy – 'N.B.' – whom it was unfortunately not possible to identify from the accounts. Perceval complained that Charles Newington refused to allow him to attend church. However, given the role of religion in Perceval's mental disorder, the unfinished state of the chapel while he was a patient, and the fear that he would attempt to escape if allowed to leave the asylum grounds, this cannot be taken as evidence of a general repudiation of the value of religious observance to moral therapy.[81] Nevertheless, since in practice it proved difficult for Ticehurst to secure the regular services of a chaplain for some years after the chapel was completed, it is clear that the chapel at Ticehurst played a far less central role in the life of the asylum than Arnold's pulpit did at Rugby School.[82]

The sanctions with which authority was backed up at Ticehurst and at Rugby were different too. In keeping with the utilitarianism of Mayo's penal philosophy, corporal punishment of the type practised at Rugby was ruled out as a means of control. The 16-year-old boy 'N.B.', whose treatment Mayo supervised at Ticehurst, was attended by two men who were instructed to use force to ensure obedience, but not such as would cause 'the slightest bodily pain'. At other times 'N.B.' was intimidated with the threat that he would be put in a strait waistcoat, but this was never actually done. Mayo believed the reality of confinement and close supervision deterred resistance; he described 'N.B.' as 'tranquillized by his utter inability to resist'.[83] Ultimately, the doctors' and attendants' power stemmed from the patients' desire for release: an inverse image of the threat of expulsion through which boys were manipulated at Rugby School.[84]

In many respects, the moral therapy advocated by Mayo conformed to what is known of the moral treatment practised in other early nineteenth-century institutions for the insane. Tuke's *Description of the Retreat* also emphasized the value of the patient's separation from their home surroundings in providing an incentive for recovery.[85] Mayo's recommendation of the importance of gaining psychological ascendancy over the patient through irresistible force rather than violence, as well as his advocacy of seclusion and a minimal use of restraint, conformed to practice at the Retreat. Although religion played a less central and pervasive role at Ticehurst than at the Quaker Retreat, Mayo would have felt comfortable with Tuke's emphasis on cherishing 'the strengthening and consolatory principles of religion and virtue' in patients' minds. Like

The asylum and moral reform

Tuke, Mayo advocated the value of exercise, varied objects of amusement, and purposeful activity or work to the patient's recovery.[86]

With logical consistency, Mayo had argued in 1829 that morally insane patients needed to be treated with authority rather than through appeals to their desire for approbation, since such desires formed part of the moral sense Mayo believed these patients lacked.[87] However, in his case-history of 'N.B.', Mayo noted the beneficial effect of praise in slowly cultivating the 'desire for esteem' which Tuke had seen as central to moral management. In addition, Mayo described the operation of a psychology of reward and punishment which was similar to that practised at the Retreat: 'N.B.' was encouraged to correspond with Mayo, but if he sent a letter which was 'insolent or wayward', his next letter would be returned unopened. The threat of mechanical restraint, the incentives of greater freedom within the establishment (such as being invited to dine with the Newingtons), and ultimately of release, also formed part of this disciplinary framework.[88]

Like Tuke, Mayo argued that the way to elicit trustworthy behaviour was to treat the patient with trust. To 'N.B.' Mayo emphasized the contractual nature of the bond between patient and physician: the restraint imposed on the patient would be inflexible until the patient learnt self-control, at which point 'strict justice will be done him, upon the terms originally stated to him'.[89] Yet Mayo's self-presentation as a man who was guided by reason needs to be critically read. He described his response to a patient who announced his recovery to Charles Newington after nearly three years in Ticehurst in these highly rational terms:

> I went over to Ticehurst, and formally stated to the patient, that I accepted with pleasure his announcement of his recovery; that nothing more remained, than that he should give himself and me some proof of the soundness of his own impression by spending a portion of time which I named, at the establishment. This patient never relapsed.[90]

Yet Perceval's account of Mayo's response to his appeals for a transfer to single care suggests that – although Mayo certainly presented himself to his patients as open to persuasion – in practice he was guided by Charles Newington's opinion of a case, and observed his patients with a less open mind than his writings imply.[91]

In other respects, Mayo acted with great moral self-confidence in assuming the right to take decisions about his patients. Thus although 'N.B.' was considered neither insane, nor an idiot, and therefore fell outside the ambit of the lunacy laws, Mayo was candid about how he had persuaded the magistrates to allow 'N.B.' to be confined because he lacked 'self-control'.[92] Perceval's impression, not only that Mayo was 'too much the ally of Mr Newington', but that he intervened to discourage the magistrates from paying serious attention to Perceval's desire for transfer to single care, thus gains plausibility from Mayo's own account of his

85

The asylum and moral reform

behaviour in 'N.B.'s' case.[93] Alongside the moral contract which Mayo described as existing between patient and doctor – that the patient could regain their liberty through co-operating fully with their treatment – there was also a less clearly articulated understanding to be reached between the physician or superintendent of the asylum in which a patient was placed, and the patient's family. Thus it was 'N.B.'s' father who consulted Mayo on how he should manage his son; and to Mayo that Perceval's mother wrote for advice on how she should respond to her son's request to be transferred to single care.[94] Since it was the patient's family who paid the physician's fees, it was primarily they, rather than the patient, whom the treatment had to satisfy.

As for the first twenty-five years of its operation, most patients in the 1820s and 1830s were referred by a close relation, and predominantly by men.[95] Beyond the assumption of this clearly defined legal responsibility, other members of the family could play an actively solicitous role in monitoring the patient's treatment: thus although Perceval's certificates were signed by his eldest brother, his mother corresponded regularly with him and with his doctors.[96] Some information is available on the kind of behaviour which led to confinement: Perceval suffered from aural hallucinations; 'N.B.' had threatened one of his teachers with a knife, and (although three years prior to his confinement) exposed himself to his sisters; the surgeon and horticulturist Joshua Mantell (1795–1865), who became a patient at Ticehurst in the mid-1830s suffered from *déjà vu* after being thrown from his horse, and became irritable and angry with his family and servants.[97] What is missing is the process of internal decision-making by which families decided to try asylum care.

The role played by doctors who referred patients is largely obscure in this period. One possibility is that copies of the prospectus were sent to physicians with a special interest in mental disorders, in the hope that they would refer patients to Ticehurst. This would help to explain why Ticehurst's catchment area widened. Certainly, from the early 1830s, several patients – including Alexander Goldsmid – were referred by Alexander Robert Sutherland (1782–1861), the physician at St Luke's who also had an extensive private practice of patients in single care. However, Sutherland was the only physician apart from Mayo who is known to have referred more than two patients to Ticehurst in this period.[98]

The problem of why families chose to send patients to an asylum rather than caring for them at home, or placing them in single care, is highlighted when it is considered that in the 1830s public confidence in the medical profession was at a low ebb.[99] It is difficult to know whether asylum care was seen primarily as a means of relieving the family of a difficult member, and with how much therapeutic optimism patients were confined. High standards of physical care, and the doctor's own confidence in his abilities could help alleviate the guilt and helplessness experienced by families who

The asylum and moral reform

no longer felt able to cope with a mentally disturbed relation. Mayo's confident assumption of a paternalist role in relation to his patients relieved families of the responsibility of caring, and taking decisions, for them.

Medically, Mayo secured the broadest possible audience through eclecticism and openness to new ideas. Thus, although he was eager to dissociate himself from phrenology's politically radical exponents, he suggested that the localization of conflicting attributes in the brain of one individual (such as benevolence and destructiveness) offered important insights into the fundamentally conflicted character of human nature.[100] Similarly, although Thomas Mayo never gave mesmerism the vociferous and wholehearted support which eventually led to his brother Herbert's relegation from the ranks of medical respectability, he believed some therapeutic potential – particularly in the treatment of hysteria – might emerge from further investigation into double consciousness, while firmly repudiating materialist explanations of how animal magnetism worked.[101] The presence of such a broad-based approach in practice at Ticehurst, as well as high standards of physical care, gave the asylum widespread appeal. It made it possible, for example, for the homoeopath and phrenologist John Epps (1805–69), who visited Joshua Mantell in Ticehurst in March 1836, to be completely satisfied with the care his former student and friend was receiving, while he pondered the role played by Joshua's large 'organ of individuality' in the case.[102]

As in the case of 'N.B.', there is no trace of Joshua Mantell's admission in the accounts: the first entries in his name were made in 1839. It therefore seems likely that both these patients were initially admitted to the Highlands, the records for which are less complete. The introduction to Epps's diary described the circumstances in which Mr and Mrs Epps saw Joshua in this way:

> They found him seated in a large, comfortable room, by a good fire, with his books and papers about him. He was delighted to see his old friend, with whom he had a long talk concerning the botany of the neighbourhood, and on other subjects of mutual interest, one of which was a book Joshua said he was about to publish.[103]

The Eppses were later told that Joshua's talk of publication was delusional, but the impression of a warm and cheerful domestic ambience at the Highlands echoed Perceval's depiction of the Asylum. Indeed, patients at the Highlands lived more intimately with the Newingtons, and were invited to share meals with the family as their condition improved. Even in the asylum, a genteel ethos underplayed the institution's confining role by, for example, concealing bolts on the doors behind panelling, in a way which may have reassured the families and friends of patients – as well as some patients – through its simulation of an ordinary domestic environment.[104]

The asylum and moral reform

Statistics of Ticehurst's cure, discharge and death rates did not become available to families or physicians until the publication of the first government statistics in 1844.[105] While the cure rate these presented of over 50 per cent was comparable to other highly regarded asylums like the Retreat and Brislington House – and at slightly less than 15 per cent the death rate was noticeably lower – these statistics differ considerably from those calculated from Ticehurst's records, which show only about 20 per cent as cured. Most of the discrepancy between the recovery rates could be accounted for by the number of patients whose condition at discharge was not listed in the accounts. However, a closer focus on the period 1 August 1817 to 31 July 1842, for which the condition at the end of treatment is given for two-thirds of first admissions, still reflected a lower recovery rate than those calculated by Parry–Jones at Hook Norton and Witney in Oxfordshire, and by Anne Digby at the Retreat (see Table 3.8).[106]

The difference in death rates between Hook Norton and Ticehurst was negligible: yet the death rate at Ticehurst cannot be accounted for by a predominance of pauper patients in poor physical health, as Parry-Jones

Table 3.8 Outcome of stay for first admissions to the asylum, 1817–42

Figures do not include admission to the Highlands
Years run from 1 August to 31 July

| Year | Died | Discharged | | | | Unknown |
		Well	*Improved*	*Not improved*	*Unknown condition*	
1817–22	20	47	6		38	6
1822–7	17	29	13	2	23	3
1827–32	14	20	11	2	22	3
1832–7	17	12	5	4	8	3
1837–42	12	5	1	3	6	7
Total	80	113	36	11	97	22
%	(22.3)	(31.5)	(10.0)	(3.1)	(27.0)	(6.1)

Sources: See Table 3.6

Table 3.9 Outcome of stay for patients resident in the asylum, 1820–40

Figures are for 31 July of each year and do not include the Highlands

| Year | Died | Discharged | | | Unknown |
		Well/ improved	*Not well/ transferred*	*Unknown condition*	
1820	21	12		13	4
1825	27	8		8	4
1830	30	5		13	
1835	40	7	2	4	2
1840	46	4	7	2	2

Sources: See Table 3.6

The asylum and moral reform

accounted for the relatively high death rate at Hook Norton. Unlike the high proportion of deaths within four weeks of admission noted at Hook Norton, most of those who eventually died in Ticehurst stayed longer than the median length of stay for first admissions.[107] Arguably, the high death rate at Ticehurst – or more accurately, the lower rate of removal and transfer – despite relatively high and increasing fees reflected a high level of satisfaction amongst Ticehurst's clients, which had nothing to do with the asylum's capacity to cure. This hypothesis is confirmed by the presence of a fairly low rate of removal or transfer, and high death rate, at the highly reputed Retreat.[108] Seen from this perspective, the increasing length of stay at Ticehurst becomes a measure of the asylum's success in the eyes of its client population.

It is one of the paradoxes of the development of private asylums that it was able to occur at a time when middle- and upper-class families were becoming increasingly insular and self-regarding. Yet private asylum care was marketed in a way which stressed its fundamental harmony with the best interests of the family. The increasing use of the word 'asylum' rather than 'house' to describe private madhouses as well as larger institutions chimed with a vision of the world outside as hostile, immoral and distracting. Private asylums sought to emulate the cosiness and tranquillity of idealized family life. Although in sending an insane person to an asylum the family's close natural bonds and self-sufficiency were temporarily disrupted, the asylum also offered to protect the family from the discord, disorder, intemperance and irrationality of mental disturbance. Mayo argued that such a separation was advisable not only because the painfulness of exclusion from the family gave the patient an incentive for recovery, but because the bad feeling aroused in the patient by the necessity for restraint might otherwise permanently damage the harmony of family relations.[109]

The extent to which disruptive behaviour came to be construed in moral terms is evident in the fact that for a time 'moral insanity' became the most frequently used diagnosis at Ticehurst. Between 1 January 1839 and 31 December 1843, almost one-third of all admissions were diagnosed as morally insane.[110] Anne Digby has also described a peak in the use of moral insanity as a diagnosis at the Retreat between 1838 and 1855.[111] Tantalizingly, nothing is known of the kind of behaviour which led to such a diagnosis at Ticehurst. What is clear is that asylums with a middle- and upper-class clientele were able through the use of the diagnosis of moral insanity to appear as part of the apparatus for moral reform; and the emphasis that such reform was primarily a problem of individual transformation from within complemented the socially conservative role of Evangelicalism in suggesting that moral regeneration from within the existing structures of church and state could mitigate the radical social problems created by industrialization.

The asylum and moral reform

It has been argued that the most crucial role played by Evangelicalism was in mediating the transition to political power of the industrial bourgeoisie.[112] Since access to private asylums was primarily determined by wealth, like public schools they helped to forge a moral consensus amongst different sectors of the upper and middle class. At the Highlands in the early 1840s the *arriviste* son of a trillionnaire Russia merchant or Manchester silk manufacturer could have talked over dinner to two baronets, and the daughter-in-law of the high sherriff of Cornwall; or alternatively to members of the upper professional middle class, like the wife of a royal surgeon and sister-in-law to a former headmaster of Eton, or the brother of Queen Victoria's surgeon–accoucheur.[113] For the Newingtons, Ticehurst was a vehicle for upward social mobility. Four of Charles and Eliza Newington's sons went to Oxford or Cambridge; and the two eldest who qualified in medicine became physicians rather than surgeons. In addition, both these sons who eventually succeeded Charles Newington married daughters of local landowners.[114] Although Thomas Mayo's future career was not so intimately bound up with Ticehurst, it followed the same pattern of a consolidated middle-class position which ultimately aspired to the privileges of the upper class. After acting as president of the Royal College of Physicians during the crucial period of the Medical Licensing Act, Mayo made an affluent marriage to an admiral's widow, and completely retired from practice.[115]

The private madhouses which prospered most in the 1820s–30s had several characteristics in common. All offered high standards of physical care in genteel surroundings and aimed to maximize confidentiality for their clientele. Brislington House and Laverstock House had laid out pleasure grounds to provide varied walks for patients before 1815, and like Ticehurst, they offered different standards of accommodation depending on fees. In 1828, William Finch complained that the Wiltshire magistrates had threatened to revoke his licence because he was unwilling to reveal the whereabouts of patients after discharge.[116] Although Perceval felt that the grounds of Ticehurst were like a 'table-top' exposed to public view, he also claimed that patients had been known by pseudonyms in the asylum, to conceal their true identities. Mayo's care in disguising the identity of cases he described from Ticehurst means that, in contrast to Perceval's descriptions, they were difficult to link to the asylum's records.[117] Although the 1828 Madhouses Act required proprietors to notify the Home Secretary of admissions, licensed houses in the provinces continued to expand after 1828. Most well-regarded asylums, like Brislington House, Laverstock House and Ticehurst placed increased emphasis on the value of religious consolation; although some proprietors, including Finch and Charles Newington, thought patients with religious delusions should be discouraged from attending services.[118]

By 1844, a majority of licensed houses took no pauper patients; but only

The asylum and moral reform

four of these were licensed for more than fifty patients, including Brislington House and Ticehurst. If Ticehurst followed Brislington House and Laverstock House in laying out pleasure grounds and building a chapel, Charles Newington led the way in discontinuing pauper admissions by 1825. Whereas the Foxes stopped being licensed for pauper patients in 1838, provision for pauper patients at Laverstock House reached a peak in 1841, and continued for ten more years. In 1816, Brislington House and Laverstock House had been highly praised by Edward Wakefield; but in the early reports of the new Lunacy Commissioners after 1845, it was Brislington House, Shillingthorpe and Ticehurst which were identified as market leaders.[119] This was partly because they offered models of good practice in terms of physical care; but Ticehurst's engagement with moral reform would also have met with natural sympathy in Evangelical members of the Lunacy Commission.[120] Although Mayo left Ticehurst in 1835 to set up a private practice in London, it was his work which laid the foundations for a strong emphasis on the diagnosis of moral insanity at Ticehurst. He also referred some of Ticehurst's wealthiest patients to the asylum in the 1820s–30s, and thus helped Charles Newington transform what had been a relatively ordinary middle-class asylum in the early nineteenth century into the elite institution it became in the mid-Victorian period.

Notes

1. *Report from the committee on madhouses in England*, July 1815 (PP1814–15(296.)IV.801–), p. 24.

2. A. Scull, *Museums of madness*, London, Allen Lane, 1979, p. 141.

3. Ibid., p. 139, note 1.

4. For Thomas Mayo, see W. Munk, *The gold-headed cane*, London, Longmans & Co., 1884, pp. 220–40; and *Dictionary of National Biography* (*DNB*). Official visits by Thomas Mayo were recorded in the Visitors' Reports, 1828–32 (QAL/1/3/E10), and VB1833–45, up to 29 September 1835. Professional consultations were recorded in, for example, BB1819–26, pp. 4, 67, 139, 145; BB1826–32, pp. 21, 51, 57, 62, 73, 81, 94, 111, 142; BB1832–9, pp. 16, 18, 29, 66.

5. [Perceval], *Narrative*, London, Effingham Wilson, 1838; and J. Perceval, *A narrative*, London, Effingham Wilson, 1840.

6. T. Mayo, *Remarks on insanity; founded on the practice of John Mayo, M.D.*, London, T. & G. Underwood, 1817, pp. 71–2.

7. W.F. Bynum, 'Rationales for therapy in British psychiatry, 1780–1835', *Medical History*, 1974, 18: 327.

8. Mayo, op. cit., note 6 above, pp. 83–4; Bynum discusses the implications of moral treatment for the theological doctrine of free will, op. cit., note 7 above, pp. 320–1, 328–9.

9. Mayo, op. cit., note 6 above, pp. 19, 26.

10. Ibid., pp. 31–2, 64–9.

11. BB1811–19, p. 114. And, for example, BB1811–19, pp. 119, 139, 155; BB1819–26, pp. 1, 14, 41, 59, 91, 114; BB1826–32, pp. 4, 38, 92, 124; BB1832–9, pp. 38, 57, 78.

The asylum and moral reform

12. Entry for Miss Jeffries, BB1819–26, p. 51.

13. C. Newington, 'An instrument invented for administering food and medicine to maniacs by the mouth during a closed state of the teeth', *Lancet*, 1826, 10: 845–6.

14. I am grateful to John Symons for directing my attention to J. Read, *An appeal to the medical profession, on the utility of the improved patent syringe* . . ., London, W. Glendinning, 1824, which contains commendations from Charles and Samuel Playsted Newington.

15. Entries for Mr Holloway and Mr Wall, BB1826–32, pp. 44, 77.

16. Perceval, op. cit., note 5 above, 1840, p. 240.

17. Quoted in H.F.H. Newington and A.S.L. Newington, 'Some incidents in the history and practice of Ticehurst asylum', *JMS*, 1901, 47: 65.

18. VB1833–45, entries for 5 October 1842, 10 June 1843, 1 September 1843, 15 June 1844, 25 January 1845, 28 May 1845 and 28 August 1845.

19. J. Perceval, op. cit., note 5 above, 1840, p. 415.

20. T. Mayo, *Elements of the pathology of the human mind*, London, J. Murray, 1838, p. 59.

21. For fees see C. MacKenzie, 'A family asylum', London University PhD thesis, 1987, pp. 485–6.

22. Mary Morris was admitted on 18 May 1819, AP1842–5. The first licence for the Highlands was granted for not more than four patients in April 1830, although a second patient had been admitted one year previously (QAL/1/1/E1).

23. W. Ll. Parry-Jones, *The trade in lunacy*, London, Routledge & Kegan Paul, 1972, pp. 252–3.

24. D. Roberts, *Paternalism in early Victorian England*, London, Croom Helm, 1979, p. 125.

25. BB1819–26, pp. 37, 127; and BB1826–32, p. 53; and BB1819–26 pp. 46, 47.

26. M.A. Lower, *The worthies of Sussex*, Lewes, G.P. Bacon for subscribers, 1865, p. 254.

27. Catherine Cobb, George Simons, George Basnet and David and Emily Martineau all reduced their fees; Eliza Wright increased hers (BB1819–26, p. 11; BB1826–32, pp. 6, 37, 46, 88, 108). For bankruptcy, see BB1811–19, p. 95.

28. Lower, op. cit., 1865, note 26 above.

29. L. Hodson and J. Odell, *Ticehurst: the story of a Sussex parish*, Tunbridge Wells, 'Courier' Co., 1925, p. 59; Visitors' Reports 19 April and 31 August 1831 (QAL/1/3/E10); VB1833–45, entry for 9 January 1833. Parry-Jones, op. cit., note 23, pp. 114, 118.

30. *Ticehurst private asylum for insane persons*, place of publication unknown, c.1828.

31. Perceval, op. cit., note 5 above, 1840, pp. 90, 92.

32. The accounts list Perceval as resident in Ticehurst Asylum from February–December 1832 (BB1826–32 p. 142; BB1832–9, p. 36). Gregory Bateson made an error in suggesting that Perceval was transferred to Ticehurst in May 1832: his Ticehurst diary began in February 1832. Bateson suggested that Perceval probably remained in Ticehurst until 1834: however, Perceval's 1840 text referred to him being in Sevenoaks in 1833. It therefore seems likely that in December 1832, Perceval succeeded in persuading his relatives to transfer him to single care, and that the remainder of his confinement was in Sevenoaks. (See G. Bateson, *Perceval's Narrative. A patient's account of his psychosis, 1830–1832*, New York, William Morrow & Co.Inc., 1974, p. vii; and J. Perceval, op. cit., note 5 above, 1840, pp. 1–2).

33. BB1826–32, p. 142; BB1832–9, p. 36.

34. Perceval, op. cit., note 5 above, 1840, p. 90.

The asylum and moral reform

35. Lower, op. cit., note 26 above, p. 255.

36. Perceval, op. cit., note 5 above, 1840, pp. 91–2.

37. Ibid., p. 92.

38. Ibid., pp. 92–3.

39. Ibid., pp. 92, 227–8.

40. Ibid., pp. 93, 97–9, 146.

41. Ibid., pp. 93, 228–30.

42. Ibid., p. 93; a brewery is shown on the ground plan of the asylum.

43. Perceval, op. cit., note 5 above, 1840, p. 416.

44. Ibid., pp. 241, 248.

45. Visitors' Reports, 1828–1832 (QAL/1/3/E10) and VB1833–45, entries 9 January 1833 – 16 September 1842.

46. See, for example, BB1819–26 pp. 16, 52, 98, 147; BB1826–32 pp. 20, 55, 104, 130; BB1832–9 pp. 18, 123, 143. And BB1811–19 p. 150; BB1819–26 pp. 16, 59, 70, 94, 116; BB1826–32 p. 116.

47. Perceval, op. cit., note 5 above, 1840, pp. 392–404, 415–16. Henry Charles Blincowe (1796–1861) from Hayes in Middlesex was the son of Robert Willis Blincowe of Bristol, and educated at University College, Oxford. In Ticehurst from February 1828 until his death in April 1861 (*Alumni Oxon.*; BB1826–32, p. 67). Charles Nunn (d. 1836) from London, in Ticehurst from September 1824 until his death in January 1836 (BB1819–26, p. 133, BB1832–9, p. 66). Alexander Goldsmith (1780–1843), a merchant from Finsbury Square in London, in Ticehurst from October 1830–August 1842, when he left the asylum (BB1826–32, p. 146, BB1840–6, p. 19). John Allsopp (1808–43), a surgeon from Linton in Kent, in Ticehurst from October 1830 until his death in March 1843 (BB1826–32, p. 120 and BB1840–6, p. 90). For fees in early 1830s see BB1826–32, pp. 30, 67, 120, 146.

48. Perceval, op. cit., note 5 above, 1840, p. 393; AP1842–5 and RA1845–81.

49. Perceval, op. cit., note 5 above, 1840, p. 415.

50. Perceval, op. cit., note 5 above, 1840, p. 210.

51. Stephen Dickenson (1758–1841), a farmer from Pembury, and deacon in the Countess of Huntingdon's chapel in Tunbridge Wells, in Ticehurst Asylum from March – May 1830, and possibly a second time from March – October 1837 (BB1826–32, p. 105 and BB1832–9, p. 91).

52. Newington and Newington, op. cit., note 17 above, pp. 62–4; and T.W. Horsfield, *The history, antiquities and topography of the county of Sussex*, vol. I, Lewes, Sussex Press, 1835, pp. 578, 588–92.

53. Ibid., p. 590.

54. By 1835, only four patients are known to have been admitted to the Highlands: Mary Morris, described as 'independent' (see note 22 above); Louisa Cay, details of whose social status are not given, was a patient from April 1829 until her death in April 1845; Lady Charlotte Poole, was a patient from January 1830 to December 1837; and Frances Prideaux, described as 'independent', was a patient from May 1833 until her death in March 1849 (QAL/1/5/E5; AP1842–5).

55. See MacKenzie, op. cit., note 21 above, p. 487.

56. Ibid., p. 485.

57. Of these, William Edgeworth was admitted from Ireland in November 1818 (BB1811–19, p. 155 and BB1819–26, p. 13); but Mrs Thelwall from Wales, Mrs Creighton from Yorkshire and Revd Probyn from Boulogne were all admitted in 1834–5 (BB1832–9, pp. 50, 64, 73). In addition, one of the patients at the Highlands, Louisa Cay, came from Sunderland (AP1842–5).

58. See MacKenzie, op. cit., note 21 above, p. 491.

The asylum and moral reform

59. *Statistical Appendix to the Report of the Metropolitan Commissioners in Lunacy to the Lord Chancellor* . . . (PP1844(621.)XVIII, 1–), pp. 115–16.

60. Six were listed as 'independent', and one as having 'no occupation'; one was a former 'butler', and three patients' former occupations were not given. Five paid four guineas a week or more; three were patients at the Highlands; two paid two and a half guineas a week; and one paid only one guinea a week (AP1842–5; BB1819–26, pp. 50, 77, 133, 139; BB1826–32, pp. 20, 73, 109, 113; and BB1832–9, p. 144).

61. An aunt and nephew, Elizabeth and William Nash, admitted to the asylum on 25 May and 3 March 1830, respectively; and Louisa Cay and Frances Prideaux, see note 54 above (AP1842–5). VB1833–45, entry for 16 January 1846.

62. Mayo, op. cit., note 20 above, pp. 107–16.

63. Ibid., pp. 112, 117, 151–2; and Mayo, op. cit., note 6 above, pp. 31–2, 46, 48.

64. A. Digby, *Madness, morality and medicine*, Cambridge and New York, Cambridge University Press, 1985, pp. 82, 128.

65. Ibid., p. 128.

66. Mayo, op. cit., note 20 above, p. 99.

67. W. Houghton, *The Wellesley index to Victorian periodicals, 1824–1900*, vol. II, Toronto, University of Toronto Press, 1972, p. 522.

68. T. Mayo, *An essay on the relation of the theory of morals to insanity*, London, B. Fellowes, 1834, pp. 41–9, especially p. 42.

69. Ibid., pp. 5–6.

70. Ibid., pp. 20, 30, 44, 46.

71. T. Mayo, *An essay on the influence of temperament in modifying dyspepsia or indigestion*, London, B. Fellowes, 1831, p. 59.

72. Mayo, op. cit., 1834, note 68 above, pp. 32, 43.

73. It is unclear whether Mayo was familiar with Prichard's earlier discussion of moral insanity in an article on 'Insanity' in J.Forbes *et al.* (eds), *The cyclopaedia of practical medicine*, vol. II, London, Sherwood, Gilbert & Piper, 1833, pp. 824, 826–31. A fuller description was given in J.C. Prichard, *A treatise on insanity and other disorders affecting the mind*, London, Sherwood, Gilbert & Piper, 1835, pp. 4, 12–26, 34–71.

74. Mayo, op. cit., 1834, note 68 above, p. 33.

75. Ibid., pp. 9–10.

76. Ibid., p. 33.

77. [Perceval], op. cit., note 5 above, 1838, p. 275; see also Perceval, op. cit., note 5 above, 1840, pp. 176–7. J. Chandos, *Boys together. English public schools 1800–64*, London, Hutchinson, 1984, pp. 248, 252; the boys' resistance to Arnold's moral persuasion is described on pp. 255–6.

78. Arnold quoted in L. Strachey, *Eminent Victorians*, London, Chatto & Windus, 1918, p. 199; and Mayo, op. cit., note 68 above, pp. 5, 11–12, 14, 31.

79. Mayo, op. cit., note 20 above, p. 132.

80. Ibid., pp. 85, 177.

81. Perceval, op. cit., note 5 above, 1840, p. 387; Mayo, op. cit., note 20 above, pp. 172–82.

82. Services were performed regularly for the first two years after the chapel opened, but were then only intermittently performed until Autumn 1847 (VB1833–45 and VB1846–69, reports up to 25 October 1847).

83. Mayo, op. cit., note 20 above, pp. 174–5.

84. Ibid., p. 99.

85. S. Tuke, *Description of the Retreat*, York, W. Alexander, 1813, p. 157.

86. Digby, op. cit., note 64 above, p. 98; Mayo, op. cit., note 20 above, pp. 99–100, 152; and Tuke, op. cit., note 85 above, pp. 96, 129, 156, 181.

The asylum and moral reform

87. Mayo, op. cit., note 68 above, pp. 4, 31, 33–4.

88. Mayo, op. cit., note 20 above, pp. 99, 175, 177–8.

89. Ibid., pp. 175–6.

90. Ibid., p. 103.

91. Perceval, op. cit., note 5 above, 1840, pp. 376–80.

92. Mayo, op. cit., note 20 above, pp. 181–2.

93. Perceval, op. cit., note 5 above, 1840, p. 377.

94. Ibid., p. 429; and Mayo, op. cit., note 20 above, p. 172.

95. MacKenzie, op. cit., note 21 above, p. 492.

96. QAL/1/3/E7; Perceval, op. cit., note 5 above, 1840, *passim*, especially pp. 215, 220, 250, 382.

97. Ibid., p. 10; Mayo, op. cit., note 20 above, pp. 172–3; Mrs Epps, *Diary of the late John Epps, M.D. Edin . . .*, London and Edinburgh, Kent and Co., 1875, pp. 195–6. I am grateful to Lawrence Pedersen for drawing my attention to the references to Ticehurst in Epps' diary.

98. The other five patients certified by Alexander Sutherland were Emma Baldwin, admitted 12 October 1831; James Halford, admitted 5 March 1837; John Churchill, admitted 1 July 1840; Revd W.W. Park, admitted 8 October 1842; and Amelia Sims, who was transferred from Sutherland's private asylum, Otto House on 3 May 1843 (QAL/1/4/E5; AP1842-5).

99. R.H. Shryock, *The development of modern medicine*, New York, Knopf, 1947, pp. 248–72.

100. Mayo, op. cit., note 20 above, pp. 58–60.

101. Ibid., pp. 38–9, 158–60; see Herbert Mayo's obituary in *Lancet*, 1852, ii: 207.

102. Epps, op. cit., note 97 above, p. 279.

103. BB1832-9, p. 140; Epps, op. cit., note 97 above, p. 196.

104. Perceval, op. cit., note 5 above, 1840, p. 92.

105. Op. cit., note 59 above.

106. Parry-Jones, op. cit., note 23 above, pp. 211–12; Digby, op. cit., note 64 above, p. 231.

107. The median length of stay for those first admissions between 1 August 1817 and 31 July 1842 who eventually died in the asylum was 2–5 years. For the median length of stay for all first admissions in the same period see Table 3.5.

108. Digby, op. cit., note 64 above, p. 231.

109. Mayo, op. cit., note 20 above, p. 99.

110. Op.cit., note 59 above, p. 140.

111. Digby, op. cit., note 64 above, p. 94.

112. C. Hall, 'The early formation of Victorian domestic ideology', in S. Burman (ed.), *Fit work for women*, London, Croom Helm, 1979, pp. 18–19.

113. John Giles Loder, admitted to the Highlands August 1841; son of Giles Loder (1786–1871); outcome unknown (Boase; QAL/1/4/E5). Henry Winkworth, admitted to the asylum August 1844; son of Henry Winkworth (d. 1869), grandson of Stephen Dickenson (see note 51 above); discharged not improved December 1846 (AP1842-5 and RA1845-81). Sir William Walter Yea (1784–1862), admitted to the asylum November 1825; educated at Eton and Brasenose College Oxford; succeeded grandfather to baronetcy 1833; died in Ticehurst (ibid., and *Alumni Oxon.*). Sir Samuel Fludyer (1800–76), admitted to the asylum and transferred to the Highlands 8 July 1842; educated at Christ Church Oxford; succeeded to baronetcy 1833; died in Ticehurst (ibid., BB1832-9, p. 160 and AP1842-5). Frances Prideaux, née Patten (d. 1849), widow of Charles Prideaux (1760–1833), son of the high sherriff of Cornwall; died in Ticehurst (Boase). Isabella Keate, née Ramus (d. 1859), admitted to the Highlands January 1842; married to Robert

The asylum and moral reform

Keate (1777–1857), former president of the Royal College of Surgeons and serjeant-surgeon to Queen Victoria, and brother of John Keate (1773–1852), headmaster of Eton 1809–34; died in Ticehurst (*DNB* and AP1842–5). Dr George Bragg Blagden (1788–1860), admitted to the asylum August 1817, brother of Richard Blagden (1789–1861), surgeon-accoucheur to Queen Victoria; died in Ticehurst (ibid.; and Boase).

114. Neither Charles Hayes nor Samuel took an MD. Charles went to Trinity College Cambridge; BA 1837 (*Alumni Cantab.*); LRCP, London, 1836. Samuel went to New Inn Hall Oxford, BA 1842; LRCP, London, 1843 (*Medical Directory*). Philip Playsted (BA Worcester College Oxford, 1842) and Frank (BA St John's College Oxford, 1845) both trained for the church, and Philip became vicar of Combe Keynes, Dorset (1860–73) and Osmington, Dorset (1873–7) (*Alumni Oxon.*). Charles Hayes married the daughter of Revd Wetherell from Pashley Manor; and Samuel married the daughter of Major Alexander Beatson (see *DNB*).

115. Annual Address to the Royal College of Physicians, *BMJ*, 1871, i: 387.

116. Parry-Jones, op. cit., note 23 above, p. 267.

117. See note 47 above.

118. Op. cit., note 59 above, pp. 6–10; Parry-Jones, op. cit. note 23 above, p. 118.

119. See, for example, *Lunacy Commissioners' Report*, 1847, p. 280.

120. See N. Hervey, 'A slavish bowing down: the Lunacy Commission and the psychiatric profession' in W.F. Bynum, R. Porter and M. Shepherd (eds), *The anatomy of madness. Vol. II Institutions and Society*, London, Tavistock Publications, 1985, pp. 98–131.

4

Madness and the Victorian family

In the 1820s–30s, some families who could afford private asylum care had nevertheless been reluctant to spend money in this way. For example, in Somerset in 1822, a Mr Goold refused to refer his suicidal wife for treatment at Brislington House because his parish would not bear the cost. Despite appeals from the local rector to Mrs Goold's husband and father, whom he believed had the means to pay, she remained at home, in this case with tragic consequences. Locked in the house alone one evening while her husband was out, her clothes caught fire and she burned to death.[1] Despite the success of asylums like Ticehurst in attracting an upper-class clientele, the private madhouse system had been able to expand partly because some licensed houses continued to take pauper patients. However, in 1845 the provision of county asylums became compulsory. Although some counties were slower than others to comply with this legislation, and pauper patients continued to be accommodated in private madhouses, from the 1850s proprietors of licensed houses increasingly depended on private patients (see Table 4.1). Institutions which already restricted their intake to private patients were best placed to survive in a more competitive market; and all proprietors may have hoped to benefit from the economic prosperity of the 1850s–60s. However, factors apart from cost influenced the willingness of Victorian families to refer patients to private asylums.

The Victorian middle classes' high evaluation of family life, and concern

Table 4.1 Number of patients in private asylums, 1850–80

Year	Private patients	Pauper patients	Total	% Private patients
1850	2,677	4,054	6,731	39.8
1860	2,948	1,352	4,300	68.6
1870	3,144	1,760	4,904	64.1
1880	3,408	1,141	4,549	74.9

Sources: LCRs 1850, 1860, 1870 and 1880

Madness and the Victorian family

with moral probity, created a climate in which segregation of the insane was likely to be an attractive option. Nevertheless, the medical profession's helplessness in the face of repeated epidemics of cholera, typhus, typhoid and influenza in the 1830s and 1840s had left public confidence in the curative capabilities of the medical profession, even of physical disease, at a low ebb. An appeal to a physical pathology of insanity provided a rationale for the medical profession's involvement in the treatment of the insane, but would not necessarily foster an acceptance of asylum treatment amongst the middle and upper classes. Despite the popularity of spas and sea-bathing resorts, treatment away from home was not the norm for acute physical illness. Emphasis on the value of a domestic ambience in moral treatment might be reassuring, but in 1846 there were further revelations of abuses in private asylums.[2] Despite the impact of moral treatment on the ethos of asylums, and regular inspection by the visitors and Lunacy Commissioners, public confidence in the good will of asylum proprietors, and the quality of private asylum care, remained poor. If the worst revelations concerned pauper patients, regular inspection by the Lunacy Commissioners from 1845 created new anxieties about the loss of privacy which might result from government regulation.

There is ample evidence from Victorian letters, diaries and auto-biographies that upper- and middle-class families feared asylums, and had low expectations of the kind of care their relatives might receive there. In July 1843, before Henry Winkworth's admission to Ticehurst, his younger sister Catherine (1827–78) visited Lancaster Prison, and noted in her diary that 'no sight can be more painful unless it be a lunatic asylum'. Her subsequent imaginative description of what she believed an asylum would be like was edited out of the published journals by her sister Susanna, but such fearful fantasies must have made it difficult for Catherine to come to terms with Henry's confinement two years later.[3] Personal inspection did not always allay families' anxieties about asylums. When the novelist William Thackeray's wife Isabella became suicidal after the birth of their third child in 1842, he contacted one of the Lunacy Commissioners, Bryan Procter (1787–1874), for advice about private madhouses. Later, Thackeray wrote to his mother that 'Procter . . . took me to his favourite place which makes me quite sick to think of even now. He shook his head about other places'; and they eventually made arrangements for private care with a Mrs Bakewell in Camberwell.[4] In 1849, the chairman of the Lunacy Commission, Lord Shaftesbury, chose to lodge his epileptic son Maurice with a protestant family in Lausanne in Switzerland. It is possible that Shaftesbury felt his position as Lunacy Commissioner would be compromised if he placed his son in care in England; but in his diary he frequently expressed fears about how Maurice would be treated in the future: 'I know well the sufferings of an unhappy creature so afflicted when removed from the vigilant eye of personal and parental affection. What

Madness and the Victorian family

will become of him if Minny [Shaftesbury's wife] and I are removed?' In 1851, he commented bluntly 'Fits are treated like madness, and madness constitutes a right, as it were, to treat people as vermin.'[5]

Alternatives to the asylum

Single confinement outside the home was only one of a possible range of alternatives available to upper- and middle-class Victorians who chose not to opt for asylum care. Patients who were eventually admitted to Ticehurst had sometimes also spent time being treated at home, often with a private nurse or attendant, or been sent on trips abroad in an attempt to cure them of their disorders. A letters book which recorded applications for admission between 1857 and 1873 occasionally noted a family's last-minute reluctance to have the patient admitted to an asylum as the reason why a prospective patient had not been admitted. Equally, patients who failed to improve might be removed to a different form of care rather than another asylum: over 40 per cent of first admissions to Ticehurst between 1 August 1845 and 31 July 1885 were discharged 'relieved' or 'not improved' rather than 'recovered'; but less than one-quarter of these were transferred immediately to another asylum or single medical care.[6]

The case-history of a patient called Washington Travers illustrates some of the non-medical options which were available. Initially admitted to a small private asylum in Guildford, Washington Travers improved sufficiently for Dr Sutherland and a Dr Benjamin Travers (no known relation) to recommend a period of travel abroad to confirm his recovery. He became a student at Queen's College, Gallway, and travelled from there with one of his professors to Koblenz; but while there he became violent, and was arrested by the Swiss police, spending a short time in an asylum on the continent before being transferred to Ticehurst. After being a patient at Ticehurst for sixteen months, he was placed in single confinement with a Revd Cawithen in Devon in January 1856. However, when he ran away to his brother's in London, went to where the Prince of Wales was bathing, laughed at him and called him names, Travers was returned to Ticehurst in July 1858. From there, he was allowed out several times on trial, spending the Christmases of 1858 and 1859 on the Isle of Man with a friend, and part of the summer of 1859 in Scotland with his cousin. In April 1860, he left for Australia with an attendant, and travelled for about eight months, coming back via Shanghai and Japan. Shortly after his return he was discharged from his certificates and went back to Australia, where he planned to stay for five years.[7] As is clear from this example, although psychological physicians advocated early asylum treatment, they might recommend travel abroad after a patient's condition had improved. More general practitioners sometimes advised patients to go abroad rather than seek asylum care. Thus in the 1870s, Herman Charles Merivale, son

99

Madness and the Victorian family

of the permanent under-secretary of state for India, claimed one of the doctors he consulted had somewhat melodramatically told him to 'Travel, . . . do anything rather than give way. If once you find yourself in an asylum, Heaven help you!'[8]

Doubts about the therapeutic effectiveness of orthodox medicine had opened the market to heterodox practitioners, such as mesmerists, homeopaths and hydropathists, who treated patients at home or in their own establishments. As Terry Parssinen has argued the people who patronized these 'medical heresies' in the 1840s were 'an affluent, urban clientele': precisely the kind of people who might otherwise have sent patients to private asylums.[9] Mayo had expressed interest in mesmerism's therapeutic potential, and the homoeopath John Epps had been satisfied with the treatment his friend Joshua Mantell received; but by 1860 the Unitarian minister George Kenrick was described as having been 'subjected' to hydropathic and homoeopathic treatment before his admission to Ticehurst.[10] Nevertheless, as spas, bathing places and new hydropathic establishments sprang up and prospered all over Europe in the first half of the nineteenth century, the luxurious pampering of incurable complaints in establishments which were run like hotels rather than hospitals provided a prototype which private asylum proprietors could emulate in their own practice.

Despite mesmerism's particular claim to the successful treatment of nervous disorders, there is no evidence of patients being treated mesmerically before admission to Ticehurst; however, in the 1840s–50s several of them attributed their disorders to mesmeric interference.[11] The therapeutic scepticism which attracted patients to unorthodox medicine could make them fear that any attempted remedies might be ineffective at best, and at worst positively harmful. In cases where the patient's symptoms did not lead to ostracism, disillusion could lead to a total rejection of treatment. To give an example, William Rathbone Greg's brother Samuel (1804–76), a reformist mill owner, suffered a nervous breakdown in 1846 when the introduction of new stretching machinery to his mill at Bollington in Cheshire led to a walk-out by staff. He suffered from debilitating depression, did not go out for nine years, and was never able to resume management of the mill. Attributing his ill-health to the phrenomesmerist experiments he had undertaken with William in the 1820s, Samuel Greg believed his nervous system had been irreversibly depleted of energy. Initially trying hydropathic treatment at Malvern and on the continent, he 'suffered many things from many physicians, but with little help or satisfaction, and came to feel that he must sit down under his burden and live with it as best he could to the end'.[12] Despite the Newingtons' successful treatment of William Greg's wife Lucy in the late 1850s, and W.R. Greg's subsequent recommendation of Ticehurst to family and friends, Samuel Greg never entered an asylum.

Madness and the Victorian family

Resignation like Samuel Greg's required tolerance and fortitude from the sufferer's family and friends. In acute cases, or when someone became suicidal or violent, it was simply impracticable. It was George Kenrick's volatile temper and attempt one night to conceal a razor in his bed (with what were presumed to be suicidal intentions), which persuaded his wife Sarah that homoeopathic and hydropathic treatment at home offered insufficient protection in his case, so that she agreed to his certification.[13] The advantage which homoeopathic and hydropathic treatment had over certification was that they could be addressed to treating whatever physical disorder was believed to be affecting the patient's mind, thereby avoiding the stigma of mental disease. In his evidence to the select committee on the lunacy laws in 1877, James Crichton Browne alleged that many insane patients were illegally confined in hydropathic establishments to avoid the stigma of certification.[14] Certainly patients who considered themselves 'nervous' rather than insane might opt for treatment at a hydropathic establishment rather than an asylum. Herman Charles Merivale sought treatment at a hydropathic establishment before being admitted to Ticehurst; and he attributed his ultimate breakdown to the enervating effects of this unsuccessful water cure, the reduced diet dictated by his disturbed liver and excessive medicinal use of chloral hydrate, as well as grief at his father's death. In his autobiographical account of his confinement at Ticehurst, Merivale described the loss of self-esteem which certification and involuntary confinement entailed for the patient, noting that 'The feelings of fear and shame – for it had in one's own despite a sort of shame about it – that the experience left behind, died slow and hard'.[15] His own feelings of shame were sufficiently acute for him to publish *My experiences in a lunatic asylum by a sane patient* (1879) anonymously, despite its blustering title; just as John Perceval had initially published his *Narrative* anonymously because he was 'ashamed of his late calamity'.[16]

The shame experienced by families when one of their members developed a mental or nervous disorder could also be very intense. Susanna Winkworth's biography of her sister Catherine described the close and affectionate relationships enjoyed in their Evangelical family. Yet although the biography was privately printed for circulation within the family only, and referred to physical illnesses and treatment experienced by various members of the family, the eldest brother Henry, who was confined at Ticehurst, was never mentioned by name. References in Catherine's diaries which circumstantial evidence suggests were to him were represented by asterisks, and he was described in the footnotes simply as 'a close connection'.[17] Lord Shaftesbury reacted with acute embarrassment when his son had an epileptic fit in public:

> [Maurice] fell yesterday in the Park and I trembled lest a vast crowd should be gathered. Sent away the children and sat by his side as

101

Madness and the Victorian family

though we were only lying on the grass, and by degrees he recovered and walked home.

It was shortly after this incident that Shaftesbury accepted doctors' recommendations that Maurice should be separated from the family. Despite the fact that, by 1850, Shaftesbury acknowledged 'solitude and separation have done nothing for [Maurice]', his son never returned home.

Although families might want to do everything they could to secure a patient's recovery, the cost of treatment could also be a source of financial embarrassment. Before Lord Shaftesbury placed his son in single care, he observed in his diary: 'We have tried an immense variety of physicians, we have expended hundreds of pounds (how shall we ever repay them?) and he is far worse. He must not be left for a moment.'[18] While Lord Shaftesbury could have afforded private asylum care for Maurice, it is likely that Henry Winkworth was removed from Ticehurst because his family could only afford the fees there for a limited period. The decline of the Winkworth family's silk-manufacturing business created financial problems; in 1859, Susanna's younger brother Stephen took over her housekeeping expenses so that she could afford to pay her doctors' bills. Although the Ticehurst accounts do not record how much was paid for Henry Winkworth (partly because some of his time was spent at the more costly Highlands), even if he had been paying average fees in the mid-1840s of three guineas a week, his annual bill would have come to more than the £100 per annum his father eventually felt able to bequeath for his upkeep in 1869.[19]

Reasons for certification

If anticipated shame and embarrassment was one reason why patients and their families might resist or postpone certification, as happened in Herman Charles Merivale's case, these emotions could also make a family eager to remove a patient from their family circle, in order to conceal their disorder. Amongst the middle and upper classes, it was families and friends who made the initial diagnosis of insanity by referring someone for treatment, and most admissions were made on the authority of one or more family member.[20] In the 1850s, lunacy reformers lobbied parliament to bring this process under the control of the courts, by adopting a system similar to the French *conseil de famille*, where the alleged lunatic's family would meet with a magistrate to decide whether certification was appropriate. However, in the absence of reform, private patients who had not broken the law were only entitled to a court hearing if their families referred their cases to the Court of Chancery. And, since long delays were common, families usually only applied for a lunatic's estate to be protected when they believed the patient's condition to be incurable. Perhaps for this reason, the protection of property was rarely at the forefront of reasons

Madness and the Victorian family

given for certification. However, although the admission certificates and histories in the case notes from Ticehurst do not make it possible to build up a detailed picture of the family's internal process of decision-making, they do give some indication of the kind of behaviour which families found so intolerable, disruptive or disturbing that they were willing to resort to certification, despite the stigma it carried.

Violence to people or property, and threats or attempts of suicide, were amongst the most common reasons given for certification, perhaps partly because danger to one's self or others was recognized in law as sufficient reason for depriving a person of their civil liberties. Thus in September 1845 Pauline Folliau, who was described as neither suicidal nor dangerous to others, was nevertheless certified after 'violent behaviour, breaking furniture, burning her clothes, accusing her parents of injustice & ill-treatment'; and Charles Rawdon was admitted in October 1846 after he had 'armed himself with loaded pistols with the intent to shoot a person besides frequent threats of the same kind against other individuals & many other similar acts of violence'. Anna Direy was confined when she slashed her arm with a razor in a suicide attempt in June 1849 because she 'cannot safely be left alone'; and in May 1856 Edward Lloyd was diagnosed as suffering from 'suicidal melancholia' two days after he had 'made an attack on his wife with a pen-knife making two wounds of a serious character'.[21]

Other patients had become unmanageable at home because of their tendency to wander away from home, or cause disturbances locally. Thus in July 1848, 78–year-old Elizabeth Winser was confined because of 'her general dislike of friends, disinclination to take food, & a constant desire to leave her house & wander about & wish to see her brothers & others who have been dead a long time'; and in August 1856 Revd Patterson had 'left his father's house in the middle of the night with only his shirt-drawers & travelled for a distance of a mile & a quarter to a neighbour's house declaring that his brother was persecuting him'. However, it was only after Patterson had also been evicted by his landlady, left by a private attendant who 'could not endure his [Patterson's] abuse', and boarded in single confinement without any improvement in his condition, that his family agreed to his being admitted to Ticehurst six months later.[22] As well as being violent, Arthur Basset, who became a patient at Ticehurst in March 1856, was described as 'wildly incoherent in his manner & conversation . . . often howling and screaming'; but violence was the more crucial factor in deciding on certification.[23] Fifteen months before James Brook's family seriously considered certifying him, his brother-in-law described Brook as looking 'half demented . . . as if he could not bear the light – and he had been howling and larking on horseback with Miss Hirst'; but the final decision to confine Brook was taken only after he had become:

103

Madness and the Victorian family

very violent, feared treachery, spoke of murder and suicide, and seemed to take a terrible horror of me [Dearman Birchall] and his uncle. He threw bread violently at Lillie calling her a murderess. He said he was W. Leigh Brook of Meltham [his father] and had twice attempted his life.[24]

Delusions and forms of behaviour which were not acutely disruptive might be tolerated for some years before certification was considered. For W.R. Greg, a unitarian and author of the widely discussed *Creed of Christendom* (1851), the fact that his wife's delusions centred on religion created social embarrassment. After her year's stay at Ticehurst, Lucy Greg was still not free of the 'delusion' that she was a Roman Catholic. While staying with the Gregs in 1859 Susanna Winkworth confided to her sister Catherine that: 'Mrs Greg is such a sweet creature . . . but evidently very weak and can't bear much talking . . . it was awkward in our talks that I don't know, and can't make out whether she is Protestant or Catholic.'[25] Mrs Greg finally openly went over to Rome in 1867; but clearly by itself this kind of embarrassment could be tolerated within her family circle. Lucy Greg had spent a short time in Brislington House in 1842, but for several years before she was confined to Ticehurst, despite her religious convictions and periodic delusions, she had lived in a cottage near her family where she was nursed by William Greg's sisters, 'occasionally enjoying the intercourse and society of her domestic circle'; and she was only certified in 1857 after she had also become violent. In chronic cases like Lucy Greg's, asylum treatment could be resorted to to protect the family from the patient's most extreme symptoms, and relieve them of the burden of caring for a chronically insane relative, rather than with strong hopes of obtaining a cure; although in Lucy Greg's case the Newingtons were able to wean her off the opiates with which she had been sedated at home, and discharge her 'recovered' at the end of a year.[26]

More basic breaches of social decorum were less easily tolerated. Dirtiness and neglect of appearance alerted some families to the possibility that a prospective patient was unable to take proper care of themselves. Thus, George Wood, who was certified in April 1853, seemed 'unconscious of eccentricities which have long prevented the possibility of his living with his relations . . . for many months he has neglected all habits of Cleanliness'; while four years later Thomas Wright was confined because he refused to eat, and was 'refusing to conform to any of the usual rules of society and neglecting to dress himself'. In April 1860 the main reason given for Eliza Gipps's certification was that 'she entertains the delusion that when obeying the calls of nature her life is passing from her and therefore retains them as much as possible & is very dirty in her habits'.[27] After over six years at Ticehurst James Brook was no longer violent, but when Dearman Birchall visited him at St Leonards, Brook:

Madness and the Victorian family

walked about laughing in a most idiotic fashion. He bites his nails, sucks his thumb and spits. His general effect affords no grounds for encouragement. He made no observation and declined a more intelligible answer to our enquiries than a grunt.[28]

However, his relatives do not appear to have considered removing him from Samuel Newington's care at this time.

Obscene language and manifestly sexual behaviour also featured amongst the reasons why patients were originally confined. Thus in 1855 Mary Turney was admitted to Ticehurst because she had delusions, refused food, and '[used] foul language'. Frances Willington was described on her certificates in 1853 as 'labouring under nymphomania'; and Henry Shepherd's 'general conduct especially towards females' was said to be 'not that of a sane person'. In 1858 Isabella Foster was certified after she 'made an attempt upon the life of one of her children, . . . [and] exposed herself naked several times'; and she was also described as 'making use of very foul language'. In some cases, expressions of sexuality were found to be particularly disturbing because they were seen as inappropriate socially: Augustus Gawen had proposed marriage to a fisherwoman; and Henrietta Golding was admitted in April 1847 after she had 'shewn strong inclinations to form an improper connection with a Person of very inferior grade'. Charles Mawley, who was later removed from Ticehurst because he annoyed other patients, was confined partly on account of his 'keeping low company' and making 'Indecent conversation in the presence of ladies'.[29] However, evidence from Ticehurst suggests that certification could not easily be resorted to by middle- and upper-class Victorians as a means of sexual and social control when no other 'symptoms' of insanity were present; but that single confinement may have been used in this way.

While staying for her health with a Dr Smith in Ilkley Wells, Henrietta Unwin, who later became a patient at Ticehurst, alleged that the doctor had sexually assaulted her while she was 'unconscious'. On hearing this, her husband removed her from Dr Smith's and took her to Brighton. From there, Mrs Unwin ran away to her mother's in Essex, where she cut off her hair and dressed in a man's clothes before travelling to London. Taken back to Essex by her husband, she again ran off to London, and from there to Paris. On the channel steamer she met a man with whom she spent the next three or four days in a hotel in Paris, before applying successfully for a position as English governess with a French family. When her husband discovered where she was, he went to fetch her, and took her back to Brighton where he attempted to have her certified. In April 1861 she was diagnosed as 'morally insane' and admitted to Ticehurst; but only one week later she was discharged 'not improved'. Subsequent notes suggested that, although two certifying doctors were listed in the admissions book, her husband could find only one doctor to sign her certificates; and this may

Madness and the Victorian family

explain her early removal. In 1864, Mr Unwin again brought his wife to Ticehurst village in the hope that he could get her admitted to the asylum; but, despite the fact that it was a common practice for prospective inmates to be certified by local doctors after they had been brought into the locality, he was unable to find two doctors who were willing to certify her. Finally in February 1866, her husband succeeded in finding two doctors to sign the necessary certificates, and Henrietta Unwin became a patient at Ticehurst for nine months, during which time the notes which were kept on her case suggest that she 'never exhibited the slightest symptom of intellectual insanity'.[30]

In 1864, when Mr Unwin could not find two doctors to certify his wife, Newington arranged for Mrs Unwin to be lodged in Ticehurst village. The exact nature of these lodgings is unclear, but although no formal certification or admission was made, according to the letters book which recorded applications for admission to Ticehurst, Mrs Unwin 'came 18th November 1864 & went to W. Balcombe'.[31] Just as the first Samuel Newington had boarded out violent and refractory patients in Ticehurst village, the most plausible explanation for his grandson Samuel Newington's involvement in finding lodgings for Mrs Unwin would be that, like other mad-doctors in private practice, he endorsed private lodgings for single patients in the local area. By the mid-nineteenth century, it was those patients whose status before the law was most ambiguous, rather than those who were most violent, who were likely to be confined in single lodgings. The very small extent of this practice in Samuel Newington's case may be gauged from the fact that in 1870 his total income from 'out-patients', who would have included former inmates sent out on trial, was only £9.4s.0d.[32]

Patients' rights and lunacy reform

Since 1845, single lunatics had been legally subject to the same regulation and inspection as patients in private asylums. However, since single lodgings were not licensed, in practice the Lunacy Commissioners had great difficulty fulfilling their statutory obligations. In 1859, Lord Shaftesbury complained that the Lunacy Commissioners did not know how many single patients were confined, despite the fact that they had spent 'years trying to learn it'. Chancery patients, including those in single care, were visited by the Lord Chancellor's Visitors in Lunacy; and it was a source of irritation to Shaftesbury that the Lunacy Commissioners were not allowed to see the Lord Chancellor's list of single Chancery patients.[33] In addition, the Lunacy Commissioners were not required (or able) to inspect single patients confined at home. As the *British Medical Journal* observed in 1879, 'There [was] no law to prevent a Mr Rochester from locking up his mad wife in the attic of his mansion, with a keeper, as described in *Jane*

Madness and the Victorian family

Eyre'.[34] Despite the evident potential for an abuse of civil liberties which arose from the lack of effective regulation of single confinement, it was this type of care which some lunacy reformers advocated as preferable to private asylum treatment; with the important difference that they wanted as many patients as possible to be voluntary.

Both Perceval and (later) Merivale emphasized in their accounts of their illnesses that they had known that they were in need of treatment, and that the sense of humiliation which resulted from being stripped of their autonomy through certification, and which persisted long after they had recovered, would not have occurred in a system which made provision for voluntary treatment.[35] As secretary of the Alleged Lunatics' Friends Society, which lobbied for lunacy reform, Perceval was also influential in persuading the society to advocate single care. As Nicholas Hervey has argued, Perceval's faith in single confinement stemmed partly from the high evaluation of confidentiality which was traditional to his class.[36] However, in 1858–9 when a select committee investigated the operation of the lunacy laws, there was some tension between Lord Shaftesbury's desire to strengthen his Commission's powers over single patients, and John Perceval's advocacy of single care because it provided greater privacy than private asylum treatment. In 1862, new legislation required the Lord Chancellor's Visitors to visit Chancery lunatics resident in private houses a minimum of four times a year; but made no other change to the position of single patients (25 and 26 Vict., *c*. 86). Voluntary admission was not included in the new lunacy legislation, but from 1862 it became legal for patients who had recovered sufficiently to be released from their certificates to stay on at private asylums as voluntary boarders (25 and 26 Vict., *c*.111); a move which was designed to go some way towards allaying fears that private asylum proprietors sometimes delayed the discharge of patients.[37]

Concern about the civil liberties of private patients placed lunacy reform back on the political agenda in the 1870s. A former private asylum patient, Louisa Lowe (1821–1907), who believed she had been wrongfully confined in 1870–1 on account of her spiritualist beliefs, founded the Lunacy Law Reform Association in 1873. Like the Alleged Lunatics' Friends Society, the LLRA was most critical of the ease with which patients could be confined in private asylums, and the difficulty in obtaining release. Unlike John Perceval, however, Louisa Lowe focused on the limitations, rather than the intrusiveness, of the law; and the fact that it did nothing to prevent her estranged husband, who had arranged her certification, working in what she saw as collusion with the mad-doctors who benefited financially from her confinement in three private asylums. One of these physicians, Henry Maudsley, was an advocate of single care for private patients. In his presidential address to the Medico-Psychological Association in 1871, while Louisa Lowe was a patient at his private asylum in Hanwell, Maudsley

Madness and the Victorian family

urged his fellow professionals to consider the advantages of medically supervised single care over asylum treatment. Even after the formation of the LLRA, Maudsley continued to recommend domestic, rather than asylum, treatment, for both recent and chronic cases. In acute cases, Maudsley favoured single medical care because he believed it would facilitate early treatment, by removing the more public stigma of certification in an asylum; but in the case of chronic patients Maudsley advocated domestic care because it offered 'the *priceless blessing of the utmost freedom* that is compatible with . . . proper care' (original emphasis).[38]

Maudsley's emphasis on the benefits of domestic care for chronic patients was naturally popular with those in his profession, like one of the Lord Chancellor's Visitors in Lunacy, John Charles Bucknill, who had been interested in easing the problems of overcrowding in county asylums through the development of a 'cottage system' where incurable quiet and harmless patients could be boarded out from asylums.[39] One implication of the boarding-out system was a recognition that chronic patients might not need more than occasional medical checks; but while this was popular with some county asylum doctors, it had little appeal for those private asylum proprietors who derived the bulk of their income from easily manageable chronic cases rather than acute admissions. Support for Maudsley's views on single care for early cases was more difficult to marshal, but some did come from the Lord Chancellor's other Visitor in Lunacy, Charles Lockhart Robertson, who favoured the closure of private asylums. In fact, the support of the Lord Chancellor's Visitors was no coincidence, since it was they who had most strongly resisted calls from Lord Shaftesbury and others for further regulation or abolition of single care.

The interest of the Lord Chancellor's Visitors in Lunacy, and public self-questioning of the medical profession, must have been influential in the decision to call a select committee to consider the operation of the lunacy laws in 1877. Nevertheless, when this committee met it was the questions raised by the Lunacy Law Reform Association which dominated the agenda: that is, the risk of wrongful confinement; the possibility that patients were treated in a way which was not conducive to cure; and any difficulties faced in securing discharge upon recovery. Although the bulk of witnesses at the inquiry were medical men, including Bucknill, Maudsley and Robertson, some former patients, including Louisa Lowe, also gave evidence.

The scope of the inquiry was not limited to private patients, but the emphasis on civil liberties meant that private cases assumed prominence in the proceedings. Private wealth was seen as providing the motive and means for relatives to seek to confine sane individuals, and the incentive for doctors to collude with them. All the individual cases examined in detail by the select committee involved patients with private means; but most had not been Chancery patients. (If they had been, the case for their confinement would already have been heard by a court, which was the kind of legal protection the LLRA hoped to secure for all patients.) Nevertheless, the extent to which the select committee took seriously the possible risk of infringement of patients' civil liberties, and where they had concluded the most serious risk lay, can be seen in their subsequent recommendation that the system of visitation to Chancery lunatics should be extended to all patients, including single patients, through an amalgamation of the Lunacy Commission and the Lord Chancellor's Visitors in Lunacy. The committee did not recommend the closure of private asylums.[40]

In examining witnesses, the select committee were assiduous in pursuing all three questions outlined earlier; but in the evidence of former patients it was criticism of the certification and discharge procedures which predominated. Both Louisa Lowe and Walter Marshall, who had been a patient at Ticehurst, objected to an apparent complicity between the two certifying doctors, who were required by law to make independent assessments of the patient's mental state. Marshall's case is interesting because it represented most of the central allegations of the LLRA: he was a member of a prosperous Leeds textile family, who had been confined after undertaking some business transactions his family disapproved of; he suspected collusion between the certifying doctors (although not the good faith of his family); and the proprietor of Ticehurst, Samuel Newington, advised the Lunacy Commisioners against a compulsory discharge when it was recommended by two independent doctors. None of the evidence conclusively suggests malpractice or bad faith, rather than errors of judgement, on the part of the Samuel Newington or his nephew, Hayes Newington, who kept Marshall's case notes. However, it is clear from the case notes that Hayes Newington, and the consultant physician William Gull, both probably misdiagnosed Marshall, who had previously been treated for syphilis, as suffering from the first stage of general paralysis; and consequently warned Marshall's family that he would 'never leave Ticehurst'. In fact, after being transferred to single care by the Lunacy Commissioners, Marshall was discharged from certificates and remained living at home and apparently well for at least six months before giving evidence to the select committee.[41]

The case of Thomas Preston, who had also been a patient at Ticehurst, highlighted some of the particular problems faced by Chancery lunatics who believed they were unjustly confined. In August 1873, Preston had written to the LLRA alleging that his brother, who had sole control of Thomas's estate under an order of the Chancery Court, would not allow him any money to appeal again to the court to establish his sanity and regain control of his affairs. A former attendant at Ticehurst, Robert Minchin, supported Preston's claim, telling the LLRA that during his time at Ticehurst Preston had appeared sane, and that he also knew 'of other

Madness and the Victorian family

persons at Ticehurst perfectly quiet and harmless'. By September 1874, Preston 'seemed perfectly sane' to Dearman Birchall, who was one of the visiting magistrates at Barnwood House in Gloucestershire to which Preston had been transferred. He was well enough to follow up Birchall's visit with a letter which Birchall described as 'very clever, containing an amusing account of Dr Newington who considers Ticehurst a paradise on earth and wonders everybody does not rush in to be confined'. Nevertheless, at the select committee only one of Preston's former fellow patients, John Thomas, was prepared to say that Preston had been 'perfectly in his senses' when he was at Ticehurst. The medical witnesses, and the Secretary to the Lunacy Commissioners, all emphasized that Preston had a history of criminal assaults on women; Preston was not called to give evidence.[42]

The select committee's conclusion that 'It would . . . tend to prevent abuse if it was required that the order [i.e. permission for admission] should be given by a near relative', suggests that they gave little credence to the likelihood that close relations, like Thomas Preston's brother, or Louisa Lowe's husband, might have ulterior motives for wrongfully confining patients; and believed that requiring two medical certificates provided sufficient safeguards. This was despite the fact that some medical witnesses had emphasized the fears and reluctance of family members to accept home a recovered patient as a factor in delayed discharge. Henry Maudsley, for example, told the inquiry that Mr Lowe had refused to agree to his wife's discharge, because one of their six children had been frightened by her mother's frequent conversations with God. The Secretary to the Lunacy Commissioners, Charles Palmer Phillips, confirmed Samuel Newington's claim that he had been unable to discharge one of the Chancery cases taken up by the LLRA, John Thomas, because his family had feared that he would cause damage to their property. The main concession the report made to concern about involuntary admission was in recommending that voluntary boarding should be allowed for new patients wanting to receive treatment, provided notice of their admission was sent within twenty-four hours to the Lunacy Commissioners.[42]

Since the select committee found little evidence of abuse of civil liberties, and did not recommend the closure of private asylums, no government legislation was introduced immediately following publication of the Report in 1878. However, both the LLRA and members of the medical profession continued to raise questions about the private asylum system. The medical debate revealed a continuing jockeying for position between the Lord Chancellor's Visitors in Lunacy and the Lunacy Commissioners. John Charles Bucknill had told the select committee that he was not in favour of the abolition of private asylums; but in a series of anonymously published articles in the *British Medical Journal*, which began in January 1879, he reviewed what he saw as the major defects of existing legislation, noting in

110

Madness and the Victorian family

his first article the fundamental principle that: 'the tradition of the Lord Chancellor's lunacy offices is opposed to the incarceration of any lunatic in an asylum, for whom due protection and the enjoyment of life can be provided outside'. By April, he was quoting John Conolly's view that 'Every lunatic asylum should be the property of the State, and be controlled by public officers.' In August, Bucknill, Lockhart Robertson and Crichton Browne (who was also a Lord Chancellor's Visitor) sent a public memo to the Lord Chancellor calling for three state asylums to be provided in preference to private asylums for those Chancery patients for whom single care was inappropriate.[44]

Bucknill revealed himself as the *British Medical Journal*'s anonymous lunacy correspondent in January 1880, when he addressed the South London District of the Metropolitan Counties branch of the British Medical Association, and insisted that: 'no change of the law can be satisfactory which does not contemplate the eventual abolition of all private lunatic asylums'. He was supported in this by a letter from John Alfred Lush, a Liberal MP and joint proprietor of Fisherton House private asylum, who had been a member of the 1877 select committee. More importantly, Bucknill took the opportunity to link the mounting dissatisfaction with the private asylum system to criticism of the administration of the Commissioners in Lunacy, and called for an extension of the authority of the Lord Chancellor's Visitors to all private patients. Following the election of a Liberal government in March 1880, lunacy reform legislation was promised in the Queen's speech. Given this, it is particularly surprising that when the quarterly *Journal of Mental Science* reported Bucknill's speech to the BMA in April, the editors suggested there was widespread support amongst members of the Medico-Psychological Association, including some private asylum proprietors, for the closure or local government administration of private asylums, provided asylum owners were adequately compensated. However, as the editors pointed out, private patients represented only about 6 per cent of all asylum inmates; and they may have hoped that closing private asylums would assuage public fears about the good faith of their profession. Understandably, they expressed disappointment when no government bill was introduced; and a private members' bill was brought forward which would have involved a magistrate, as well as two doctors, in the certification process.[45]

Although this bill was not passed, members of the Lunacy Law Reform Association must have felt that their cause finally had some chance of being vindicated. Following the select committee's report, advocates of lunacy reform had tried, with some success, to maintain public interest. Herman Merivale's *My experiences in a lunatic asylum by a sane patient*, was published in 1879. Unlike Walter Marshall or Louisa Lowe, Merivale believed that he had needed treatment. However, he had first been deterred by his doctor from seeking asylum treatment because it required certification;

Madness and the Victorian family

and then, when his condition worsened, he had been traumatized by the experience of involuntary confinement.[46] In 1878, Louisa Lowe had helped an amateur singer and fellow-spiritualist, Georgina Weldon, who was separated from her husband, elude the doctors he had sent to certify her; they had even called at the LLRA's offices in London hoping to carry out the interviews which were necessary before certification. After finding two doctors who were willing to attest to her sanity, Mrs Weldon joined Louisa Lowe on the platform at public meetings called to draw attention to the defects in existing legislation. In 1879–80 she held twice-weekly 'at homes' in Tavistock Square, at which she told 'How I escaped the Mad Doctors' and performed a repertoire of songs. She was in fact a skilled and determined publicist. She advertised in newspapers, sold her auto-biography to the *London Figaro* (who were subsequently sued by her husband), and ultimately took her case to the courts.

Grateful that she had been urged to become a singer by 'Ma Mie', one of the spirits with whom she believed she was in communication, Georgina Weldon recognized that the publicity she gave the issue of lunacy reform might cut both ways. Unexpectedly invited in the autumn of 1879 to sing at a series of promenade concerts in Covent Garden she replied ironically to the organizer: 'I'll do my best to get accused of murder. What brings money and crowds are people accused of crime. That is what really fetches the public.' When Louisa Lowe expressed doubts about the damage such flagrant sensation-seeking might do to the LLRA, Mrs Weldon assured her:

> It is a great thing . . . Mr Gladstone taking it up. In time we'll do wonders, and you must not *curb my audacity*. Remember that when the storm rages fiercely the best way to save the ship is to steam full steam and full sail through the tempest. The captain may sleep if the man at the wheel has his nerve (original emphasis).[47]

Nevertheless, when Dillwyn's bill failed, Gladstone's government did not immediately introduce alternative legislation. In 1883, Louisa Lowe quietly published a renewed attack on the private asylum system, called *The Bastilles of England*; but when the Lord Chancellor, Lord Selborne, attempted to introduce a lunacy bill to the House of Lords in the same year he was forced to withdraw it because of lack of support. The sensationalist publicity given to Georgina Weldon's lawsuits for alleged libel, assault, wrongful arrest, false imprisonment and trespass, in 1884, however, led to the successful tabling of a Lords' motion that 'the existing state of the lunacy laws . . . constitutes a serious danger to the liberty of the subject'; and, despite opposition from Lord Shaftesbury, Selborne was able to reintroduce his bill in 1885.[48]

Selborne's bill responded to public sympathy with Mrs Weldon, and opposition to the private asylum system: a magistrate would be required to approve certification; and no new licences would have been issued for

Madness and the Victorian family

private asylums. However, the defeat of Gladstone's government in the Commons in June led to the bill being withdrawn. By the time a new bill was introduced by the re-established Liberal government in 1886, there was a new Lord Chancellor, Baron Herschell, who had been a member of the 1877 select committee. In its main principles, Baron Herschell's bill was similar to Lord Selborne's, but he went further in suggesting that the Lunacy Commissioners should be empowered to close private asylums; and that existing asylums should not be allowed to expand their numbers. Now that Lord Shaftesbury was dead, Herschell also proposed to extend the interests of the Lord Chancellor's Visitors by outlawing the single confinement of any patients except Chancery ones; and giving the Lord Chancellor powers to amalgamate the offices of the Lunacy Commissioners, the Lord Chancellor's Visitors, and the Masters in Lunacy (barristers who represented the legal, rather than medical, interests of Chancery patients).[49]

Herschell's bill was thrown out at its second reading on 11 June 1886, and the subsequent defeat of the Gladstone administration meant that it was not reintroduced. However, it had raised the prospect that, despite the conclusions of the 1877 select committee, private asylums might eventually be abolished. While this can only have been good news for members of the LLRA, at Ticehurst on 1 June, the Lunacy Commissioners found that:

> The bill before parliament for the amendment of the Lunacy Laws was on the lips of many, and one lady especially inveighed against the abolition of private asylums, in which she has herself (here & elsewhere) passed many years of her life.[50]

The possibility that private asylums might be abolished, and that the courts might be routinely involved in certification, was not necessarily welcomed by patients or their families who placed a high premium on privacy.

As well as reflecting public concern about patients' civil liberties, the debate about lunacy reform in the 1850s–80s demonstrated the lack of consensus amongst doctors and government administrators with responsibilities for the insane. For families and patients seeking to make a choice about treatment, this posed a series of dilemmas. Care at home involved least regulation, but it also made it difficult for the family to keep what was happening private in their locality. Certification enabled wealthy lunatics to be accommodated at some distance from their homes. This minimized the risk of gossip, like the news Dearman Birchall passed on to his sister-in-law in 1885:

> I have been at Barnwood [in Gloucestershire] this week. *Entre nous* we have another well known Yorkshire man, Johnston Scott of Woodhall, Wetherby, brother of Lord Abergavenny's wife. . . . I am dreadfully sorry to hear that his eldest son, and of course nephew to

113

Madness and the Victorian family

our patient, is also out of his mind. Is it not sad to have such a skeleton in the closet?[51]

Since voluntary admission was not possible, decisions concerning treatment remained the responsibility of the patient's family in consultation with doctors; and it seems likely that, given their concern for privacy, middle- and upper-class families would have preferred this to a court hearing. However, while most doctors recommended separation of the patient from the family, medical opinion was divided on whether single care or asylum treatment offered the best chance of recovery. The families of wealthy patients faced the scrutiny of the Court of Chancery and the Lord Chancellor's Visitors, who were publicly critical of private asylums. It is worth exploring how the controversial image of private asylums, and allegations that some patients' relations had confined them for mercenary reasons, affected the decisions of families who were considering referring a patient to a private asylum.

Choosing private asylum care

Statistically, there is evidence that the madhouse business began to decline in the 1850s. The number of licensed houses, and patients confined in them, reached a peak in 1848–9.[52] The decrease in pauper admissions to licensed houses masked a continuing increase in the number of private patients confined in private asylums; but nevertheless, as provision for private patients was expanded in registered, county and borough asylums, the proportion of private patients confined in licensed houses declined (see Table 4.2). In contrast, although cases in single care were not always reported to the Lunacy Commissioners, the number of patients who were registered as being in single confinement more than doubled, from 212 to 441, between 1865 and 1875. There were more men than women in all types of private care except single confinement which suggests that middle-class families were willing to spend more on the treatment of male breadwinners.[53] Nevertheless, despite the increased prosperity of the 1850s–60s, and the growth of the middle classes, private asylum proprietors were relatively unsuccessful in capturing the expanding market for private care. From the early 1880s, when the campaign against private asylums reached its peak, the number of patients confined in licensed houses began to decline (see Table 4.2). Increasingly, middle-class families who chose asylum care opted for fee-paying provision in county, borough and registered hospitals, rather than licensed houses. It was mainly these institutions which catered for the growing lower-middle classes. If private asylums were to prosper in an increasingly competitive market, they needed to respond sympathetically to the requirements and feelings of a higher-class clientele.

114

Madness and the Victorian family

Table 4.2 Percentage of private patients in private asylums, 1850–1890

Year	Total*	In private asylums	Percentage in private asylums
1850	3,774	2,677	70.9
1860	4,927	2,948	59.8
1870	5,372	3,144	58.5
1880	6,594	3,408	51.7
1890	7,379	3,035	41.1

*Not including private patients in naval, military and criminal asylums, or single care
Sources: See Table 4.1; and *LCR* 1890

The decision to confine a relative or friend, even when it was believed that this would be in the individual's best interests, could lead to strong feelings of guilt. Walter Marshall, whose case was subsequently investigated by the select committee, had been depressed for many years before he became a patient at Ticehurst in May 1876. Immediately prior to his admission, he had become excited campaigning for the Liberals during an election. He spent money backing business deals which his family believed were bad investments. His wife Annie, other family and friends were concerned by his change of character. Marshall assured the select committee that he was confident his wife had acted in good faith in agreeing to his certification. However, while he was confined in Ticehurst, it appears that he may have accused his wife of complicity in a plot to confine him illegally. Following William Gull's diagnosis of GPI (general paralysis of the insane), Marshall's cousin, the psychical researcher Frederic Myers (1843–1901), wrote to his friend Henry Sidgwick (1838–1900): 'Gull has seen W. & expresses a very unfavourable opinion. [N]ewington tells me he thinks he will never leave Ticehurst. W. is now angry and complaining of plots etc. wh. much distresses A.'[54] The situation was compounded by the fact that for several years Myers had been in love with Annie, and although they had agreed not to allow their relationship to become a sexual one, they were close friends. Prior to Louisa Lowe's certification, she evidently suspected that her husband was having an affair, and may have believed this to have been his true motive for wanting her confined. Alan Gauld has rightly dismissed the suggestion of a genuine conspiracy between Myers and Annie as unfounded; in fact they reacted to news of the putative seriousness of Walter's illness by deciding that it would be better if they stopped seeing each other. In August, Myers left for Norway, while Annie remained in the Lake District with her five children. After a family conference, at which Annie asked to be relieved of the responsibility of taking decisions concerning Walter's welfare, she confided to Myers' mother that she believed she had been wrong to agree to her husband's certification. A few days later she committed suicide by drowning herself in Ullswater, after having failed in an attempt to cut her throat with a pair of nail scissors.[55]

Madness and the Victorian family

It seems likely that Annie's decision to have Walter certified was precipitous. Her fears for his sanity may have been coloured by her experience of having had two sisters who died insane, and her knowledge that one of Walter's brothers was incapable of managing his own affairs. Exhaustion from living with his intense activity and volubility, as well as his sleeplessness (he woke regularly at 5.00 a.m.) may have contributed to her decision. Her subsequent suicide testifies to how fragile her own state of mind was. What is striking is the ease with which she was able to find doctors to certify him, despite the fact that although Walter had some physical symptoms indicative of a nervous disorder, he was neither delusional, nor dangerous to himself or others. The certificates emphasized reports by his relatives of his recent change of character, and of his recklessness with money.[56] Certifying doctors and asylum proprietors had to balance the social needs of patients' families against the require- ments of the law. Once a patient had been admitted, the continuing trust and confidence of the family depended on the ability of the asylum keeper to negotiate the difficult feelings aroused by the patient's mental distress or disorder, and the decision to resort to certification. In many cases, describing mental disturbance in terms of individual organic pathology alleviated families' feelings of responsibility, although in Walter Marshall's case the pessimistic prognosis, and Walter's hostility to confinement, created additional and ultimately unbearable strain for Annie.

In the case of female patients, mental disorders were often perceived by families and doctors as resulting from gynaecological problems. Thus before the Countess of Durham was certified in 1885 she had been taken to Cannes for a rest by her sister-in-law, and to consult the eminent gynaecologist, Matthews Duncan, before a psychological physician, George Fielding Blandford, was consulted. In this case, too, an examination by Sir William Gull had directed the course of treatment, when he advised the Countess of Durham's family that her malady was physical rather than mental in origin. Medical evidence given in camera during her husband's suit for divorce apparently centred on a debate over whether the Countess had been imbecile from childhood (in which case the marriage could have been annulled), or whether her case was one of 'post-connubial insanity'. Unlike one *Times* editorial on the case, editorials in the *British Medical Journal* and the *Lancet* did not speculate on whether, if it were a case of 'post-connubial insanity', the Duke's behaviour could have precipitated his wife's breakdown.[57]

The 'supposed causes' of insanity listed in the admission notes at Ticehurst rarely pointed to family relationships as a source of stress. Rather, they attributed mental disturbance to accidents ('blow on the head', 'a fall'), physical ill-health ('influenza', 'fever'), natural processes ('childbirth', 'her age'), or the environment ('tropical climate', 'long residence in India'). Or it was attributed to the individual's role in society

116

Madness and the Victorian family

('excitement from business', 'overwork in the ministry'), an adverse change of circumstances ('loss of property', 'business failure'), or the individual's lack of moderation and self-control ('intemperance', 'irregular living', 'self-abuse'). Where mental disturbance was seen as resulting from the family, the stress referred to was generally one beyond the family's control ('bereavement', 'sudden illness of adopted daughter'). The only other emotional circumstance seen as commonly affecting mental stability was rejection in love ('disappointed affections', 'disappointment in love'). The one patient whose breakdown was attributed to an 'unhappy marriage' was referred by her mother rather than her husband. 'Heredity' was very rarely given as the supposed cause.[58]

Certification could protect the family from the patient's bizarre or extreme behaviour. As well as removing patients from their home environments, asylum doctors sought to regulate the degree of contact patients were allowed to have with the outside world, for example, censoring patients' letters.[59] However, since 1828 the person who signed the admission order had been legally bound to visit the patient once every six months; and, apart from the statutory visitors, they could also determine who was allowed to see the patient. In contrast to most doctors, the Commissioners in Lunacy actively encouraged families to stay in close contact with private asylum inmates; recommending in 1879, for example, that relatives and friends should sometimes stay with patients in licensed houses. Despite feeling embarrassed by his son's disorder, Lord Shaftesbury had regularly visited Maurice in Switzerland, and was able to draw comfort from the fact that, although 'his intellect, through a terrible succession of fits, had sunk exceedingly' Maurice retained his 'spiritual strength'. At Ticehurst, some families came and lodged in neighbouring houses, maintaining daily contact with patients for at least part of their confinement.[60]

Difficulties arose, however, when families were not in agreement about the patient's treatment. For example, in 1878 the family of Captain Hope Johnstone MP were in evident dispute. During his confinement, Johnstone had been visited by his mother, brother, sister, aunt, uncle and great uncle. He rode out regularly on Saturdays with his favourite brother; but on 20 May, his mother, who had signed his admission order, wrote to Dr Newington:

> After hearing my dear son say to you 'cannot you stop my relations invading me, very hard that a fellow having a little change because under supervision has no power to stop them' he again after you left complained to me. So I have promised this shall be stopped. I now find I have the *power to order* that no relations are to be admitted to see him, beg you will carry this out. . . . P.S. My son says you are on *no account* to let his Uncle Jack join the fishing party to Stockbridge.

On 23 May, Johnstone's uncle arrived unexpectedly with Dr Bucknill, but they were not allowed to see the patient. In this case, the disagreement

Table 4.3   Length of stay of patients resident in Ticehurst, 1845–1915

*Figures are for 31 July of each year and include the Highlands **

Length of stay	1845	1855	1865	1875	1885	1895	1905	1915
4+–13 wks			1	1			1	
13+–26 wks	1		1	2	3		1	3
26+ wks–1 yr	1	2	3	4	2	1	2	2
1+–2 yrs	3	1	2	5	1	5		4
2+–5 yrs	3	1	10	9	10	4	3	5
5+–10 yrs	3	3	4	4	1	2	7	7
10+–20 yrs	13	11	5	13	15	17	12	22*
20+–35 yrs	20*	19*	12*	11*	16*	20*	29*	21
35+–55 yrs	16	18	16	26	27	25	21	11
55+ yrs	4	3	3	4	3	2	2	2
Unknown								2
Total	64	58	57	79	78	76	78	79

*Median length of stay
** From 1852 the House (asylum) and Highlands were on one licence
Sources: RA1845–81, RA1881–90, RP1890–1906, CR1907–19, RDD1845–90, RRDD1890–1906, RDT1907–30, RD1907–30

Madness and the Victorian family

about treatment appears to have been due to Johnstone's history of violent threats: he had been admitted after threatening to shoot himself; and Bucknill questioned him about allegations that he had said he wanted to kill Lord Beaconsfield and the Prince of Wales. These threats were taken sufficiently seriously for the Home Secretary to send two doctors to examine Johnstone before he was allowed out on trial.

On 15 June, the Commissioners in Lunacy were outraged to learn that Bucknill had been visiting Johnstone, who was not a Chancery case, and reporting to his uncle, but not his mother, the local visitors or themselves. Coming shortly after the select committee had recommended that the system of visitation of Chancery lunatics should be extended to all private patients, this breach of protocol suggests that the rivalry between the Lord Chancellor's Visitors and the Lunacy Commission was sometimes fought out through patients. During his confinement, Johnstone had threatened that 'he would make the locking up of lunatics a more difficult matter'; and complained that he 'considered this incarceration a poor return for his ten years soldiering, & his four years in Parliament'. The Lunacy Commissioners did not recommend a transfer to single care; but agreed that Johnstone might travel abroad under certificates, as he apparently hoped to do once he had resigned his seat in the House of Commons. On 24 June, Johnstone told the visiting magistrates that he would prefer to stay at Ticehurst; but he was nevertheless removed by his mother on 10 July.[61] For families who chose to stay in close contact with asylum inmates, as the Lunacy Commissioners recommended, certification did not necessarily ease the distress and conflict caused by the patient's illness. Perhaps for this reason, some families visited only occasionally.

Nancy Tomes has argued that:

> Hospitalization justified the removal of a disruptive individual while at the same time promising medical treatment and a possible cure. Hospital treatment thus addressed the powerful sense of guilt and helplessness expressed by so many families when dealing with an insane relative.[62]

Yet, as noted above, real confidence in the capabilities of the medical profession was limited; as was asylum doctors' actual ability to cure. When the patient population of Ticehurst is taken in profile at any one time, the prognosis most patients and their relatives or friends could look forward to appears bleak. From 1845, the median length of stay for patients resident in Ticehurst fluctuated around twenty-five years (see Table 4.3). Between 60 and 80 per cent of those resident could expect to die in Ticehurst, and only between 2 and 11 per cent could expect to be discharged 'recovered' (see Figure 4.1). Statistics like these have led Andrew Scull to conclude that:

> the rich could buy greater attention and more eminent psychiatrists

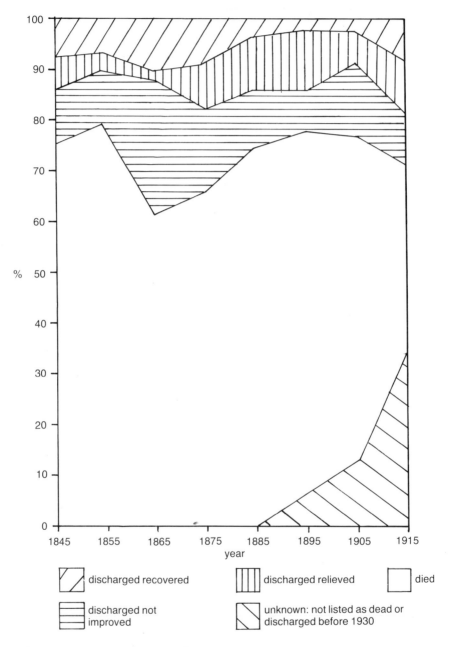

Figure 4.1 Outcome of stay: profiles, 1845–1915.
Note: Outcome of stay for those resident in Ticehurst on 31 July of every tenth year, represented as successively cumulated percentages.

Madness and the Victorian family

for their crazy relatives, but not more cures; so that for all the lavish expenditure of funds, private asylums remained in Bucknill's words 'institutions for private imprisonment'.[63]

Looking instead at the outcome for patients grouped by date of admission, this picture is inverted. As Laurence Ray found for the county asylums at Brookwood and Lancaster, and Anne Digby noted at the Retreat, the median length of stay for patients admitted to Ticehurst between 1845 and 1885 was around one year (see Table 4.4).[64] By 1875–85 the median length of stay for first admissions was only one-third of the median length of stay in 1845–55. Between 60 and 80 per cent of those admitted could expect to be discharged, although only between 16 and 39 per cent 'recovered' (see Figure 4.2). While this rate of recovery modifies Andrew Scull's assessment of the rate of cure as 'abysmally low', more importantly the discharge of almost half of all admissions when they were not improved or recovered undermines the image of private asylums (like public ones) as dumping grounds for social misfits.

Certainly Scull is right to argue that money could not buy health: Ticehurst's recovery rate was less good than, for example, the Retreat's. Only just over one-quarter of first admissions to Ticehurst between 1845 and 1885 were discharged 'recovered', although clearly there must have been an element of subjective judgement by doctors in deciding whether to list a patient as 'recovered' rather than 'relieved', or 'relieved' (albeit slightly) rather than 'not improved'.[65] However, given the therapeutic resources available to mid-Victorian physicians, the criterion of cure is an unrealistic one by which to assess the success or failure of asylums, despite the fact that it formed part of the reformers', and the medical profession's, rhetoric in calling for asylums to be built, and to be staffed by medical men. No doubt many patients and their families initially approached asylum doctors hoping for a cure, even if they had been given pessimistic prognoses elsewhere. For many, considering asylum treatment came at the end of a pragmatic search for help from homoeopaths, hydropathists and gynaecologists; or after attempts at self-help through holidays abroad and increased rest and relaxation. Consulting a range of physicians, as the Countess of Durham did, was not cheap. In 1869, Lord Shaftesbury grumbled that a single consultation with William Gull had cost him 70 guineas.[66] Nevertheless, many families exhausted other options before contacting an asylum.

Merivale noted that, in the mid-1870s, Ticehurst was regarded as an asylum which was 'chiefly for "incurables" '.[67] As was clear in Walter Marshall's case, the Newingtons felt little reservation in telling a patient's family when they believed there was no hope of recovery, suggesting that the ability to cure was not of primary importance to their role as private asylum physicians. In the case of James Brook, Samuel Newington

121

Table 4.4   Length of stay of admissions to Ticehurst, 1845–1915

Figures include admissions to the Highlands **
Numbers in brackets represent known readmissions
Years run from 1 August to 31 July

Length of stay	1845–55	1855–65	1865–75	1875–85	1885–95	1895–1905	1805–15
Up to 7 days	2	3	2	1	1	1	6
8 days–4 wks	1	12	4 (1)	5 (3)	3	3 (1)	4
4+–13 wks	6	8 (3)	14 (4)	31 (8)	15 (1)	10 (1)	7
13+–26 wks	3 (1)	15	16 (5)	30 (13)	14 (3)	18 (2)	13 (2)
26+ wks–1 yr	7 (2)	10 (3)*	29 (5)	19 (5)*	10 (6)	12 (3)	24*
1+–2 yrs	7*	11	21 (2)*	15 (5)	12 (4)*	11 (3)*	13 (1)
2+–5 yrs	8 (1)	6 (3)	22 (3)	21 (3)	10 (1)	16 (3)	13 (4)
5+–10 yrs	3 (1)	4	7 (1)	5	5 (1)	7 (2)	6 (1)
10+–20 yrs	6	2	9 (1)	10 (1)	11 (2)	5 (1)	3 (1)
20+–35 yrs	4	7	5 (1)	8	3	8 (1)	(1)
35+–55 yrs	3 (1)	1	10 (1)	4 (1)	2	1	
55+ yrs			1				
Unknown					3	4 (2)	12 (4)
Total	50 (6)	79 (9)	140 (24)	149 (39)	89 (18)	96 (19)	101 (14)

*Median length of stay
** From 1852 the House (asylum) and Highlands were on one licence
Sources: RA1845–81, RA1881–90, RP1890–1906, CR1907–19

Madness and the Victorian family

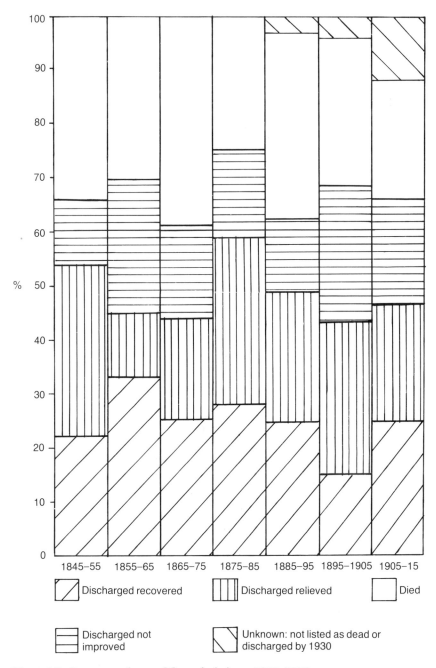

Figure 4.2 Outcome of stay of first admissions, 1845–1915.
Outcome of stay for first admissions to Ticehurst, represented as successively cumulated percentages. Years run 1 August – 31 July.

Madness and the Victorian family

consoled Dearman Birchall three years after Brook's certification that, although the case was incurable, 'Jimmy past abusing himself is taking large doses of Bromide of potassium and may live a good age'; and Birchall at least became reconciled to the incurability of Brook's complaint.[68] Given the limitations of mid-Victorian therapeutics, and repeated exposures of abuses in private asylums, it would be wrong to underestimate the importance to a patient's family of knowing that, in the absence of a cure, their relative would be well fed, tenderly nursed and regularly entertained in a luxurious and tranquil environment. In order to prosper, elite asylums needed to reassure prospective clients that inmates continued to enjoy many of the benefits of their privileged social position despite their illness. It was this which formed the criterion by which the Lord Chancellor's Visitors assessed the appropriateness of care for Chancery cases.

Social embarrassment was one reason why patients like Brook were confined; yet Henrietta Unwin's case, and the findings of the select committee of 1877, suggest that many of the ALFS's and LLRA's fears about wrongful confinement in asylums were unfounded. Family disagreements were more likely to lead to confinement in unreported single care than certification in an asylum. Despite continuing Victorian middle-class concern for moral probity, 'moral insanity' was not used frequently as a diagnosis at Ticehurst in the 1850s–70s.[69] A high evaluation of family life made removal of the acutely mentally disturbed likely; but the reluctance of many Victorian families to discard their relatives permanently because of the embarrassment and distress they caused was reflected in the high discharge rate of patients who were 'not improved' or only 'relieved', to continue their search for health elsewhere, or to live at home. However, the Ticehurst records show that individual patients' disturbances often were part of a wider pattern of family problems. Removing a patient from home could ease family tensions, and it was partly this social need which asylums fulfilled. The rate of discharge of patients who were not recovered or relieved suggests that in many cases temporary removal was sufficient. Ray is right to argue that there was a more fluid interchange between the Victorian asylum and the outside world than is suggested by Scull's emphasis on the accumulation of chronic cases. The next chapter explores who Ticehurst's clientele were; and what kind of treatment was offered at the asylum which Merivale dubbed 'Pecksniff Hall'.[70]

Notes

1. H. Coombs and P. Coombs (eds), *Journal of a Somerset rector 1803–34*, Oxford, Oxford University Press, 1984, pp. 186–8, 216–18.

2. W. Ll. Parry-Jones, *The trade in lunacy*, London, Routledge & Kegan Paul, 1972, pp. 58–9.

3. S. Winkworth, *Letters and memorials of Catherine Winkworth*, 2 vols, Clifton, for the author, 1883 and 1886, vol.I, p. 67.

Madness and the Victorian family

4. G.N. Ray, *The letters and private papers of William Makepeace Thackeray*, 4 vols, London, Oxford University Press, 1945, vol. II, p. 81.

5. G. Battiscombe, *Shaftesbury*, London, Constable, 1974, pp. 259; G.B.A.M. Finlayson, *The seventh Earl of Shaftesbury*, London, Eyre Methuen, 1981, pp. 335–6.

6. LB1857–73, entries for 31 May 1858 and January 1864. Nineteen were transferred to other private asylums, seven into single care, five to registered hospitals and one to a county asylum (RDD1845–90, RDD1890–1906).

7. Admission certificates for Washington Travers, QAL/1/4/E6; CB5, pp. 9–11, 44, 71, 80–1.

8. [H.C. Merivale], *My experiences in a lunatic asylum*, London, Chatto & Windus, 1879, p. 84.

9. T.M. Parssinen, 'Professional deviants and the history of medicine: medical mesmerists in Victorian Britain', in R. Wallis (ed.), *On the margins of science: the social construction of rejected knowledge*, Keele, Keele University Press, 1979, p. 109.

10. CB9, p. 47.

11. See, for example, admission certificates for Dorothy Davis and Mary Hills, QAL/1/4/E6.

12. S. Greg, *A layman's legacy*, London, Macmillan, 1877, pp. 17, 21–3, 33.

13. CB5, pp. 146–9.

14. *Report from the select committee on lunacy laws; together with the proceedings of the committee, minutes of evidence, and appendix*, PP1877 XIII.1–, p. 75.

15. [Merivale], op. cit., note 8 above, pp. 71–2.

16. J. Perceval, *A narrative*, London, Effingham Wilson, 1840, p. xi.

17. Winkworth, op. cit., note 3 above, vol. I, dedication and p. 78.

18. Battiscombe, op. cit., note 5 above, pp. 208–9; and Finlayson, op. cit., note 5 above, p. 323.

19. Winkworth, op. cit., note 3 above, vol. II, p. 267; Henry Winkworth (d. 15 May 1869), first codicil to his will, 23 May 1861.

20. See C. MacKenzie, 'A family asylum', London University PhD thesis, 1987, p. 509.

21. Admissions certificates for Pauline Folliau, Charles Rawdon, Anna Direy and Edward Lloyd, QAL/1/4/E6).

22. Ibid., certificates for Revd Patterson and Elizabeth Winser, CB4, p. 48.

23. Admissions certificate for Arthur Basset, QAL/1/4/E6.

24. D. Verey (ed.), *The diary of a Victorian squire. Exracts from the diaries and letters of Dearman and Emily Birchall*, Gloucester, Alan Sutton, 1983, pp. 3, 5.

25. Winkworth, op. cit., note 3 above, vol.II, p. 265.

26. CB4, pp. 71–2, 74–5, 114.

27. Admissions certificate for Eliza Gipps, QAL/1/4/E6.

28. Verey, op. cit., note 24 above, p. 51.

29. Admissions certificates for Mary Turney, Frances Willington, Henry Shepherd, Isabella Foster, Henrietta Golding and Charles Mawley, QAL/1/4/E6.

30. Local doctors who certified many admissions included Charles Adey from the East Sussex Infirmary in St Leonards (18); James Combs from Burwash (12); William Mercer, medical officer of the Wadhurst District of Ticehurst Union (45); John Taylor, medical officer of the Ticehurst Union (39); Charles Trustram, who practised in Tunbridge Wells (14); John Wardell, who also practised in Tunbridge Wells (9); and Francis Ayerst Young from Hawkhurst (31) (RA1845–81 and RA1881–90). Case no.199, RA1845–81; CB11, p. 105.

31. LB1857–73, entry for 17 October 1864.

32. Ticehurst asylum audit, 1870.

33. K. Jones, *A history of the mental health services*, London, Routledge & Kegan Paul, 1972, p. 16.

Madness and the Victorian family

34. *BMJ*, 1879, i: 245.

35. [Merivale], op. cit., note 8 above, pp. 44–6; Perceval, op. cit., note 16 above, pp. 95, 268–9.

36. N. Hervey, 'Advocacy or folly: the Alleged Lunatics' Friends Society, 1845–63', *Medical History*, 1986, 30: 256.

37. See Parry-Jones, op. cit., note 2 above, p. 238.

38. Op.cit., note 14 above, pp. 239–42. H. Maudsley, 'Presidential address', *Journal of Mental Science*, 1871–2, 17: 311–34; Maudsley quoted in A. Wynter, *The borderlands of insanity and other allied papers*, London, R. Hardwicke, 1875, p. 143.

39. See Parry-Jones, 'The model of the Geel lunatic colony and its influence on the nineteenth-century asylum system in Britain', in A. Scull (ed.), *Madhouses, mad-doctors and madmen*, London, Athlone Press, 1981, pp. 208–9.

40. *JMS*, 1877–8, 23: 283

41. A. Gauld, *The founders of psychical research*, London, Routledge & Kegan Paul, 1968, p. 121; PB1846–1904, entry for 21 August 1876; op. cit., note 14 above, p. 422.

42. Verey, op. cit., note 24 above, pp. 71–2; L. Lowe, *The bastilles of England; or the lunacy laws at work*, London, Crookende, 1883, pp. 20–5; op. cit., note 14 above, p. 282.

43. *JMS*, 1877–8, 23: 284.

44. *BMJ*, 1879, i: 94, 566; ibid., 1879, ii: 180.

45. *JMS*, 1880–1, 26: 74

46. Lowe, op. cit., note 42 above, p. 20; [Merivale], op. cit., note 35 above.

47. E. Grierson, *Storm bird. The strange life of Georgina Weldon*, London, Chatto & Windus, 1959, pp. 173–6, 180.

48. Jones, op. cit., note 33 above, p. 172.

49. *JMS*, 1886–7, 32: 74–6.

50. VB1869–87, entry for 1 June 1886.

51. Verey, op. cit., note 24 above, p. 187.

52. Parry-Jones, op. cit., note 2 above, pp. 31, 55.

53. *LCRs* 1865, p. 29 and 1875, p. 51.

54. Gauld, op. cit., note 41 above. Gauld quotes this letter as reading 'Trewington tells me . . .', but this was probably a misreading of the manuscript original.

55. Ibid., p. 122.

56. Ibid., p. 117 and CB22, pp. 93–5, 104.

57. *The Times*, 11 March 1885, p. 9.

58. RA1845–81 and RA1881–90, for example, case numbers 92, 110, 129, 164, 232, 296, 336, 476, 556, 591, 617, 711.

59. For example, Florence Stannus was confined to the grounds after attempting to post a letter which had not been approved by the Newingtons (CB32, p. 246).

60. Parry-Jones, op. cit., note 2 above, pp. 232–3. When Maurice died in 1855, Shaftesbury had his tombstone inscribed with the text, 'It is good for me that I have been afflicted'; E. Hodder, *The life and work of the seventh Earl of Shaftesbury, K.G.*, London, Cassell & Co., 1886, pp. 524–5.

61. PB1846–1904, entries for 15 June to 27 July 1878; and CB24, pp. 119–20, 123, 127.

62. N. Tomes, 'The persuasive institution: Thomas Story Kirkbride and the art of asylum-keeping, 1841–83', University of Pennsylvania PhD thesis, 1978, p. 13.

63. A. Scull, *Museums of madness*, London, Allen Lane, 1979, p. 208.

64. L. Ray, 'Models of madness in Victorian asylum practice', *Archives of European Sociology*, 1981, 22:261–2; A. Digby, *Madness, morality and medicine*, Cambridge, Cambridge University Press, 1985, p. 219.

Madness and the Victorian family

65. Ray, op. cit., note 64 above, p. 231.
66. Finlayson, op. cit., note 5 above, p. 504.
67. [Merivale], op. cit., note 8 above, p. 41.
68. Verey, op. cit., note 24 above, p. 7.
69. See Chapter 5, this volume, Table 5.5.
70. [Merivale], op. cit., note 8 above, p. 28.

5

Mid-Victorian prosperity

Patients at 'Pecksniff Hall'

Merivale's lampooning of Victorian Ticehurst as 'Pecksniff Hall' was not misplaced. Former occupations are known for all except one of the thirty-six men and twenty-eight women who were patients at Ticehurst on 31 July 1845. Three-quarters of these were listed as 'independent', including all female patients except the one whose former occupation was not given. The fifteen male patients who were not living on private capital were members of the middle classes: professionals, merchants or manufacturers, and clerks. Fees ranged between £50 and £500 p.a., with an estimated average of £150 per year.[1]

Only one-quarter of these patients were ever discharged from the asylum; and of these, only five 'recovered' (see Figure 4.1, p. 120). The median length of stay for patients resident in the asylum at this time was between twenty and thirty-five years (see Table 4.3, p. 118). Almost one-third of the patients had already been at Ticehurst twenty years or more. The oldest, 72-year-old John Daniel Lucadon, had been there for over fifty years, since 1793. Of the seven patients who had been there longest, six were diagnosed as suffering from 'imbecility' or 'imbecility, amentia', and only one as suffering from 'delusions'. A brother and sister, George and Caroline Simson, who had been admitted in 1820 and 1830, lived until the 1870s–80s, having paid the increasingly nominal sum of £50 per year each since 1841.[2]

Nearly half the patients might have dimly remembered a former prime minister's son who had been a resident for a short time in the early 1830s. Of those patients with whom Perceval had become personally acquainted, only Henry Charles Blincowe remained, and it would be another sixteen years before he died of 'nervous exhaustion consequent on palsy'.[3] Alexander Goldsmid's nephew, Revd Louis de Visme, an Anglican minister, was now a patient in the asylum; and the Methodist Stephen Dickenson's grandson, the 21-year-old Manchester silk manufacturer,

Mid-Victorian prosperity

Henry Winkworth, was the youngest patient in the asylum. Together with the youngest female patient, 22-year-old Sophia Lindsell, these were three of the patients who eventually left Ticehurst: Louis de Visme was transferred in 1867, after a stay of twenty-seven years, to West Malling Place in Kent; Henry Winkworth was discharged 'not improved' after only two years; and Sophia Lindsell recovered and left the asylum six months after her admission, in November 1845.[4]

In line with national trends in private asylums, more men than women were admitted to Ticehurst between 1 August 1845 and 31 July 1885, and there were generally more men than women resident in the asylum (see Tables 5.1 and 5.2). As at the Retreat, most male and female admissions to Ticehurst were single. However, admissions to Ticehurst of both sexes were older on average than admissions to the Retreat – 35–44 years old,

Table 5.1   Admissions to Ticehurst, 1845–1915

Figures include admission to the Highlands *
Numbers in brackets represent known readmissions
Years run from 1 August to 31 July

Years	Men	Women	Both	Total
1845–55	26 (6)	24	50 (6)	56
1855–65	40 (3)	39 (6)	79 (9)	88
1865–75	84 (9)	56 (15)	140 (24)	164
1875–85	74 (12)	75 (27)	149 (39)	188
1885–95	48 (11)	41 (7)	89 (18)	107
1895–1905	46 (10)	50 (9)	96 (19)	115
1905–15	56 (8)	45 (6)	101 (14)	115
Subtotal	374 (59)	330 (70)	704 (129)	833
Total	433	400	833	

*From 1852 the House (asylum) and Highlands were on one licence
Sources: RA1845–81, RA1881–90, RP1890–1906, CR1907–19

Table 5.2   Number of patients resident in Ticehurst, 1845–1915

Figures are for 31 July of each year and include the Highlands *

Years	Men	Women	Total
1845	36	28	64
1855	36	22	58
1865	31	26	57
1875	44	35	79
1885	42	36	78
1895	39	37	76
1905	43	35	78
1915	41	38	79

*From 1852 the House (asylum) and Highlands were on one licence
Sources: See Table 4.3

Mid-Victorian prosperity

rather than 25–34 years old; reflecting the extent to which asylum treatment was regarded as a last resort by upper-class families.[5] Despite this, Ticehurst was able to prosper in the competitive market of the 1850s–80s, expanding to take nearly eighty patients by 1875.

The geographical area from which admissions were drawn continued to widen. Occasionally, and increasingly, patients came to Ticehurst from countries outside the United Kingdom. This mirrored not so much a further expansion of the asylum's reputation, as the growth of Britain's interests overseas, and in the number of personnel who managed the Empire. Some patients had worked on plantations, or in the Indian civil service, before being certified and sent to Ticehurst (see Table 5.3). Others had been travelling abroad in an attempt to shift their disorders, and were confined to an asylum only after this attempted remedy proved unsuccessful.[6]

Within England, patients travelled from all over the country to be admitted to Ticehurst (see Figure 5.1). In part, this reflected the increasing ease of travel brought about by the development of the railways, but it was also a product of the Newingtons' growing ability to be selective in their choice of patients, and the high-class clientele of the asylum. Despite the Newingtons' charity to a few long-stay, nominal fee-paying patients like the Simsons, local families who were eager for their relatives to be treated at Ticehurst were sometimes turned away. Thus in January 1863, a Mr Hudson applied through one of the visiting magistrates for a relative of his to be admitted, but he was refused because the fees he offered were too low. In August of the same year, a letter of application from a man in Cranbrook 'relative to a lady' was speedily followed by his arrival the same day with his insane sister and two medical men 'but neither the terms nor the patient would suit', and they were sent away.[7]

Some of those who journeyed furthest within Britain to become patients at Ticehurst were related to former patients, like Stephen Dickenson's grandson, Henry Winkworth, who came from Manchester. Others may have heard of the asylum through friends, as it is possible William Rathbone Greg, whose wife Lucy travelled from Westmoreland to become a patient at Ticehurst in 1857, did from Henry Winkworth's sister Susanna. A woman who came to Ticehurst from Scarborough in Yorkshire in 1856 was there on the authority of her son, who was a surgeon; and two other admissions, from Yorkshire and Scotland respectively, were medical men, including the former superintendent of North Riding Asylum, Samuel Hill. This suggests that, although Ticehurst was not advertised in the *Medical Directory* as many private asylums were, its reputation was widespread and high within the medical profession, including those who specialized in the treatment of insanity.[8] Another factor influencing a family's willingness to send patients some distance to Ticehurst was a desire for confidentiality. Several of the most aristocratic admissions to Ticehurst

Mid-Victorian prosperity

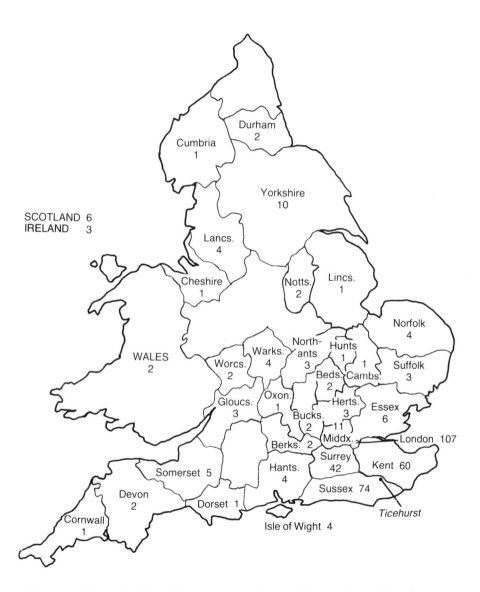

Figure 5.1 Place of origin of first admissions from within the United Kingdom, 1845–85.

Mid-Victorian prosperity

Table 5.3 Former occupations of admissions to Ticehurst, 1845–85

Figures include admission to the Highlands ***
Numbers in brackets represent known readmissions
Years run from 1 August to 31 July

Women	1845–55	1855–65	1865–75	1875–85
Independent:	9	7 (1)	3 (1)	4
Gentlewoman	8	29 (5)	33 (12)	8 (2)
No occupation/none	3		9 (1)	13 (6)
Lady			5 (1)	7 (6)
Living at home				1
Wife/spinster:		1		2
Clergyman's daughter			2	
Colonel's wife				1
Barrister's wife			1	
Solicitor's wife				1
Merchant's wife/daughter		1		1
Publisher's wife		1		
Butcher's daughter	1			
Employed:				
Lady's companion	1			
Teacher/governess			1	2 (1)
Hotel keeper			1	
Servant	1			
Unknown	1		1	35 (12)
Total	24	39 (6)	56 (15)	75 (27)

Men	1845–55	1855–65	1865–75	1875–85
Independent:	1 (2)	6 (2)	6 (3)	1 (1)
Gentleman	2 (1)	9 (1)	18	6
No occupation/none	1		2	2 (1)
Church: Clergyman	7 (1)	2	8 (3)	4
Clerk in Holy Orders		1	3	3
Dissenting minister		1		
Deacon	1		1	
Priest				1
Student				1
Army/navy:	1	2	2	
Major/Commander		1		2
Cavalry officer			1	
Colonel	1		3	1
Captain	1	2	5	5 (1)
Lieutenant	1			2 (1)
Student		1		
Medicine: Physician		1	3	1
Medical man				4
Asylum superintendent			1	
Surgeon	1	1		1
Surgeon-Dentist			1	
Student				1

132

Mid-Victorian prosperity

Men (cont.)	1845–55	1855–65	1865–75	1875–85
Law:	1			
Barrister		2	5	1 (3)
Solicitor			2 (1)	
Student	1	1	1	
Civil Service:				
Diplomat				2
Indian Civil Service				1
War Office clerk			1	
Judge's clerk			1	(2)
Agriculture:				
Coffee planter			1	
West Indian planter				1
Squatter				1
Merchants and manufacturers:				
Merchant	2	3	5	4
Wine merchant				1
Cornfactor	1			
Maltster				1
Manufacturer			1	
Silk manufacturer	(2)			
Snuff manufacturer				1
Varnish manufacturer			(1)	
Lime manufacturer			1	
Cotton spinner				1
Finance and commerce:				
Gentleman Dept Public Banks		1		
Gentleman banker			1	1
Banker			1	
Stockbroker		2		
Secretary joint stock co.			1	
Underwriter	1	1		
Business/commerce				2
Engineers:				1
Civil engineer			2 (1)	1 (2)
Education:				
Tutor		1		
Junior fellow, Cambridge			1	
Student at Oxford			1	
Student	1		1	2
Pupil	1			
Other:				
Wharfinger		1		
Polyglott and oriental printer			1	
Bookseller		1		
Hotel clerk	1			
Unknown		2	2	17 (1)
Total	26 (6)	40 (3)	84 (9)	74 (12)

* From 1852 the House (asylum) and Highlands were on one licence
Sources: RA1845–81, RA1881–90

Mid-Victorian prosperity

came from estates at some distance from Sussex: the Earl of Carlisle's son, a daughter of the Earl of Macclesfield, two brothers of the Marquis of Tweeddale and the Countess of Durham. (Although in the last instance, the Duke's highly public and unsuccessful divorce suit rendered such discretion futile.)[9]

Although the geographical area from which the Newingtons drew their patients expanded, three-quarters of all first admissions between 1 August 1845 and 31 July 1885 still came from London or the home counties (see Figure 5.1). The dramatic increase in admissions from London and Surrey reflected the growth of the metropolis, and of new outer suburbs like Herne Hill, Norwood and Peckham. Many admissions to Ticehurst came from the increasingly prosperous middle classes who could afford to build detached villas in these semi-rural suburbs. As Ticehurst's fees rose, the proportion of admissions from Sussex and Kent to Ticehurst declined. In the 1840s–50s, members of the Newington family were involved in providing further accommodation for private patients in Kent and Sussex: one of Charles Newington's sons, Samuel, who worked at Ticehurst, briefly licensed his home in Frant in 1847–9; a nephew, Samuel Wilmot Newington, opened a small private asylum called Tattlebury House, and took single patients at his home, in Goudhurst; and another nephew, Jesse Henry Newington, took single patients in Tenterden.[10]

Just over 15 per cent of first admissions to Ticehurst between 1 August 1845 and 31 July 1885 were transferred from other asylums, including two patients who were transferred from registered hospitals, and one who was transferred from Sussex county asylum. Most patients were transferred from private asylums in London run by established metropolitan physicians: Blacklands House, Chelsea (run by the Sutherlands); Brooke House, Clapton (run by the Monros); Manor House, Chiswick (run by Harrington Tuke); the Priory, Roehampton (run by William Wood); and Sussex House, Hammersmith (run by Forbes Winslow). Patients were also admitted from private lodgings, such as those supervised by Alexander John Sutherland in Alpha Road, Regents Park, and by Forbes Winslow in St Leonards.[11]

Fewer patients than were transferred to Ticehurst were discharged from there to other asylums in this period. Amongst these, too, patients were frequently sent to Brooke House, the Priory and Manor House, although no patients were transferred to Blacklands House or Sussex House. Patients were also transferred to other licensed houses, including Camberwell House, Moorcroft House and Northumberland House in London, and West Malling in the provinces. Perhaps surprisingly, only five patients were discharged from Ticehurst to a registered hospital or county asylum: two to Barnwood House in Gloucestershire, two to Northampton Asylum and one to Bodmin Asylum in Cornwall. Although it was a registered hospital, Barnwood House took only upper- and middle-class

Mid-Victorian prosperity

fee-paying patients.[12] The lower transfer rate from Ticehurst than to it suggests a high degree of satisfaction among its clientele. In addition, the negligible proportion of chronic patients who left private care, even if they left Ticehurst, reflected how securely moneyed that clientele was.

Throughout the period covered by this chapter, fees tripled, from an estimated average of £150 p.a. in 1845, to an estimated average of £450–£500 p.a. by 1875. Within this overall increase, the lowest fees stayed at only £50 p.a., while the highest fees rose from £500 to £1,500 p.a. by the early 1880s.[13] To some extent this mirrored a general increase in retail prices associated with the growth of consumerism generated by the expansion of the middle classes in the 1850s–70s. After 1875, fees in the middle range plateaued, although the highest fees continued to rise. To place these fees in perspective, average fees at Ticehurst cost less than half what the Royal Commissions on Oxford and Cambridge in the 1850s estimated was needed to support a student at one of these universities for a year; and about four times what it cost in 1868 to send a pupil to Rugby School for a year.[14]

What proportion of their income were middle- and upper-class Victorians prepared to spend on health care? J.A. Banks' otherwise detailed and thorough study of the mid-Victorian middle class makes no estimate of what percentage of their income was disbursed in this way. In the 1840s, a man who wanted to support a dependant at Ticehurst on average fees of £150, and have left over sufficient funds to support a respectable middle-class lifestyle, would have needed a secure middle-class income of £300 p.a. or more. This made short-term treatment affordable for middle-class families like the Winkworths, who might be unable or unwilling to expend a high proportion of their income on long-term asylum care. By the 1870s, however, a man who wanted to support a dependant at Ticehurst on average fees of £450–£500, and have left over the £700 Banks estimated as the minimum necessary to maintain a family in the 'paraphernalia of gentility', would have needed an above average upper-class income of *c.* £1,200. It is hardly surprising that the letters book recording applications for admission between 1857 and 1873 gave the inability to pay fees like this as the most common reason for turning people away. Nevertheless, although upper-class patients who paid £1,000 p.a. or more belonged to a small elite, some middle-class patients continued to be admitted at the lower end of the range.[15]

Looked at from the point of view of first admissions rather than patients resident in the asylum at any one time, 27 per cent of first admissions between 1 August 1845 and 31 July 1885 were discharged 'recovered', and a further 23 per cent were discharged 'relieved'; the median length of stay was just over one year (see Figure 4.2 (p. 123) and Table 4.4 (p. 122)). While results like these hardly made Ticehurst a secure investment, families who were dependent on a male breadwinner for a high income

135

Mid-Victorian prosperity

may have felt it was worth staking a considerable proportion of their financial resources on the chance of a cure: the not infrequent admissions of merchants, medical men, barristers and financiers would suggest that this was so (see Table 5.3). The relatively high proportion of admissions who were clergymen reflected not only the upper-class nature of the church as a profession, but also the fact that the church was the only profession where chronic disability did not lead to redundancy: several long-term inmates at Ticehurst, like Revd James Maxwell, Revd Joseph Jefferson and Revd Henry Sulivan remained the incumbents of prosperous livings.[16]

Earned income was only one source of finance from which fees at Ticehurst were paid. The most succinct way of defining the social class of patients in Ticehurst – particularly those who were able to stay as long-term patients – is to call them 'capitalist'; they were people who were able to derive a secure middle-class income or more from invested capital. By 1 January 1875, almost one-quarter of patients resident in Ticehurst had been found lunatic by inquisition, and were living on the proportion of their capital set aside for their upkeep by the Chancery Court.[17] These patients accounted for most of those paying the highest fees at Ticehurst; and the activity of the courts in laying aside large sums of money for their maintenance, and of the Lord Chancellors' Visitors in Lunacy, provided some of the momentum for increased fees. Revd W.G. Howard, who was a Chancery case, paid Ticehurst's highest fees of £650 p.a. when he was admitted in 1846. However, other Chancery patients, like Sir Samuel Fludyer, whose case was later taken up by the LLRA, overtook him and were paying £800 p.a. by 1850. It was only after Howard became the eighth Earl of Carlisle in 1864 that his fees increased, first to £1,000 p.a., and then to £1,500 p.a. by 1880.[18]

The chronically insane who were very wealthy posed a dilemma to those who were responsible for their care in Victorian England. On the one hand, the desire to protect the lunatic's property and the reputation of their families prompted their removal to single care or an asylum. On the other, there was a desire to protect the insane from a breach of fortune. Once their property was protected, families might feel guilty that lunatic heirs were not enjoying the privileges of wealth which were seen as rightfully theirs. James William Brook, the heir of a Yorkshire mill-owning family, was a minor when he was admitted to Ticehurst in 1866. When he came of age in 1868, a commission of lunacy was held, and a committee appointed to take charge of his affairs. Dearman Birchall, a Leeds cloth merchant whose baby daughter Clara was James Brook's future heir, was one of this committee. Initially paying twelve guineas a week, by 1875 Brook's fees had risen to almost £1,000. Nevertheless, Birchall's diary reflected how sensitive he could be to any suggestion that James Brook was not receiving the best possible care. In February 1875, James Brook's aunt went to stay with Dearman Birchall in Gloucestershire:

Mid-Victorian prosperity

When [Mrs Brook] went home I travelled as far as Cheltenham with her in company of Mr Addison who most strongly urged our taking James William away from Ticehurst, thinking that as he had derived no benefit from Dr Newington's treatment it was time to try some other. I said I had not the slightest opinion that any treatment we might advise would cure him, but that as the cost was about £1,200 per annum I thought he was entitled to greater attention, better apartments and more luxury. I promised to see if [Dr] Needham could recommend any better place.[19]

It seems likely that Dr Needham, medical superintendent of Barnwood House, would only have been able to echo the opinion of James Crichton Browne, who visited Brook in August 1875, that, 'at Ticehurst [James Brook] commands advantages as regards accommodation, comfort and medical skill unobtainable in any other private asylum in the country.'[20] Nevertheless, in 1877 Brook's fees were actually increased to nearly £1,200 p.a.[21]

It is difficult to imagine what this money could have been spent on. As William Rathbone Greg wrote in an essay on the increasing cost of living in the *Contemporary Review* in 1875, 'to live in remote districts or in an isolated fashion' was a way of avoiding expenditure; and, removed from the social and domestic commitments people of their class normally maintained, that was effectively what patients at Ticehurst did.[22] Birchall's reference to 'greater attention, better apartments, and more luxury' summarizes the way in which high fees were justified. In 1852, a fire had destroyed much of Ticehurst's main building, including the chapel and some of the patients' rooms. Despite the rebuilding this necessitated, in the 1850s–70s additional houses were added to Ticehurst's licence, and the main building was extended. Although the number of patients resident increased, individual patients were able to have exclusive use of larger and finer apartments. From the late 1860s, two houses were rented for convalescent patients at St Leonards. Other novelties included new walkways and fountains in the asylum's grounds, and the addition of an entertainments hall.[23]

By December 1877, Ticehurst employed 150 servants and attendants, and twelve lady and gentlemen companions, to cater to the needs of sixty-three patients. Attendants' wages in 1879 were from £34–£100 p.a. for men, and £25–£30 p.a. for women; so that even if Brook and the Earl of Carlisle enjoyed the exclusive attention of several attendants, their wages can only have accounted for a small part of these patients' bills.[24]

Apart from what patients were charged for rent and medical attendance, the remainder somehow had to be spent on the best meats, good wine, fine clothes, excursions to Brighton and St Leonards and other luxuries. It is of some significance here that the right to wear patients' cast-off clothing was listed in a Lunacy Commissioners' report as one of the material benefits enjoyed by attendants at Ticehurst.[25]

Mid-Victorian prosperity

Although Dearman Birchall and James Brook's maternal uncle, Edward Armitage, were keen to provide the best for Brook, in 1881 they balked at the predictable suggestion of the Lord Chancellor's Visitors that Brook should 'have a carriage and pair, be taken away from Ticehurst and set up in an establishment in London'. After a meeting with their solicitor in London they agreed:

> This recommendation [was] ... most reckless and unsuitable. Edward and I [Birchall] each sent an affidavit conveying our objections. The Judges almost immediately said they thought the Visitors had been misled. They granted £250 for the purchase of carriage and horses and extra £500 for expenses; but insisted on his remaining at Dr Newington's.[26]

By 1881, the blue landau Birchall and Armitage bought for James Brook was only one of many carriages at Ticehurst. Whereas in 1860 only seven or eight patients had carriages of their own, by 1877 these numbers had trebled to a total of twenty-two carriages and thirty-three horses which were kept at Ticehurst, including some kept by Samuel Newington for the patients' exclusive use.[27]

Of the sixty-eight patients who were resident on 31 July 1880, more than half had been at Ticehurst for less than ten years, and a third for less than five. Only five patients who had been resident on 31 July 1845 were still there, including Caroline Simson. Two patients who were over eighty might still have remembered Perceval; and another two had been admitted before Goldsmid left the asylum in 1842. All five who had been there more than thirty-five years had been diagnosed as suffering from 'delusions' rather than 'imbecility' or 'amentia', and one had been admitted on a warrant from the Secretary of State after shooting a policeman. Unusually, equal numbers of men and women were resident in the asylum. The patients' former occupations had not changed significantly since 1845: about two-thirds were described as 'gentlemen', 'gentlewomen' or 'independent', but no former occupations were given for eight patients. None of the female patients whose 'former occupation' was given had been in employment. The male patients who were not independent included five clergymen, five lawyers, a merchant, a banker and a physician.[28]

Just over one-quarter of these patients were ultimately discharged, but only four 'recovered'. Of the forty-seven patients who eventually died in Ticehurst, twenty-six lived to see in the new century, and twelve to witness the start of World War I.[29] The patient population in 1880 was younger than that in 1845. In terms of social class, its composition had not changed significantly, but the expectations of patients who had grown up in the prosperous 1850s–60s were greater. Those responsible for their care demanded better apartments, more attendants, carriages and holidays by the sea. As fees rose, expenditure on close attendance, improved

Mid-Victorian prosperity

accommodation and luxurious facilities did not prevent Ticehurst from becoming increasingly profitable. In 1863, the asylum's annual income was just over £14,000; but six years later this total had more than doubled, to over £30,500. By 1870, the Newingtons' annual profit had risen to 34.7 per cent; and they were able to draw annual salaries of £1,800.[30] The subsequent downturn in the national economy led to a rise in consumer prices which increased the asylum's outgoings; and together with the death of several high-fee-paying patients, this caused Ticehurst's annual profit to fall to 18.75 per cent by 1880.[31] Nevertheless, by the late 1870s Ticehurst enjoyed an unrivalled reputation, amongst the Lunacy Commissioners and the medical profession, which enabled the Newingtons to weather the less hospitable economic climate of the 1880s. The next section considers the moral and medical treatment which underpinned this reputation.

Psychophysiology in practice

During these months I had the advantage of living in a castellated mansion, in one of the prettiest parts of England. . . . With carriages to take me out for drives, closed upon wet days, open on fine; with cricket and bowls and archery for the summer, and a pack of harriers to follow across country in the winter . . . with five refections a day whereof to partake . . . with a private chapel for morning prayers or Sunday service . . . with little evening parties for whist or music amongst 'ourselves', and a casual conjuror or entertainer from town to distract us sometimes for an evening.

[H.C. Merivale], *My experiences in a lunatic asylum by a sane patient*, 1879, pp. 7–8

In the 1840s, two of Charles Newington's sons returned to Ticehurst to assist their father in managing the asylum. The visiting physicians who succeeded Thomas Mayo from 1836 played a less active role in the treatment of patients at Ticehurst.[32] As Oxbridge-educated physicians, Charles Hayes and Samuel Newington were less inclined to consult outside opinion. However, following Charles Hayes Newington's death in 1863, Samuel appointed an assistant medical officer who kept the patients' case notes and took day-to-day decisions concerning treatment.[33] Treatment continued to combine elements of medical and moral therapy; and also incorporated new principles drawn from Victorian physiology.

Charles Newington worked within a humoral framework, describing patients on admission as being of a particular temperament. The trend towards cautious use of depletion, and a more supportive regimen had continued. In the late 1840s and early 1850s, no patients were bled on account of their mental condition, although one patient suffering from retention of urine and partial paralysis had eleven leeches applied to his

Mid-Victorian prosperity

left temple.[34] Patients were routinely purged, but with relatively mild laxatives. From the early 1850s, some patients who had been purged to quell excitement and decongest their systems were afterwards given unspecified doses of the tonic 'Quince disulphate', or quinine, to counteract physical weakness as their mental condition improved.[35] These changes reflected a trend in general medicine away from heroic depletion, particularly blood-letting, and towards a more supportive system, which would stimulate the body's natural capacity for health through increased nourishment.

Before the increased prescription of tonics, physically feeble patients were given a supportive diet which sometimes included stimulation with alcohol. Thus Captain Mello, who suffered from scrofula, was fed on 'porter, port wine, jellies etc.' in an attempt to restore his bodily health, at the same time as he was given enemas. Patients who were vegetarian were encouraged to include meat in their diet. Mayo had argued that patients of 'sanguine' or 'bilious' temperament could withstand greater depletion than those of 'nervous' or 'serous' temperament, but in the late 1840s the Newingtons suggested of the 'bilious' surgeon Mr Crommelin 'that his mind will recover its tone as his body acquires strength', and they encouraged him to eat meat, which he had not done for two years.[36] The evidence from Ticehurst would suggest that, just as John Harley Warner has argued that the abandonment of blood-letting in clinical practice in Edinburgh occurred before its rejection in medical theory, heroic depletion ceased to be part of treatment at Ticehurst while the medical model of insanity employed by the Newingtons was still one of plethoric congestion. Given the timing of this shift, and the fact that it did not reflect an outright rejection of medical therapy, it makes more sense to see this as part of the general trend in physical medicine, rather than as a response to the critique of heroic methods in moral therapy.[37]

Bodily strength was also fostered through encouraging patients to take regular exercise. A secondary gain was that physical activity tired the patients, minimizing their restlessness. Thus in 1850, Miss Gordon walked about five miles a day 'which we find the best sedative'. Although Mayo had recommended milder narcotics than opium, the only clear instances of chemical sedation in these years were of a woman patient who was given (unspecified) 'small doses' of opium to procure sleep, and of a male patient who took half a grain of morphia each night for the same reason. Despite more moderate purgation, and the relative absence of chemical sedation, for over four years between March 1846 and May 1850, no mechanical restraint was used. Only one patient was restrained for general restlessness, 'to keep her from constantly getting out of bed' at night.[38]

Apart from being physically tiring, walks around the varied grounds were expected to stimulate the patient's interest in the external world.

Mid-Victorian prosperity

Other outdoor activities were also intended to soothe the patient, or absorb their mental attention: fishing, bowls, cricket and hunting with a pack of harriers were amongst the sports and games pursued. Patients who were too physically weak to walk far were taken for carriage rides, to benefit from the air and varied scenery. Since 1832, the Foxes had kept lodging houses and baths in Weston-super-Mare for patients from Brislington House. Ticehurst was not able to emulate this until the 1860s, but Charles Newington's sisters took several female patients on day excursions, and one male patient was sent to the seaside 'for a change'. Inside the asylum, reading and playing musical instruments were encouraged, and staff and the Newington family played games like draughts, chess and billiards with the patients. An interest in attending parish services was noted as a sign of improvement in patients, but the Newingtons could be fairly relaxed in their attitude to formal religion, as when they noted that one patient, Revd W.G. Howard, 'much delighted in pretending to perform service from the pulpit in the chapel'.[39]

Although organized activities were believed to be morally therapeutic, in other respects moral treatment was primarily a question of astute psychological management. A patient called Henry Borrer was told that he had been confined by the magistrates rather than his father 'it being thought advisable to tell him so, his feelings already being most vindictive towards his father'. When another patient called Mr Debary threatened Samuel Newington with violence, Newington ' walked up to him & told him if he attempted anything of the kind I wd. call in a dozen servants, whereupon he quietly walked to his sofa'. More persistently violent patients, or those who were eager to escape, were constantly attended by more than one person. Thus William O'Kelly, who had been confined on a warrant from the Secretary of State after shooting a policeman 'often attempts to escape from his attendants, & wd. be violent when restrained in these attempts if he had but one attendant'.[40] The numerous staff at Ticehurst helped to reduce the incidence of mechanical restraint.

Despite this, the transition of authority from Charles Newington to his sons in 1852 was associated with a temporary increase in the use of mechanical restraint. Since this trend began before the fire, it cannot be attributed to difficulties of accommodation after that event. The increase was not in the number of patients restrained, but in the frequency with which a small proportion of patients were restrained. For example, when Eliza Hawes was transferred to Ticehurst in 1854, she bit and scratched her attendants and herself, and her hands were restrained. A week later, the Newingtons experimented by giving her the free use of one hand, but after she behaved in the same way again she was kept in almost continual restraint for over eighteen months.[41]

Entries in the case books and medical journals in the early 1850s reflected a new self-consciousness about the use of mechanical restraint.

Mid-Victorian prosperity

The medical journals stressed the gentleness (and gentility) of the methods employed, especially when they were used on female patients. 'Velvet bracelets', a 'velvet belt' and 'soft straps' were among the instruments with which women were restrained. Male patients were restrained by 'loose sleeves' which encased the patient's hands as well as arms, and were fastened by straps to the patient's shoulders and thighs; or at night their wrists were fastened by 'soft straps' to the sides of the bed. It is worth noting that all of these methods left the patients' legs free, so that those whose arms and hands were restrained during the day were able to continue to take exercise walking in the grounds. More restrictive means of restraint, such as strait waistcoats, were used occasionally in cases of extreme violence; and from 1858, a camisole was used to restrain patients while they were being force-fed.[42] Seclusion, in the sense of leaving the patient alone in their own room, with the shutters closed, in the hope that they would calm down, was commonly tried before mechanical restraint was applied. Patients who were noisy or violent to property were sometimes secluded in a room at some distance from the other patients' rooms, where a grille protected the window from being broken. However, even after the asylum had been re-built in 1853, there was no specially constructed seclusion room or padded cell; and in reply to a questionnaire from the Lunacy Commissioners on seclusion and restraint, the Newingtons suggested that seclusion 'can scarcely be said to have ever been resorted to in this establishment'.[43]

The Newingtons' self-consciousness about the use of mechanical restraint reflected their awareness of opposition to the use of restraint from the Lunacy Commissioners, and many patients' families, rather than their own distaste for the use of force when they believed it was necessary. This sensitivity embraced any situation in which physical force might be used. Thus in 1853 they asked Lord Dartmouth's approval for having resorted to force to get his sister Lady Beatrix Legge out of bed. Although deference to this patient's aristocratic status made the issue particularly sensitive, even with middle-class patients the Newingtons were reluctant to override a family's wishes. In 1865, Samuel Newington asked one anorexic patient's parents to remove their daughter from the asylum, after the parents had insisted that no force was to be used in feeding her. In this case, the parents' refusal to allow their daughter to be fed with the stomach pump resulted in the patient being mechanically restrained for the first time, when she was placed in a camisole while she was fed with a spoon.[44]

Despite public sensitivity to the use of mechanical restraint, there can be little doubt that the Newingtons not only found it practically useful, but that they believed it to be therapeutic in some cases. Although violence was still the prime reason why patients were restrained, another reason which was given for the first time in June 1852 was masturbation. The two male patients who were most continuously restrained in the early 1850s, Henry

Mid-Victorian prosperity

Oxenden and Frederick Goulburn, were restrained for this reason. Medical and popular belief that masturbation was physically damaging and caused insanity, meant that this reason for mechanical restraint might have been accepted as a valid one by the Lunacy Commissioners and patients' families. When Henry Oxenden's parents visited, the Newingtons made a point of noting in the medical journals that 'His [Oxenden's] father requests that mechanical restraint may be placed upon him'. By the early 1860s, some families ascribed their relatives' insanity to masturbation, when asked of any known cause by certifying doctors.[45] Having grown to maturity in the morally straitened atmosphere of the 1820–30s, Charles Hayes and Samuel Newington shared these beliefs. They also believed that the value of mechanical restraint was not only that it prevented physical depletion or damage through masturbation or violence, but that used continuously over a period of time it broke established patterns of behaviour, and created a new habit of abstinence. This belief had foundations in the work of Victorian physiologists like William B. Carpenter and Thomas Laycock, who argued that a habit repeated often enough becomes automatic and reflexive.[46]

Reflex physiology suggested that, in long-established and recalcitrant cases like Henry Oxenden's and Eliza Hawes's, appeals to the patient's voluntary co-operation through moral therapy would necessarily be ineffective, but mechanical restraint might work. After being continually restrained for more than eighteen months, Eliza Hawes had 'discontinued biting her fingers & tearing her face in consequence of wearing leather gloves she appears to have got rid of the habit', and she was released from routine restraint.[47] Used in this way, mechanical restraint could be perceived as part of medical therapy, since the route by which change was believed to be effected was physiological and not simply disciplinarian; and it could be seen as complementary to moral therapy, rather than as antagonistic to it, although it did nothing to enhance the patient's voluntary control.

It is important to emphasize that patients who were routinely restrained over long periods of time represented a tiny proportion of cases at Ticehurst. Perhaps because of the unfashionability of mechanical restraint, the practice of using it to prevent masturbation declined. From the early 1860s, the introduction of potassium bromide, with its anaphrodisiac properties, meant that patients who behaved in a manifestly sexual way were more likely to be chemically than mechanically restrained. More moderate physical restraint –, for example, by a sheet tucked tightly over the patient in bed – was sometimes used, and combined with close watching by an attendant. In addition, from the early 1870s local applications were made to patients' genitals to discourage masturbation: of alum (a drying agent) in the case of women, and of liquor epispasticus (a blistering agent) in the case of men.[48]

143

Mid-Victorian prosperity

In 1854, the treatment the Newingtons recommended to minimize the need for mechanical restraint was moral:

> A patient, cheerful, and respectful behaviour on the part of an attendant, indulgence towards harmless caprices, but steadiness in not permitting what would prove injurious, change of attendant, where an obvious antipathy has arisen . . . will often accomplish what no amount of mechanical restraint will effect.[49]

The emphasis here on the attendant's relationship to the patient is instructive, although it is an aspect of treatment of which it is difficult to form a full picture. What little is known paralleled the attitude which Mayo recommended doctors to assume towards the insane: that is one of firmness, and a refusal to be roused to anger. Complaints of maltreatment and physical abuse of patients were extremely rare at Ticehurst, and none were upheld on investigation, suggesting that the Newingtons were able to recruit staff of high quality. Just as Mayo had argued that one reason for confining patients away from home was that treatment at home could lead to ill-feeling within the family, when patients at Ticehurst were secluded, a different attendant was substituted for their regular one 'lest a feeling of dislike should be engendered' in the patient.[50]

Wages paid to attendants at Ticehurst compared favourably to average wages for domestic servants. Attendants could take two weeks holiday a year; and married attendants were allowed to sleep at home. Although unmarried attendants generally slept in the room of the patient for whom they were responsible, male attendants were allowed three hours of relaxation every day, and female attendants 'short periods' of relaxation two times a week, and one full day a month. Job satisfaction, relative to other employment opportunities locally, was reflected in a low staff turnover, particularly on the male side, where wages were highest. In 1879, the magistrates commented that one male attendant had been employed at Ticehurst for forty-eight years. Attendants and domestic servants who married each other sometimes stayed on to work at the asylum. For unmarried attendants, as much as for chronic patients, Ticehurst could become their home, and the patients their life companions. One female attendant who worked with the same patient, I.S., from 1871 stayed on as her companion long past retirement age until the patient died at the age of 107 in 1939: a total of sixty-eight years. Despite this sustained proximity, however, and the attendants' need at times to assume authority over the patients, the little evidence there is suggests that these relationships were formal, and that attendants were expected to defer to their upper-class patients. Thus John Perceval referred to his attendant at Ticehurst as his 'servant', and by the 1880s regulations at the asylum insisted that attendants must 'salute' the patients.[51]

In contrast to the day-to-day contact between patients and their

Mid-Victorian prosperity

attendants, the Newingtons' relationships with their patients became progressively more distant. Case notes from the 1840–50s suggest that it was not uncommon for Charles Hayes and Samuel Newington to spend hours talking to male patients, and walking in the countryside with them; and female patients were sometimes befriended by 'Miss Newington', probably the doctor Newingtons' cousin Elizabeth, who was later employed as female superintendent of the asylum.[52] John Perceval had resented being expected to confide in a jumped-up surgeon like Charles Newington, and advocated greater involvement by the clergy (and other gentlefolk) in the treatment of insanity, because he believed it was more appropriate for 'gentlemen to heal the minds of gentlemen'; but as Oxbridge-educated physicians, Charles Hayes and Samuel Newington were better qualified than their father to approach upper-class patients as equals, offering consolation and advice, or simply a listening ear, to their high-class clientele.[53]

The Newingtons' intimacy with their patients was guided by principles of moral treatment. Thus when a patient called James Coles complained that he was being ill-treated, the Newingtons tried to shift the conversation to another topic, as they would whenever a patient was in danger of becoming excited. Visits from patients' families were also closely regulated to protect the patient from over-excitement. When a visit was considered inadvisable, relatives were allowed to watch the patient from a window to see that they were safe, but not to talk to, or be seen by, the patient.[54] Mayo's belief that the painfulness of exclusion from the family provided a powerful incentive for recovery was incorporated within the asylum in the decreased access patients were allowed to the Newingtons, and an everyday domestic environment, if their behaviour deteriorated. The system of graduated inclusion with, and exclusion from, the Newington family was well illustrated by a letter to the Lunacy Commissioners concerning a patient called Louisa Manning in 1861 which stated that:

> On her arrival . . . Miss L.M. . . . gave way without reason to the most exaggerated paroxysms of passion . . . throwing herself into theatrical and indelicate attitudes. On . . . our [Charles Hayes Newington] mentioning that if she continued to make such unseemly noises she would be removed from the Highlands House . . . Miss L.M. immediately refrained from these exhibitions. . . . She now enters into the society of our families & attends the service at the Parish Church.[55]

In the early 1860s, a teenage epileptic patient called Timothy Brett, whom Samuel Newington described as a 'very affectionate' and 'religious' boy was invited to play with Samuel Newington's children on two consecutive evenings. This patient's subsequent statements that Ticehurst was 'a butcher's house', that he was being interfered with by electricity, and that 'he is God almighty & may do just what he likes' meant that despite Samuel

Mid-Victorian prosperity

Newington's initial liking for him, he was not invited again.[56] Rather than inviting patients into his own home, after Charles Hayes' death Samuel Newington more frequently dined with quiet and convalescent male patients in the common room of the main building.

From 1859, on the advice of the Lunacy Commissioners, a lady companion was appointed to assist female patients with music, drawing and sewing. This woman, and the assistant medical officers who were appointed after 1864, presided over the dining tables in the main building at which patients were allowed to sit only if they behaved with some self-control.[57] By 1879, five other lady companions, and six gentleman companions, some of whom were medical students, worked at the asylum, and the Newington family had very little social contact with the patients, except for when they invited well-behaved patients to afternoon tea on Sundays, or attended the asylum's organized entertainments.[58] The appointment of an assistant medical officer meant that even Samuel Newington's medical involvement in the treatment of patients was lessened. The extension of the asylum's buildings, and increased number of patients, created a longer medical round. From the 1860s, medical journals and case books were kept by the assistant medical officer.

Despite a temporary decline in entries recording the use of mechanical restraint in the early 1860s, in June 1869 the Lunacy Commissioners' inquiries about an apparent recent increase in restraint led them to discover that for 'a long time past' the housekeeper at Ticehurst had been giving female attendants permission to restrain patients without telling Samuel Newington or the assistant medical officer, and consequently without an entry being made in the medical journals. Three female patients had their feet tied together and to the bed, and a sheet pulled tightly over their chests and fastened to the bed, in addition to wearing camisoles. An entry had been made on this occasion only because on one of his rounds the assistant medical officer, Dr Dixie, had found on examining one of the patient's feet that they were tied together, and asked if any other patients were similarly restrained. The Lunacy Commissioners reprimanded Dr Dixie for even then making no report of what had occurred to Samuel Newington. Although there is no direct evidence to link the two events, Dr Dixie left Ticehurst in June 1869, and was the only assistant medical officer who appears to have left not only asylum practice, but also the medical profession after leaving Ticehurst.[59]

Anne Digby has suggested that at the Retreat the asylum's expansion in size, and the continuity of families who were involved in working there over several generations, led to an institutionalization of its previous familial ambience, and a rigidification of the early, fresh principles of moral treatment into moral management.[60] At Ticehurst, more limited expansion occurred through the addition of new houses each of which formed a small unit, but a similar process of routinization can be observed. A rapid

Mid-Victorian prosperity

turnover of assistant medical officers in the 1860s–70s inevitably meant, for long-stay patients at least, a less close and personal relationship with their physician. Central to this shift was Samuel Newington's loss of interest in the business which he had inherited, whose high standards needed maintaining but which offered only limited scope for new initiatives. Only one new project in the 1870s was personally cherished by Samuel Newington: an attempt to involve patients in gardening as a form of therapy. Newington was a keen amateur horticulturist; and in 1874, after reading of recoveries which had been achieved on the continent through the employment of the insane in gardening, he had three acres of land laid out as allotments for both male and female patients. In practice, only male patients took up the opportunity to garden, under the supervision of a professional gardener who had been employed specially for the purpose. Although this project continued for at least three years, the difficulties of persuading patients to take a consistent interest eventually proved insuperable. Following his stay at Ticehurst in 1875, Merivale remembered Samuel Newington as a remote figure, who spent more time pottering in his greenhouses than with his patients.[61]

The fundamental principles of moral treatment, in terms of seeking to combine health-giving physical exercise with mental absorption in the outside world, were continued in the 1860s–70s. Cricket, running with the harriers, and to a lesser extent bowls remained prominent activities, to which croquet and archery were added. Increasing numbers of patients had their own carriages, and for those who could not afford this luxury the Newingtons kept carriages and donkey chaises for the patients' use. The renting of two houses at St Leonards meant that convalescent and quiet chronic patients could spend time by the sea, to go bathing and for donkey rides. From Ticehurst, patients were taken to village fetes and flower shows, and on picnics. As they improved they were allowed to spend days with their families in nearby towns like Tunbridge Wells. Convalescent patients who were still under certificates were allowed out on trial for weeks or months at a time, and in such cases a continuation of the certificates was believed to exert a 'moral control' over the patient, since if they failed to keep their self-control they could be returned to the asylum. Thus in 1870 a formerly alcoholic patient, William Green, was allowed out on trial on condition that he did not drink any alcohol; an agreement which this patient managed to keep.[62]

Inside the asylum (and outside in summer), patients were encouraged to spend their time constructively in reading, drawing, painting, sewing (for women), singing and playing musical instruments. Fortnightly concerts were given by a brass band made up of male attendants who had enhanced chances of employment if they could play a musical instrument; and popular lectures on scientific subjects, such as geology, were given by guest speakers. At St Leonards, patients were allowed to go to the theatre.

Mid-Victorian prosperity

Increasingly in the second half of the nineteenth century, patients were encouraged to take an active part in entertainments, singing and playing at concerts (on the piano and violin rather than brass instruments), and giving talks on subjects which interested them, as Revd Cotton did in May 1867 on bees. This meant that patients were occupied in preparing and rehearsing, as well as attending, these events.[63] Indoor games like chess, draughts, cribbage and billiards continued to be played between patients, and with their companions. Dances and whist- parties were organized, and convalescent patients were encouraged to hold parties of their own. Mayo had suggested that mentally disturbed patients could derive mental strength from association with people who were mentally well, and in 1854 the Newingtons argued that: 'the example of the more tranquil and docile patients is of great use to those who are intractable, and the association of patients used with discrimination is of essential service'.[64] Although an interest in attending church, and attention to the content of the sermon, were seen as signs of improvement, no strong pressure was placed on patients to be religiously observant.

Which aspects of patients' behaviour did the Newingtons feel it was important to regulate, and which were they prepared to rank as 'harmless caprices'? Their concern to prevent patients masturbating has already been documented. Other overtly sexual behaviour – like the propositions of a male patient called Revd Patterson to his male attendant – also led to a firm and pragmatic response; in this case to the patient being bolted in his room at night while the attendant slept outside. The Newingtons' case notes revealed a general concern with sexual propriety, referring even in this medical context to semen as 's——n', and taking care to avoid any possible sexual innuendo, as when Charles Hayes Newington described a female patient who had 'exposed herself to [crossed out] not taken proper precautions against damp ground'.[65] However, since it was not uncommon for patients to remove their clothes in public the scope for a possible misunderstanding here was real, and could have had a material effect on what happened to the patient in the future. Patients' ability to conduct themselves with sexual propriety was one of the Newingtons' central concerns when considering temporary or full discharge.

Swearing and obscene language were also disapproved of. This partly reflected a strong sense of the kind of behaviour which was appropriate to a patient's social position. Thus Charles Hayes Newington described one female patient's language as so 'outrageous and coarse . . . that, as a lady, it was surprising where she could have heard it'; while Revd Patterson cursed in 'language such as no clergyman in his senses wd. have used at any time, much less so on Sunday'.[66] However such behaviour by itself did not prevent patients from attending communal meals, entertainments, or chapel services, although obscene language or behaviour was one reason for patients not being permitted to leave the grounds of the asylum in their

Mid-Victorian prosperity

walks, or attend the parish church. This demonstrated the strength of the Newingtons' conviction that more disturbed patients could benefit from mixing with convalescent or quiet patients, rather than a fear that better-behaved patients' condition might deteriorate if they associated with patients who were noisy and disruptive. Only one patient, Letitia Walker, was asked to leave because she was persistently antagonistic to other patients; and a male patient called Charles Mawley was removed because he was 'much disliked by other patients', but only after he had also encouraged another patient to leave the grounds of the asylum with him.[67]

Some physical rough-and-tumble was tolerated, so long as it did not become too violent or malicious in intent. Thus in April 1860 Revd Louis de Visme was described as 'very fond of striking when in close quarters', and over two years later as 'not dangerous, though he often hits very hard in his play'; but five years later after he broke a wooden poker over the assistant medical officer, Thomas Belgrave's, shoulder and threw a chair at him, de Visme's relatives were asked to remove him.[68] Outbursts which were seen as an attempt to provoke the attendants and doctors were sometimes thought best ignored, as when a patient called Mrs Welstead 'used every expedient to excite & rouse me [Thomas Belgrave]. She abused, taunted & sweared, then tossed a plate at my head, also a book & finally hit me a blow on the nose!'; but this behaviour did not lead to the patient being restrained, or any other special treatment.[69] With many patients, a visible reminder that they were outnumbered by attendants was sufficient to inhibit violence. Thus in 1855, when a patient called Mary Turney threatened violence, she:

> immediately exercised self-control upon the appearance of three attendants in her room & she remarked 'I shd. like to knock that candlestick out of yr. hand but I see it is no use trying it here, where I have been before I have always screamed & been able to get my own way. I can't do that here so I shall be quiet.[70]

Apart from the generous staff: patient ratio, generally low levels of mechanical restraint for violence were maintained by a policy of refusing admission to very violent or suicidal patients, and transferring patients who were persistently violent after admission. In 1869 the commissioners recommended that Samuel Newington should issue guidelines to his staff on the only circumstances in which mechanical restraint ought to be employed, to prohibit 'excessive' restraint like that which had recently been discovered, which Newington did; but his own preferred solution in the long term was to limit the number of acute admissions so that the incidence of violence was kept as low as possible.[71]

Great care was taken to keep faecal smearers, and those who were so depressed that they completely neglected themselves physically, as clean as possible. In 1858, a partially paralysed woman called Anne Farquhar

149

Mid-Victorian prosperity

was admitted to Ticehurst after having been in bed for three years at home. Although this woman was said to have been attended by 'most of the eminent medical men in England' (her certificates were signed by John Conolly), she had refused to be washed or to allow her bed-linen to be changed, and on admission her hands and arms were 'begrimed with dried faeces' and she was covered in boils. However, within three days of Mrs Farquhar's admission to Ticehurst, where she was washed, the windows of her room were kept open, and she was encouraged to sit up and read, she declared 'that there is nothing so delightful as a good wash & plenty of fresh air'. This transformation was represented by Charles Hayes Newington not only as one which was beneficial to Mrs Farquhar's physical health, but as a moral one, from a state of polluted and idle animality to one of virtuous and busy humanity. At first Mrs Farquhar had eaten 'more like an animal than a human being . . . chews her animal food & then spits it out' and she was 'without . . . any rational employment'; but a week later she took 'her dinner at the table in a cleanly manner . . . reads religious books & the newspapers' and was 'very amiable & grateful'.[72]

However, it was primarily dirt which was believed to carry the threat of disease which was seen as morally unwholesome, and some messiness and damage to property were tolerated, although a preference for tidiness and care with appearance were always seen as signs of improvement in a patient's condition. Before he was transferred, Charles Mawley was allowed to spend hours mixing grease and cigar-ash, to make what he described as 'hair-dye'; and in May 1865 the commissioners criticized Samuel Newington for allowing a patient called George Wood to draw all over the floor of his sitting-room with white chalk. Another patient, Fritz Steiner, sketched a landscape on the walls of his room, which he hoped would be removed and hung at the Royal Academy. In this case the doctors' initial tolerance somewhat back-fired, since when Steiner's room was redecorated three weeks later he created a disturbance when he next saw the assistant medical officer, Francis Wilton, shouting 'Where is my drawing, you bugger'.[73]

Within the boundaries set by the desire for cleanliness, physical safety and sexual restraint, considerable freedoms were allowed to patients. Apart from being able to keep their own horses and carriages, they were permitted to have pets with them in the asylum, like the former editor of the *Provincial Medical and Surgical Journal*, William Harcourt Ranking (1814–67), who kept a dog at Ticehurst in the 1860s. Their freedom of physical movement may be gauged by the fact that, despite close attendance, in the 1850–60s two patients managed to escape. In 1857 a patient called Thomas Wright was able to give his attendant the slip, and walked all the way to London without being apprehended. He was only recaptured when, pretending to be unable to talk as he often did, he handed the guard at London Bridge railway station a note saying 'I belong

Mid-Victorian prosperity

Table 5.4 Supposed causes of insanity in first admissions to Ticehurst, 1845–1915

Causes	1845–55	55–65	65–75	75–85	85–95	95–1905	1905–15
Unknown	30	23	37	52	20	14	17
Moral	8	26	41	38	32	30	29
Physical	9	22	38	42	28	30	35
Mixed			4		1	6	14
None given	3	8	20	17	8	16	6

Sources: See Table 5.3, RP1890–1906 and CR1907–19

to the Ticehurst Asylum & want to go there but have no money'. More tragically, in 1861 a patient who had been admitted after he had amputated his penis, and who suffered from increasing depression as his rationality returned, was able to walk off the grounds of the asylum and drown himself in a local pond.[74]

An analysis of the 'supposed causes' of insanity given in the admissions books shows that in one-third of cases the supposed cause was given as 'unknown', and that in those cases where a specific cause was given there was an almost equal distribution between 'moral' and 'physical' causes, with a slightly decreasing emphasis on 'moral' causes (see Table 5.4). Anne Digby has documented a similar decline at the Retreat; and Ticehurst was like the Retreat too in the fact that there was a decrease in the proportion of cases assigned to heredity. Just as Quakers were sensitive to the issue of hereditary insanity because of their high rate of inter-marriage, the Newingtons were reluctant to assign 'heredity' as a cause to their upper-class and aristocratic patients. Mayo had suggested that families were more loath to admit to insanity than consumption in the family, but histories given in the case notes make it clear that the Newingtons and their assistant medical officers were often aware of a family history of insanity, but did not necessarily assign 'heredity' as a cause in the admissions books. Indeed, since in some instances several generations of the same family had been patients at Ticehurst, the Newingtons could not have been kept ignorant of those families' histories.[75]

Degenerationist ideas were used by liberal critics of inherited privileges to argue for more open access. Thus in *Fraser's Magazine* in 1868 W.R. Greg wrote:

Not only does civilisation as it exists among us enable rank and wealth, however diseased, enfeebled or unintelligent to become the continuators of the species in preference to larger brain . . . but that very rank and wealth, thus inherited without effort and in absolute security, tends to produce *enervated and unintelligent* offspring. To be born in the purple is not the right introduction to healthy living (original emphasis).[76]

151

Mid-Victorian prosperity

Yet Greg was less willing to countenance the possibility of an hereditary factor in insanity amongst the middle classes. Greg's wife Lucy had been a patient at Ticehurst, there had been rumours that her father, the Manchester physician and chemist William Henry (1774–1836) had been insane before he committed suicide partly because of his anxiety at Lucy's illness, and her sister Charlotte had been mentally defective. Nevertheless Greg, whose own brother Samuel was also incapacitated by chronic depression, attributed the prevalence of mental and nervous disorders amongst the middle classes, like the increase in heart disease, to the stress of their position in society.[77] Anne Digby has rightly suggested that the increase in the proportion of cases whose insanity was said to have been caused by 'anxiety' or 'overwork' in the 1870s should not be attributed simplistically to an increase in stress in the depressed economy, but it seems important to place these assigned causes within the self-perceptions of the Victorian middle classes. One of the first admissions to Ticehurst whose breakdown was attributed to 'over-pressure of duties' by the former medical officer of Lincoln Asylum, Thomas Belgrave, was Samuel Hill, the former superintendent of a large county asylum in Yorkshire.[78]

Compared with admissions to county asylums only a small proportion of cases at Ticehurst were attributed to alcohol abuse. The Newingtons had a strong faith in the therapeutic value of alcohol, which might have mitigated against a willingness to see alcohol consumption as a causal factor in the onset of mental disorders. Those whose insanity was sympathetically attributed to 'anxiety' or 'overwork' included some heavy drinkers, and it seems likely that, just as the Newingtons were reluctant to highlight a possible hereditary factor in their patients' insanity, they chose to describe alcoholism as a symptom of an earlier moral cause rather than as a physical disease.[79] More importantly, by choosing not to emphasize the role of alcohol abuse, which could be seen as a vice rather than a disease, they minimized any manifest moral condemnation of their patients. Although the evangelical moral values of the 1830s continued to be incorporated in some aspects of treatment at Ticehurst, at the point of admission the Newingtons were sensitive to prospective patients' families' own perceptions of what had precipitated the mental disorder, and largely echoed them.

Evidence from outside Ticehurst would suggest that it was not uncommon for Victorian doctors to rely on what their patients or the patient's family told them of possible causes of the disorder. When H. Sieveking, who presented a paper to the Royal Medico-Chirurgical Society on the causes of epilepsy in 1857, was asked why he had not included masturbation as one of the causes, his somewhat embarrassed reply was that:

> it was not the assigned cause in any instance by the patient. The difficulty really was to arrive at the truth with respect to the influence

Mid-Victorian prosperity

of this cause in the production of the disease, and he confessed he did not know how to proceed to determine it in the case of females.[80]

Thus, when Timothy Brett's insanity was attributed to 'self-abuse' in 1863, it was because his father had given it as the cause. Less close relations may have been more willing to countenance the possibility that heredity had played a part. The 'supposed cause' of insanity given on James Brook's certificates was 'congenital, aggravated by self-abuse', and Samuel Newington candidly told Brook's brother-in-law Dearman Birchall that 'the children of an epileptic father nearly always go wrong'. In addition, Newington counselled Birchall that in order to avoid the twin hereditary taints of insanity and consumption (of which Birchall's wife had died at the age of 21) affecting his daughter Clara, Birchall should 'not excite the brain until fully developed, . . . [or] call for any mental exertion until a child is near ten years of age'.[81]

The almost equal stress placed on 'moral' and 'physical' causes of insanity neatly reflected the Newingtons', and their assistant medical officers', belief in the close interdependence and interaction of body and mind. The attribution of 'moral' rather than 'physical' causes did not imply a non-physiological pathology, or a more optimistic prognosis; any more than the attribution of 'physical' causes necessarily implied a pessimistic prognosis. As Bruce Haley has emphasized, in Victorian psychophysiology mental unease and physical pathology, of bodily as well as mental disorders, were seen as mutually aggravating. Thus in 1861 the disorder of a patient who was described on her certificates as 'morally insane' was said to be due to 'cerebral disturbance'; while William Harcourt Ranking and Samuel Hill, who both suffered from progressive paralysis, had their disorders attributed to 'excess of mental occupation' and 'over-pressure of duties', respectively. In both these cases, the patients' paralysis was listed as a 'bodily disorder', but in most cases 'general paralysis' was given as the patient's mental disorder, particularly after the introduction of 'General Paralysis of the Insane' as a diagnosis.[82]

The influence of reflex physiology in emphasizing the whole nervous system, rather than just the brain, in the physical pathology of mental disorders, was reflected in both the 'supposed causes' and the diagnoses made at Ticehurst. Thus, Anne Farquhar's paralysis and mental disorder were attributed to falls during pregnancy which were believed to have 'affected spine, nerves of spine & spinal marrow'. While in 1861 Ann Hopkinson's 'dementia senilis' was attributed to a 'womb and spinal disorder communicating with the brain'.[83] Although neither Charles Hayes nor Samuel Newington received a formal education in mental pathology, the admission books after 1850 included a wider range of diagnoses than their father had used. These differentiated several types of 'mania' ('acute', 'hysterical', 'paroxysmal' and 'puerperal'), and included 'monomania'. In

153

Mid-Victorian prosperity

Table 5.5 Diagnoses of first admissions, 1845–85

Diagnoses	1845–55	1855–65	1865–75	1875–85	Total
Delusions	27	51	39	20	137
Mania	6	7	37	61	111
Melancholia	9	6	25	40	82
Dementia	1	2	15	9	27
Nervous disorders		2	4	10	16
Imbecility	4	2	2	2	10
Moral insanity				2	2
None given	3	9	18	5	35

Sources: See Table 5.3

addition, Charles Hayes Newington diagnosed a patient in 1855 as suffering from 'chorea'; and nervous disorders like 'general paralysis' and 'epilepsy' began to be clearly differentiated. As at the Retreat, 'imbecility' and 'weak-mindedness' were less freqently used as diagnoses. However, 'delusions', the subject of which was sometimes specified, remained the preferred diagnosis until after the arrival of the assistant medical officers, who took over responsibility for keeping the admission books from Samuel Newington (see Table 5.5).

The medical therapies employed by Charles Hayes and Samuel Newington were primarily supportive. No patients were venesected, although until the mid-1860s patients continued to be leeched to alleviate 'nervous irritation', particularly in cases of epilepsy or hysteria. Thus in April 1862, Frances Hoffman had twelve leeches applied to her temples after a particularly severe epileptic fit, which Samuel Newington described as 'apoplectic' in character; and in May 1863 Miss Jenney had two leeches applied to her spine to relieve 'spinal irritation'.[84] Although the Newingtons continued to purge patients, they also prescribed an increasing range of tonics, mostly iron and zinc compounds, including 'iron & strychnia', or the chalybeate Charles Newington had refused to prescribe to John Perceval. Patients were also given a 'full' diet, although in cases of 'nymphomania' this might be based on milk and cereals rather than meat. The persistence of the belief that patients with nervous and mental disorders had feeble constitutions and needed extra nourishment can be seen from the fact that in the 1870s the most common reason given for medical treatment was 'debility'.[85]

Alcohol was prescribed as part of these supportive and nourishing diets; a practice which had been endorsed by W.B. Carpenter in 1850 when he argued that alcohol was particularly nourishing to nervous tissue. Although the value of alcohol therapy became controversial in the 1860s when some physiologists argued that, contrary to the idea that alcohol built up nervous tissue, it was rapidly and totally eliminated from the body, it continued to be prescribed at Ticehurst. Two of the keenest opponents of

Mid-Victorian prosperity

the total elimination theory, F.C. Anstie and J.L.W. Thudichum, were amongst doctors who referred patients to Ticehurst in the 1860s. Even in cases where a patient was admitted suffering from delirium tremens after a bout of heavy drinking, alcohol in moderate quantities was prescribed, both for its putatively beneficial physical effects, and to cultivate a habit of moderation in the patient.[86] In addition, alcohol was valued as a sedative, particularly as Samuel Newington remained dissatisfied with the use of opium for this purpose.

In their *Manual of psychological medicine* (1858) J.C. Bucknill and D.H. Tuke referred to opium as the 'sheet-anchor' of asylum doctors. However, although the Newingtons prescribed it both as a sedative and as an anti-nauseant, it was never their treatment of choice.[87] When Lucy Anne Greg was admitted in 1857 she had been routinely sedated with opiates by her husband's sisters while she was cared for by her family; but the Newingtons gradually reduced the amount she took, and regarded it as a sign of imminent recovery when she was able to sleep without a sedative. Similarly, when Mary Anne Foster was admitted in 1864 in a state of acute mania, she had not slept for six days and nights without morphia, and she had been restrained, bled and given no food. On arrival at Ticehurst she was bathed and given clean clothes, and then given food and an unspecified quantity of port wine, which enabled her to sleep for nine hours without morphia.[88] The concern to find an alternative sedative to opiates informed Samuel Newington's only medical articles, on the sedative effect of mustard baths and mustard packs.

In these papers in 1865, Newington described several cases of acute mania in which the patient had been calmed by a mustard bath or mustard pack.[89] Despite the Newingtons' mistrust of hydropathy, baths formed part of the treatment offered to patients at Ticehurst. In states of mania, some patients were placed in a warm bath, while cold water was applied to their heads, to direct the blood away from the brain and towards the rest of the body. Mustard baths and mustard packs were used at Ticehurst; but restrictions introduced by the Lunacy Commissioners on the number of hours for which wet packs could be applied meant mustard packs were subsequently virtually abandoned. Despite the use of mustard baths to soothe maniacal patients, morphia continued to be used to sedate patients in acute states of mania. The most common use of baths was in treating women who suffered from amenorrhoea, who were given warm hip baths to draw blood to the pelvic region. In severe cases, these patients were also given aloes, as an emmenagogue rather than a purgative. The conviction that suppressed menstruation contributed to insanity stemmed from the belief that insanity was caused by a congestion of blood in the brain, which it was hoped restored menstruation might alleviate. Although this was a long-standing belief, and Mayo's writings and early case notes at Ticehurst make it clear that Charles Newington attempted to regulate female

Mid-Victorian prosperity

patients' menstrual cycles, in the 1860s a renewed emphasis began to be placed on the importance of women's reproductive physiology.[90]

The development of a profession of gynaecology, and new surgical techniques from the mid-1860s, meant that, if the doctors' assumption of a close link between women's minds and their reproductive organs proved correct, new heroic strategies of treatment might be developed. In the 1860s, a young medical man with the prospect of a promising career in asylum medicine might opt instead to become a gynaecologist: the first assistant medical officer at Ticehurst, Dr Edis, later developed a lucrative practice in Wimpole Street as a consultant gynaecologist, from which he visited patients at Ticehurst in the 1870s.[91] Increasing numbers of female patients and their families, like the Countess of Durham, consulted gynaecologists in their search for health and well-being before they consulted asylum doctors. To have a minor anatomical or physiological disorder, one peripheral symptom of which was some emotional disturbance, was less stigmatizing than to have a frankly mental disorder. The belief that disorders of the uterus or ovaries could cause mental disorders was based by the 1860s primarily on the idea that local 'irritation' of those organs could create excessive 'irritation' in the whole nervous system and brain. Thus in 1867, a patient at Ticehurst called Mrs Welstead, whose acute mania was attributed to her prolapsed uterus, was mechanically restrained while she was fitted with a pessary. Her condition showed no sign of improvement, and after she removed the pessary herself the next day, she was not fitted with another. However, patients continued to be fitted with pessaries in an attempt to alleviate their mental condition until the late 1870s.[92]

Another group of disorders which received attention in the 1860s were those which were characterized by fits, including epilepsy. In the 1850s the Newingtons treated epilepsy with the anti-periodic quinine, with alcohol or by bleeding. However, from 1863 they began to experiment with the use of bromides. Interest in potassium bromide had been aroused in 1857 by the claims of Queen Victoria's physician Dr Locock that he had treated several epileptic patients successfully with potassium bromide. Initially attracted to the drug for its anaphrodisiac effects, and unaware of its anti-convulsant properties, when Locock found that the patients to whom he prescribed bromides suffered fewer fits as well as stopping masturbating, he believed that he had proved conclusively that masturbation caused epileptic fits. C.B. Radcliffe introduced the use of bromides at the National Hospital for Nervous Diseases in 1863, and it was Brown-Séquard, a consultant from there, who advised Samuel Newington to treat Frederick Goulburn with 'large doses' of potassium bromide in October 1863. A few months later, Newington observed gloomily that this course had been 'persevered in without any beneficial result'.[93] Nevertheless, bromides continued to be prescribed at Ticehurst not only in cases of epilepsy, but

Mid-Victorian prosperity

in cases of 'nymphomania' and 'satyriasis', and most importantly as a general sedative. In the late 1860s, very large doses were prescribed to some patients at Ticehurst. Thus Jimmy Brook was given 90 grains a day; and in 1867 Henrietta Unwin was prescribed up to 60 grains a day, despite the fact that she was pregnant. However, from the early 1870s bromism (which had been described in 1868) began to be watched for in patients who were given bromides, and doses were reduced to 60 grains or less a day, since this was the level at which there was believed to be a danger of bromism. Patients who suffered an adverse reaction to even low doses of potassium bromide were given potassium iodide instead.[94]

Although Merivale was dosed fairly heavily with potassium bromide during a period of mania at Ticehurst, like Perceval he remembered the asylum as a place where little medication was given. It is possible that Merivale's memory of his illness was incomplete, or that he was given medicine without being aware of it. Whichever explanation is correct, Merivale also noted, in contrast to Perceval, that doctors at Ticehurst were willing to give patients any medicine they asked for. Yet this ought not to be taken at face value. It is clear from case notes in the 1860s that hypochondriacal patients, as Merivale was, were readily given placebos to calm their anxieties about their health.[95] Altogether, expenditure on medicines in 1880 amounted to £81.10s., which was significantly more than that described by Anne Digby at the Retreat.[96]

In a letter to Samuel Newington in 1861, the proprietor of Manor House, Harrington Tuke, described one patient's medical treatment prior to her admission to Ticehurst as having been directed 'to local symptoms and to the general health', and this is a concise summary of what Samuel Newington believed medical treatment could achieve.[97] Yet as Bruce Haley has argued, Victorian psychophysiology taught that 'If the disease begins with a state of psychic disorder, the restitution of health might begin with a natural and orderly physical life'.[98] While moral therapy was the only specialist treatment asylum physicians had to offer, the claim of asylum doctors to a special expertise in treating the insane stemmed not only from an assertion that insanity was a brain disease, but from the belief that as general physicians they had a specialist knowledge of how to regulate the whole body, which was the physical vehicle of the mind. Despite the limitations of Victorian therapeutics, asylum doctors were confident that the mind and body had a natural tendency to recover and heal, which could be promoted by an appropriate regimen.

The most persistent problem the Newingtons faced in the mid-Victorian period was finding a way to calm and control violent and maniacal patients which would not offend the Lunacy Commissioners or patients' families. Despite their avowed commitment to moral therapy, physical restraint and chemical sedation formed a continuous backstop when moral management failed. Nevertheless, by the 1870s Ticehurst's reputation was unequalled.

Mid-Victorian prosperity

Speaking in defence of private asylums in his evidence to the select committee in 1877, Lord Shaftesbury commented that 'To abolish such a house as Ticehurst, for instance, would be a positive loss to science and humanity'.[99] Despite therapeutic limitations, the Newingtons offered exceptionally high standards of nursing care in luxurious facilities; and achieved some good results such as longer-than-average life expectancy for general paralytics.[100] As they moved away from the strong emphasis on moral insanity which had characterized Ticehurst in the 1830s, and asserted the relevance of medical developments in the 1850s–60s, they succeeded in satisfying the requirements of the Lunacy Commissioners, as well as the social demands of their high-class clientele.

Notes

1. RA1845–81, cases 1–58 (House) and 1–6 (Highlands); BB1840–6, *passim* and especially pp. 18, 44, 87.

2. RA1845–81, cases 1–17 (House) and 1 (Highlands), especially cases 1–5 and 15–16 (House); BB1840–6, pp. 43, 44; RDD1845–90, 12 December 1879 and 12 March 1881.

3. Ibid., 11 April 1861.

4. RA1845–81, cases 45, 53, 57.

5. See C. MacKenzie, 'A family asylum', London University PhD, 1987, p. 496; A. Digby, *Madness, morality and medicine*, Cambridge and New York, Cambridge University Press, 1985, pp. 175–7.

6. MacKenzie, ibid., p. 497; RA1845–81, for example, cases 101, 236, 392. Other examples of patients who had been on journeys abroad before being certified were Herman Charles Merivale and the Countess of Durham (see Chapter 4, this volume).

7. LB1857–73, 23 January and 7 August 1863.

8. RA1845–81, cases 53, 210, 241.

9. Ibid., cases 67, 153, 205, 537, 590.

10. *LCR*, 1847, pp. 5–6; N. Hervey, 'A slavish bowing down: the Lunacy Commissioners and the psychiatric profession, 1845–60', in W.F. Bynum, R. Porter and M. Shepherd (eds), *The anatomy of madness*, vol. II, London, Tavistock Publications, 1985, p. 116; I am grateful to Nicholas Hervey for the information concerning Jesse Henry Newington. For other provision in Kent and Sussex, see MacKenzie, op. cit., note 5 above, pp. 195–7.

11. RA1845–81, cases 11, 13, 77, 79, 83, 84, 97, 107, 131, 134, 139, 148, 275, 325; and, for example, certificates for William Raikes, 25 February 1851, previously lodged in Alpha Road; and Lady Beatrix Legge, 15 December 1853, 'previously under Dr Forbes Winslow & William Duke, St Leonards' (QAL/1/4/E6). RA1845–81, cases 287, 303, 537.

12. RDD1845–90.

13. See note 1 above; and PBB1870–5, *passim* and PBB1882–8, for example, p. 75.

14. J.A. Banks, *Prosperity and parenthood. A study of family planning among the Victorian middle classes*, London, Routledge & Kegan Paul, 1954, pp. 185–6, 188.

15. Ibid., pp. 95, 110; LB1857–73, for example, 26 July 1860, 14 September 1869, 13 July 1872 and December 1873.

16. Revd James Maxwell, rector of Thorpe Bishop, Norwich 1813–57, patient

Mid-Victorian prosperity

at Ticehurst, 1843–57; Revd Joseph Dunnington Jefferson, vicar of Thorganby, Yorkshire, 1832–80, patient at Ticehurst, 1869–80; Revd Henry William Sulivan, rector of Yoxall, Staffordshire, 1851–80, patient at Ticehurst 1870–3 and 1874–80.

17. *LCR*, 1875, p. 93.

18. Samuel Fludyer also paid over £1,000 by 1863 (BB1846–54, p. 62); PBB1876–82, pp. 83, 485.

19. Ibid., 1870–5, p. 290; D. Verey, *The diary of a Victorian squire*, Gloucester, Alan Sutton, 1983, p. 75.

20. Ibid., p. 77.

21. PBB1876–82, p. 24.

22. W.R.Greg, 'Life at high pressure', *Contemporary Review*, 1875, 25: 633.

23. *The Times*, 23 April 1852, p. 7; VB1845–69, 29 April 1863; VB1869–87, 26 April 1870, 27 October 1871, 17 June 1872 and 23 March 1874.

24. VB1869–87, 25 June 1879.

25. Ibid.

26. Verey, op. cit., note 19 above, p. 121.

27. VB1845–69, 20 November 1860; and VB1869–87, 7 December 1877.

28. RA1845–81; RDD1845–90.

29. Ibid.; RRDD1890–1906; RDT1907–30 and RD1907–30.

30. Ticehurst asylum audits, 1869, 1870 and 1875.

31. Ticehurst asylum audit, 1880.

32. VB1833–45, 16 January 1836, and VB1845–69, 21 December 1846, appointment Thomas Thomson, MD Paris 1816, LRCP London 1817, FRCP 1843; and John Bramston Wilmot, son of Robert Montagu Wilmot (see Chapter 2, this volume), MB (Cantab) 1828, MD (Cantab) 1834, FRCP London 1835 (see *Munk's Roll*).

33. 1864–6, Arthur Wellesley Edis (1840–93), MRCS 1862, MB London 1863, MRCP 1867 and MD London 1868, opened a Wimpole Street practice 1875; president of the British Gynaecological Society, 1889; published gynaecological books and articles. 1866–8, Thomas Bowerman Belgrave, MRCS and LSA 1858, MD Edinburgh 1864, resident assistant medical officer, Lincoln County Asylum, 1865–6, resident physician, Munster House, Fulham, 1867–8, member of the Medico-Psychological Association; emigrated to Australia 1875. 1868–9, Wolstan Fleetwood Dixie MRCS 1855, LSA 1857, St George's London, MD St Andrew's 1857; practised in Leamington Spa before working at Ticehurst; Dixie was listed as of unknown address from 1870. 1869–71, John Alexander Easton, LRCS Edinburgh 1862, MD Glasgow 1862, house surgeon Glasgow Royal Infirmary; then practised in Petworth in Sussex. 1871–82, Francis Wilton MRCS 1855, LM 1856; assistant medical officer, Gloucester County Lunatic Asylum, 1856–65; medical superintendent Joint Counties Asylum, Carmarthen 1866–9; member Medico-Psychological Association. (*Medical Directory* and *Munk's Roll*).

34. CB1, p. opposite 23.

35. Ibid., p. opposite 63(b).

36. Ibid., pp. opposite 19, 47, 72.

37. J.H. Warner, 'Therapeutic explanation and the Edinburgh bloodletting controversy: two perspectives on the medical meaning of science in the mid-nineteenth century' *Medical History*, 1980, 24: 241–58, especially pp. 246–7.

38. CB1, pp. 24, opposite 30, 34, 42.

39. Ibid., pp. 5, 6, 12, opposite 13, opposite 28, 65, 68, 83; VB1833–45, 30 August 1844 and VB1845–69, 8 July 1850 and 8 January 1851. For the Foxes' seaside houses see H. Coombs and P. Coombs (eds), *Journal of a Somerset rector 1803–34*, Oxford, Oxford University Press, 1984, p. 440.

40. CB1, pp. 4, opposite 5, 8, 71.

Mid-Victorian prosperity

41. CB2, pp. 169–76.

42. MJ1845–53, 20 January 1851; MVB1853–75, 27 November 1853 and 25 September 1854; and, for example, 25 February and 9 March 1858, 28 March 1864 and 6 March 1865. *LCR*, 1854, p. 200.

43. For cases where seclusion was tried before restraint, see CB2, pp. 112–14, 152 and CB4, p. 52; MJ1845–53, 27 April 1852 and 31 January 1853. *LCR*, 1854, see note 42 above.

44. CB2, pp. 131, 150; CB10, pp. 139, 143–2 (sic).

45. As Peter Gay has noted, the Victorians' 'persistent panic over masturbation is far easier to document than to explain', P. Gay, *The bourgeois experience. Victoria to Freud. Vol. I, Education of the senses*, Oxford, Oxford University Press, 1984, p. 309. See, for example, H.T. Engelhardt, 'The disease of masturbation: values and the concept of disease', *Bulletin of the History of Medicine*, 1974, 48: 234–48; I. Gibson, *The English vice. Beating, sex and shame in Victorian England and after*, London, Duckworth, 1978, pp. 31–2, 136; E. Showalter, *The female malady. Women, madness and English culture, 1830–1980*, New York, Pantheon Books, 1985, pp. 75–8. MJ1843–53, 5 September 1853; CB2, pp. 123–4.

46. The role of habit in establishing automatic movements was most clearly articulated by Carpenter in an article on R.B. Todd's *Physiology of the nervous system* in the *British and Foreign Medico-Chirurgical Review*, 1850, 5, i: 1–50.

47. CB2, pp. 122–3, 176.

48. See, for example, CB13, p. 145; CB15, p. 44; CB16, p. 135; CB24, p. 231 and CB36, p. 15.

49. *LCR*, 1854, p. 200.

50. Ibid.; PB1846–1904, 4 April 1879.

51. VB1869–87, 25 June 1879; tape of conversation with Herbert Francis Hayes Newington's grandson, Walter Newington; J. Perceval, *A narrative*, London, Effingham Wilson, 1840, p. 143; Attendants' book, loose letter inside front cover.

52. Censuses for 1861 and 1871, RG9.570 and RG10.1046.

53. [J. Perceval], *Narrative*, London, Effingham Wilson, 1838, pp. 276–7; and op. cit., note 51 above, pp. xx–xxi.

54. CB1, p.opposite 68; CB4, p. 118.

55. CB6, pp. 78–9.

56. CB8, pp. 134, 136.

57. VB1846–69, 24 October 1859.

58. VB1869–87, 25 June 1879; [H.C. Merivale], *My experiences in a lunatic asylum*, London, Chatto and Windus, 1879, p. 8.

59. MVB1853–75, 7 June 1869; *LCR*, 1870, pp. 45–6. See note 33 above.

60. Digby, op. cit., note 5 above, pp. 55–6, 85–6.

61. VB1869–87, 23 March 1874, last reference to patients gardening 7 December 1877; H.F.H. Newington and A.S.L. Newington 'Some incidents in the history and practice of Ticehurst asylum', *JMS*, 1901, 47: 72; [Merivale], op. cit., note 58 above, p. 73.

62. CB1, p. 87; VB1845–69, 19 December 1857, 29 April 1863, 18 June 1864, 14 July 1869; VB1869–87, 17 June 1872 and 27 July 1879. Moral control of certificates was described in ibid., 23 January 1884; William Green's case was described in CB16, p. 48.

63. VB1845–69, 8 July 1852, 15 October 1857, 18 June 1864, 11 December 1866; VB1869–87, 5 December 1870, 14 October 1878 and 29 May 1880; DCB1866–7, 23 May 1867.

64. *LCR*, 1854, p. 200.

65. CB1, p. after 10; 2, p. 121.

66. CB4, pp. 110, 139.

160

Mid-Victorian prosperity

67. Ibid., p. 40 and opposite p. 153.

68. CB9, pp. 16, 76.

69. CB11, p. 78.

70. CB3, p. 33.

71. VB1845–69, 1 December 1869.

72. It is clear from the LB1857–73, 31 May 1858, that some of Anne Farquhar's family opposed her being placed in an asylum; CB5, pp. 1–6.

73. CB4, p. 59; CB25, p. 68. PB1845–1904, 26 May 1865.

74. CB10, p. 132; CB4, p. 70; CB5, p. 126; CB6, p. 92.

75. Digby, op. cit., note 5 above, pp. 208–9; RA1845–81, cases. 9, 10, 11, 18, 21, 45, 53, 88, 91, 153, 161, 163, 164, 184, 193, 205, 227 had near relatives who were also in Ticehurst; of these, only case 91, Lord Henry Beauclerk's, insanity was attributed to heredity.

76. W.R. Greg, 'On the failure of natural selection in the case of man', *Frasers' Magazine*, 1868, 78: 355.

77. See W.V. Farrar, K.R. Farrar and E.L. Scott, 'The Henrys of Manchester. Part 2. Thomas Henry's sons: Thomas, Peter and William', *Ambix*, 1974, 21: 188–207, especially p. 191, note 49. After her own recovery, Lucy Greg considered sending her sister Charlotte Henry to Ticehurst, LB1857–73, 20 August 1858.

78. Digby, op. cit., note 5 above, p. 212; RA1845–81, case 210.

79. P. McCandless, ' "Curses of civilisation": insanity and drunkenness in Victorian Britain', *British Journal of Addiction*, 1984, 79, 1: 51; for example, RA1845–81, case 308; CB18, p. 97.

80. *Lancet*, 1857, i: 528.

81. Verey, op. cit., note 19 above, pp. 7, 10.

82. B. Haley, *The healthy body and Victorian culture*, Cambridge and London, Harvard University Press, 1978, Chapter 2. Admission certificates for Henrietta Unwin, April 1861, QAL/1/4/E7; RA1845–81, cases. 166, 188, 197, 210, 219, 443.

83. Certificates for Anne Farquhar 2 July 1858 and Ann Hopkinson 30 October 1861, QAL/1/4/E6 and E7.

84. CB7, p. 115 and CB9, p. opposite 167.

85. CB10, p. opposite 32; CB11, p. 103; MVB1853–75, for example, entries for February 1874.

86. Warner, op. cit., note 37 above, pp. 250–3; RA1845–81, cases 172 and 203; CB10, pp. 56, 58.

87. CB2, p. opposite 170; CB9, p. 78; CB10, pp. 30, 146 and CB11, p. 6.

88. CB4, pp. 74–5, 77; CB10, pp. 28–9.

89. S. Newington, 'A new remedial agent in the treatment of insanity and other diseases', *Lancet*, 1865, i: 621; and 'On a new remedial agent in the treatment of insanity and other diseases', *JMS*, 1865, 11: 272–5.

90. Newington and Newington, op. cit., note 61 above, p. 71;, for example, CB2, p. 146; CB11, p. 6; CB13, p. 3; CB14, pp. 4, 72; CB15, p. 62; CB24, p. 265; CB25, pp. 140, 243 and CB26, pp. 129, 143.

91. See note 33 above.

92. For example, CB11, pp. 5, 69, 103; CB24, p. 266 and CB25, p. 56.

93. CB1, p. 44; CB3, pp. 119–20; CB8, p. 84; R.H. Balme, 'Early medicinal use of bromides', *Journal of the Royal College of Physicians*, 1976, 10, 2: 205–8.

94. CB13, p. 3; CB24, p. 313

95. CB21, p. 25; [Merivale], op. cit., note 58 above, p. 9. For placebos see DCB1866–7.

96. Ticehurst asylum audit, 1880; Digby, op. cit., note 5 above, pp. 125–6.

97. CB9, p. 77.

161

Mid-Victorian prosperity

98. Haley, op. cit., note 82 above, p. 27.
99. *Report from the select committee on lunacy laws*, PP1877.XIII.1–, p. 546.
100. Newington and Newington, op. cit., note 61 above, p. 68.

6

The fourth generation

The Newingtons

When Samuel Newington died in July 1882 there was no shortage of heirs to his estate, or possible successors to his work at the asylum. In 1875, one of Charles Hayes' sons, Herbert Francis Hayes Newington, who was medically qualified, had returned to Ticehurst as co-proprietor (see Figure 6.1). Two of Samuel's sons, Alexander Samuel and Theodore, were also medically qualified and worked at Ticehurst as assistant physician and resident medical officer, respectively; and another of Samuel's sons, Walter James, managed the asylum's seaside extension at St Leonards. In addition, one of Samuel's daughters, Helena, was married to a former assistant medical officer at Ticehurst, George Montague Tuke (see Figure 6.2).[1] Although the prosperity of the 1860s–70s meant that the estate Samuel left was almost twice that of his brother Charles Hayes' nearly twenty years earlier, at just over £10,000 it scarcely enabled him to make lavish bequests to his wife and twelve surviving children. Indeed, when his fortune is compared with that of another of his brothers, Alexander Thurlow, who worked as secretary to the asylum but had no children, and left nearly £24,000 to his nieces and nephews in 1898, it seems likely that much of the £1,800 annual salary which Samuel had paid to himself by the 1870s went on raising and educating his children.[2]

In his will, Samuel named Alexander Samuel and Theodore as successors to his work at the asylum, but established a family trust to whom the profits from his half of the business were to be paid, and who were empowered to appoint other medical superintendents if they wished. This trust had the responsibility of ensuring that the complex division of Samuel's share of the asylum's profits into three hundred parts, to be distributed in varying proportions to his twelve children, depending on their marital status and whether or not their mother was still alive, was carried out as he had wished. In his desire to be equitable to all his children, Samuel thus created an unwieldy financial structure which opened the way to disunity in the asylum's administration.

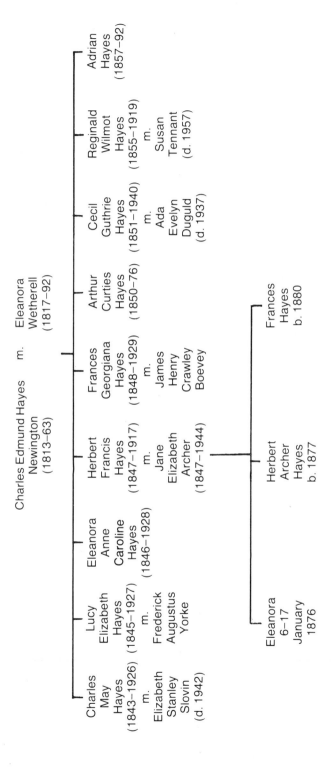

Figure 6.1 Newington family tree: Charles Edmund Hayes Newington and Eleanora Wetherell.

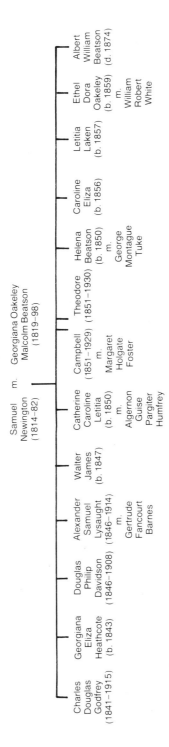

Figure 6.2 Newington family tree: Samuel Newington and Georgiana Oakeley Malcolm Beatson.

The fourth generation

Both Alexander Samuel and Theodore had taken degrees at Cambridge before studying medicine at St Thomas's, and working as assistant medical officers at Bethlem.[3] In the late 1870s, William Rhys Williams (1837–93), the resident physician and medical superintendent at Bethlem, and lecturer on insanity at St Thomas's, acted as a consultant at Ticehurst. Amongst the Newingtons' other colleagues at Bethlem was a young assistant medical officer, George Henry Savage (1842–1921), who later became a prominent consultant medical psychologist in London, and referred many patients to Ticehurst.[4] Alexander also worked as a house physician at St Thomas's, and wrote a thesis on 'Puerperal insanity', although he does not appear to have been awarded an MD. Through this work he became friendly with the prominent gynaecologist and obstetrician Robert Barnes (1817–1907), and married Barnes's daughter Mary.[5]

In contrast to his cousins' gentlemanly educations, Herbert Francis Hayes Newington took the less expensive course of studying for his MRCS at University College London. He then worked as an assistant medical officer at Morningside Asylum in Edinburgh while studying for his LRCP. In the early 1870s, Hayes Newington contributed several papers to the *Journal of Mental Science*, which was jointly edited by Thomas Clouston, whose senior assistant physician he became at Morningside; and he later succeeded Clouston as president of the Medico-Psychological Association in 1889–90. As co-partner to his uncle from 1875, Hayes Newington was entitled to a salary of £1,800 p.a., in contrast to the £200 p.a. paid to Theodore as resident medical officer in 1881; and he appears to have had a relatively free hand in managing his side of the family's share of the business.[6] In these circumstances, it is hardly surprising that it was Hayes Newington who dominated the asylum's administration during the last thirty-five years that it was managed directly by the Newingtons. In 1893, the assistant medical officer, James Henry Earls, took over as resident medical officer, and Theodore retired from work at the asylum. Since he had not married, and there was no financial necessity for him to work, the simplest explanation might be that, like his father, he lacked a profound interest in mental disorders, and found as time went on that he preferred to spend his time on other things. With his brother and cousin to supervise the running of Ticehurst there was little scope for a third superintendent.

By the early 1900s, Hayes Newington was faced himself with the difficulty of deciding how best to secure the future of the family business. Neither Alexander, nor Theodore (who lived until 1930), had any children; and Hayes Newington's son was not qualified to succeed his father as medical superintendent. Although Herbert Archer had gone to Cambridge to study medicine in 1895, his own ambition was to be a soldier. Like his uncle Alexander, who had won shooting prizes at Cambridge, Herbert Archer became a Captain of the University Rifle Corps, but failed

The fourth generation

his first MB.[7] The trust created by Samuel Newington's will had restricted Hayes Newington's independence in running Ticehurst. In his presidential address to the MPA, Hayes Newington had sketched a utopian asylum in which:

> the Committee of Management should be a small one, and only composed of those who by their aptitude and capacity for continuous work are . . . qualified to help. A large Committee would undoubtedly prejudice . . . a delicate and novel experiment if, as often is the case, the work were done by the few, while the remainder only interfered on important and critical occasions, just when they would be least qualified to record their votes.[8]

Speaking of the reasons why Hayes Newington's will had established a new family trust to manage Ticehurst, Walter Newington suggested that his grandfather had become tired of the trustees 'continually warring, almost, with each other . . . jealous of those who did the work and complaining about low dividends'. On the advice of his son, who had eventually qualified as a solicitor, Hayes Newington established a small business trust, the proceeds of which were to be divided between four branches of the family: the 'Herberts', the 'Hayes', the 'Samuels' and the 'Alexanders'. As Walter Newington disarmingly admitted, this was a 'racket' in which Herbert Archer and his sister Frances were able to claim double dividends as both 'Herberts' and 'Hayes'.[9] Amongst those who were appointed trustees in 1917 was Samuel Newington's son-in-law, George Montague Tuke, who had been an assistant medical officer at the asylum in the 1870s. The resident medical officer in 1917, Colin F.F. McDowall, was appointed resident medical superintendent. Managed by this trust, Ticehurst never regained the opulence of the 1860s–70s; but it was sold by the family as a viable business in the 1960s.

Patients

Admissions remained fairly constant throughout the period 1885–1915, but there are some indications that the economic downturn, and a decline in therapeutic optimism, may have affected business. A decreasing percentage of admissions travelled from outside Sussex, Kent or London, and particularly from abroad, to become patients at Ticehurst (see Figure 6.3). In 1885 Hayes Newington complained that 'in the case of the wealthy it is well known that an asylum is generally the last thing thought of'; and although he advocated early treatment as offering the best chance of recovery, between 1895 and 1915, for the first time since 1845, the median age of first admissions rose from 35–44 to 45–54, suggesting that Ticehurst's clientele were becoming more, rather than less, reluctant to commit their relatives to licensed houses.[10] It is difficult to assess, however,

The fourth generation

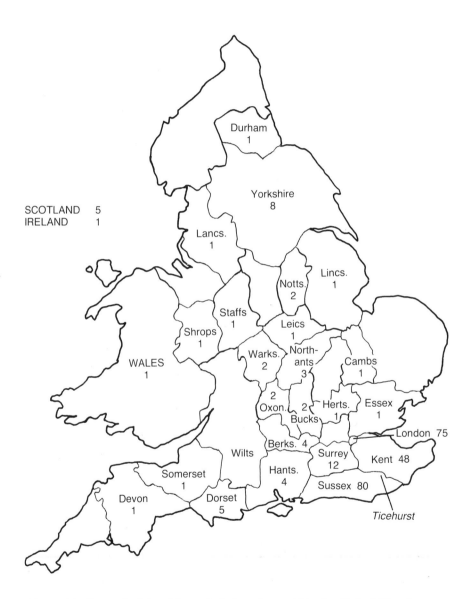

Figure 6.3 Place of origin of first admissions from within the United Kingdom, 1885–1915.

The fourth generation

how far the restriction on expansion of the private asylum system in the 1890 Lunacy Act also affected admissions. As licensed houses filled with chronic cases, it seems likely that a queue for admissions would have formed, particularly at prestigious institutions like Ticehurst. Nationally, a rise in the number of patients confined at home or in single care, reflected a shortfall of private beds for the kind of clientele who were unwilling to accept treatment in the private wards of county asylums. However, the fact that the majority of single patients continued to be women suggests that, as hitherto, those who could afford to pay for private asylum treatment were more willing to do so for a male breadwinner, and probably hoped that a cure would result.[11]

The class of patients admitted to Ticehurst remained high, with an increasing percentage coming from the plutocracy of the commercial and financial world, as well as the professions, trade and manufacturing. It is noticeable, however, that a decreasing proportion of admissions to Ticehurst came from the medical profession, perhaps reflecting some decline of confidence in the Newingtons, if not in private asylum care as a whole (see Table 6.1). Locally, a small number of doctors continued to certify a disproportionate number of admissions. Thus Augustus Woodroffe, who had succeeded John Taylor as medical officer of Ticehurst Union certified twenty-six admissions between 1885 and 1917, and Charles Herbert Fazan, who followed William Mercer as medical officer of the Wadhurst District of the Ticehurst Union, signed certificates for nineteen admissions in the same period, making it clear that some patients were still brought to Ticehurst to be certified, rather than arriving with certificates. In London, apart from G.H. Savage's twenty-seven admissions, the most frequent signer of certificates was Robert Percy Smith, who succeeded Savage as resident physician of Bethlem in 1888, and certified seventeen admissions to Ticehurst before 31 July 1917. Most patients continued to be confined on the authority of a close male relative.[12]

Despite the fall in the asylum's profits associated with the economic depression of the 1880s, what profits there were continued to be reinvested in the fabric of the asylum. In the 1880s, accommodation at Ticehurst was renovated and expanded, and a new purpose-built house, Westcliffe, was opened at St Leonards in place of the houses which had been rented there. Although the 1890 Lunacy Act forbade the issuing of new licences or any expansion of numbers in existing licences, in 1893 an extension was built onto Hayes Newington's new house, the Gables, and included in the licence. However, this expansion of space did not lead to an increase in the number of patients resident in the asylum. Between 1 August 1885 and 31 July 1915 the number of patients resident in the asylum, remained fairly constant (see Table 5.2, p. 129). As Hayes Newington explained in 1900: 'our numbers have slowly increased as additions have been made, but disproportionately, for each patient requires more space as years go on'.[13]

169

The fourth generation

Table 6.1 Former occupations of admissions to Ticehurst, 1885–1915

Years run from 1 August to 31 July
Numbers in brackets represent known readmissions

Men	1885–95	1895–1905	1905–15
Independent:			
Prince		1	
Gentleman	5 (3)	7 (2)	2
Magistrate KC			1
MA Oxford			1
No occupation/none	1 (1)	5 (1)	9 (3)
Church: Bishop	1		
Doctor of divinity			(1)
Clergyman	2		1
Clerk in Holy Orders	1 (1)	8 (3)	2
Priest	1		
Army/Navy:			
General	2		
Major/Commander			1
Officer	2	2	
Colonel	1		2
Lieutenant-Colonel		1	
Captain	1 (1)	2	2
Lieutenant	1		1
Midshipman			1
Lieutenant (RNLI)	1		
Medicine: Physician	1		
Medical Practitioner			1
Law:			
Barrister	1 (2)	(1)	3
Solicitor	1	2 (1)	2
Conveyancer	1		
Civil Service:			
Diplomatic Service	1		
Indian Civil Service			1
War Office clerk			1
Clerk		1	
Police Supt Ceylon			1
Agriculture:			
Planter		1	
Land steward	1		
Australian farmer			1
Farmer			1 (1)
Student	1		1
Merchants and Manufacturers:			
Merchant	1	1	2
Merchant and ship-owner			2
Wine merchant	1		
Wine and cigar merchant			1
Tobacco merchant	1		
Corn and brick merchant		1	

The fourth generation

Men (cont.)	1885–95	1895–1905	1905–15
Coal owner	(1)		
Manufacturer	1		
Brewer		3	
Button manufacturer			1
Worsted spinner			1
Finance and commerce:			
City gentleman	1		
Banker	1	2	
Stockbroker	1		1 (1)
Insurance broker		1	
Insurance promoter			1
Ship broker			1
Fur broker			1
Produce broker			1
Commission agent			1
Accountant		1	
Business/commerce	1		
Manager Orient SS Co.			1
Engineers:			
Civil engineer	1 (1)	(1)	(1)
Mechanical and sanitary		1	
Naval architect			1
Other: Architect			1
Chemist		1	
Literary man	1		
Printer			1
Gentleman clerk		1	
Clerk			1
Unknown:	12 (1)	4 (1)	3 (1)

Women	1885–95	1895–1905	1905–15
Independent:			
Gentlewoman	11 (1)	7 (2)	1
No occupation/none	1	16 (3)	26 (4)
Lady		5	
Wife/spinster:		1	4 (1)
Housewife		1	
Medical practitioner's wife		1	
Merchant's wife		(1)	
Stockbroker's wife		1	
Insurance broker's wife		1 (1)	
Bank manager's wife		1	
Employed:			
Teacher/governess		1	1
Hospital nurse		1	
Missionary worker		1	
Unknown:	29 (6)	13 (2)	13 (1)

Sources: RA1881–90, RP1890–1906 and CR1907–19

The fourth generation

In the early 1900s an English duke had exclusive use of Samuel Newington's former house, Ridgeway; and the sole occupant of the new extension to the Gables was an Egyptian prince, Ahmed Saaf ed Din. Despite the increased space made available to patients, most patients' fees remained at a similar level of £300–£400 p.a. throughout these 30–35 years, but a minority of very wealthy patients paid far more. Thus in the early 1900s Prince Ahmed paid over £2,000 p.a.[14]

Therapeutic pessimism

The medical philosophy which informed treatment at Ticehurst in the late-Victorian and Edwardian period was less optimistic that the body and mind had a natural tendency to revert to health. As a young trainee physician at Morningside, Hayes Newington worked under David Skae, who had developed a system of classification of insanity which was influenced by the ideas of the French degenerationist psychiatrist Benedict Morel (1809–73). While Morel's work stressed the importance of hereditary transmission in a manner which was more strongly taken up by other British medico-psychologists such as Henry Maudsley, Skae's system of classification linked the onset of mental disorders to specific organic pathologies or the physiological crises of the normal life cycle. Thus he classified insanity either in terms of a distinct physical disease or diseased organ – syphilis, rheumatism, anaemia, diabetes, Bright's disease, goitre, uterine insanity, etc. – or by the stage of life which the individual had reached – young childhood, puberty and adolescence, pregnancy, lactation, the climacteric and senility. This physiological schema did not include moral insanity, and emphasized that alcoholic insanity was a form of toxic insanity, like lead poisoning; although in Morel's degenerationist theories such physiological corruption could initiate a downward spiral of mental and moral deterioration which would be passed from one generation to the next.[15]

In choosing to write his first papers on cases in which an underlying organic pathology was clearly indicated – syphilitic insanity, hemiplegia in the insane and stupor – Hayes Newington was evidently seeking to root himself in this physiological tradition. His paper on 'A case of insanity dependent on syphilis' presented a multifactorial analysis of the aetiology of the disease which was characteristic of the 'clinical method'. Thus no hereditary predisposition was ascertainable in the case of 'Mrs J.H.', although Hayes Newington made it clear that if such a predisposition had been present it would have been considered the prime cause; instead, a syphilitic infection received early in her adult life was seen as having lain dormant for over thirty years until the physiological stresses of the climacteric precipitated the growth of a syphiloma in the brain which was believed to have caused her present insanity. Although this aetiology was

The fourth generation

mainly physiological, environmental stresses and the patient's former behaviour were also seen as having a role to play in the possible sequence of causes. Thus Hayes Newington saw 'Mrs J.H.'s' ability to rear four of her eight children to adulthood, despite being separated from her violent husband, as evidence that the original syphilitic infection had been limited in extent, since such 'a life of struggling . . . would certainly find out mental defect'.[16] However, even when symptoms were perceived as being mental in origin, their effects were sometimes traced through physiological causes.[17]

More importantly, the patient's behaviour before the outbreak of insanity, and vulnerability to stresses and temptations in the environment, were seen as a product of the patient's inherited constitution. Thus the onset of the two types of stupor differentiated by Hayes Newington could be precipitated by, in the case of what he called 'anergic' stupor, a sudden and intense shock, convulsions, acute mania or prolonged nervous exhaustion; and in the case of what he called 'delusional' stupor by melancholia, general paralysis or epilepsy; but both were seen as requiring a 'very marked' hereditary predisposition.[18] The hereditarian aspects of Morel's psychiatric schema were more extensively taken up by Skae's successor at Morningside, Thomas Clouston, whose emphasis on the hereditary transmissibility of mental, as well as physical, characteristics influenced Hayes Newington. In a paper which was read to the Medico-Psychological Association in Edinburgh in 1875 on Hayes Newington's behalf by a colleague of his at Morningside, James McLaren, Hayes Newington stressed that 'mania-à-potu', defined as 'a transient and violent mental disturbance . . . occasioned by a dose of alcohol utterly inadequate to upset a sane person' generally afflicted individuals who 'had a brain constitution that would not allow [them] to be steady . . . and may be said never to attack a person who has led anything like a moral life up to the time of seizure'.[19]

While degenerationist theories thus provided biological rationales for moral precepts, Clouston's hereditarianism stopped short of a fatalism which would have restricted psychiatry's potential to a purely descriptive science, and psychiatrists' role in society to one which was merely custodial. W.F. Bynum has rightly argued that as well as addressing areas of social concern 'hereditarianism appeared to some psychiatrists as more genuinely scientific because it offered the possibility of aetiological nosologies';[20] and the intention behind taking more detailed case-histories was ultimately the hope that they would shed light on the prophylaxis and cure of mental disorders. Clouston's work from the 1880s onwards increasingly focused on what could be done through education and mental hygiene to prevent the development of insanity.[21] However, the new emphasis on heredity as a causal factor in mental disorders challenged the kind of optimistic outlook which had informed Samuel Newington's work at Ticehurst, that there was a natural tendency to health in the patient. In

173

The fourth generation

its place, hereditarianism posited an innate potential for disease, which it was the physician's responsibility to inhibit or, when a mental disorder had already developed, undermine.

However, since the manner in which patients were affected by their heredity was construed firstly in terms of a deficiency of nervous strength, and secondly in terms of a natural tendency to form bad habits, the treatment Clouston prescribed for patients at Morningside was a combination of supportive medical treatment and moral therapy which had much in common with the treatment of patients at Ticehurst in the early 1870s. As Margaret Sorbie Thompson's history of Morningside has shown, Clouston paid great attention to the physical comfort and cheerfulness of the patients' environment; and he arranged outings and entertainments to divert their minds. Although he used some drugs, notably bromides, he was particularly sceptical of the value of opium. The most fundamental precept of the medical treatment he advocated was the importance of nutrition: 'Fatten your patient and you will improve him in mind'.[22] The only way in which treatment at Morningside differed from therapy at Ticehurst was that Clouston's lower-class patients were encouraged to work in the asylum.[23] Hayes Newington's descriptions of treatment in his early papers confirm this general framework: only 'Mrs J.H.' was given potassium bromide and potassium iodide; while stuporous patients were prescribed tonics (such as iron and aloes), force-fed if necessary, and given porter and ale as stimulants. In addition, Hayes Newington emphasized the importance of moral treatment, suggesting that 'no medical treatment is of use unless it is well backed up by moral pressure'.[24] His emphasis on the rather automatic way in which stuporous patients imitated those around them, and the importance of providing people who displayed 'industry and correct habits' as models, suggests that the way in which he understood how moral treatment might be effective continued to be informed by reflex psychology.[25]

Treatment at Ticehurst

The first case-history which Hayes Newington published from Ticehurst, in 1877, reflected a continuing commitment to an exploration of cases with an evident organic pathology, as well as the ease with which he could work within the traditions of treatment which had been established at Ticehurst. His description of a 'Case of an extraordinary number of convulsions occurring in an epileptic patient' gave an aetiological account of the patient's disorder, which stressed that her poor heredity meant that she had been 'an emotional and wayward girl' even before the onset of epileptic seizures 'slowly carried' her 'mind . . . on to insanity'. Hayes Newington's description of her fits was rich in clinical detail in a way which contrasted with Samuel Newington's case notes; but he did not hypothesize about

The fourth generation

what might be happening in 'Miss X.Y.'s' brain or nervous system.[26] Nor is it clear whether he was familiar with Hughlings Jackson's earlier work on epilepsy. Instead, Hayes Newington focused on what kind of therapeutic response best aided epileptic patients, suggesting that medicines, including bromides, were of little value, and emphasizing the benefits of supporting the patient's ability to withstand convulsions through nourishment. Since Elizabeth Beeching suffered from severe stomatitis, so that feeding by mouth was impossible, she was fed with a nutrient enema of 'one egg, one ounce of brandy, and one ounce of a strong mixture of Liebig's extract' every five hours, surviving eight days of mild epileptic fits occurring every 2–5 minutes. On the basis of this case Hayes Newington argued that many lives were needlessly lost through an absence of sufficient nourishment, when with due care not to irritate the bowel by changing the composition of the enema or including chemical agents such as hydrochloric acid or pepsine, patients' bodily strength could be maintained even when feeding by mouth was no longer possible.[27]

In 1879, while he was at Bethlem, Theodore Newington designed an instrument for feeding patients by the nose. Like his grandfather Charles, Theodore emphasized that the method of force-feeding he had devised was 'the cleanest and quickest way' involving 'least struggling on the part of the patient and medical attendant'. He recommended that, while patients were being fed, they should be fastened in bed with a sheet, the medical man 'steadying [the patient's] head with a towel over the forehead and kneeling on the ends of the towel'.[28] In the genteel ambience of Ticehurst, however, most patients who refused food continued to be fed with the stomach-pump rather than through the nose. Only those cases where the refusal of food was perceived as wilful were fed with a nasal tube. Thus in 1895, K.M., who shortly after admission had warned Alexander Newington that she would 'give all the trouble [she could] . . . it [was] merely a matter of who would last longest', one day after she had begun to refuse food, 'expressed great disappointment that she was not fed by the stomach tube. The nasal tube . . . [was] more unpleasant'; and after being force-fed one more time she started to '[take] her food well', although she now refused to talk, or wash or dress herself, and had to be carried everywhere because she would not walk.[29]

In addition to force-feeding patients who refused food, the Newingtons were keen to make sure that patients were able to digest and get full benefit from their food. A paper by the assistant medical officer at Ticehurst, Francis Wilton, published in April 1880 described the treatment which had been pursued in 'A case of obstinate constipation and inactivity of the liver'. 'M.D.' – Marianne Dalton – was force-fed as well as being given several enemas, since her sluggish digestion meant that she sometimes had little appetite for food. This case is interesting since it makes clear that medicines were sometimes given without the patient's knowledge, with food. Thus in

The fourth generation

addition to enemas, Marianne Dalton was prescribed a sedative, the tasteless liquid chloral hydrate, which was given to her on a piece of bread and butter; and a cholagogue, podophyllin, which was put in the three glasses of port wine which she was encouraged to drink each day. Although this means of administering medicine to patients who refused it was more subtle than the forcible medication described by Anne Digby at the Retreat, it suggests a similar departure from the emphasis placed on respect for the patient in moral therapy; and from the direct coaxing of patients to take medicine which Perceval described at Ticehurst in the 1830s. Even patients who became voluntary boarders under the 1890 Lunacy Act were sometimes given medicine concealed in food: thus when one voluntary boarder, L.B.T., refused any medicine in September 1911, an aperient was mixed with her next meal. An experienced patient, who had been in and out of Ticehurst for over twenty years, L.B.T. refused the food as well. She was not force-fed, but a few days later, after she had thrown a glass of lemonade at Hayes Newington and threatened her attendant with a knife, she was certified.[30]

What impact did a more biologically determined view of mental disorders have on moral therapy? As Anne Digby's study of the York Retreat has shown there could be strong institutional reasons why a gentle fostering of patients' desire for esteem should have become routinized into a more coercive manipulation of privileges and punishments. Although there was no ward system at Ticehurst into which patients could be graded depending on their behaviour, patients continued to be transferred from the smaller houses to the main building, and within the main building, if their behaviour deteriorated. Throughout the 1880s–90s seclusion was occasionally used, but the only mechanical restraint applied was the mustard pack, which was believed to be therapeutic.[31] The case of Emma Osborne illustrates some of the tactics which were used to discourage violence and encourage co-operative behaviour. On admission in 1880, she was excited and violent, smashing cups and glasses and refusing food. She was purged with calomel, and sedated with morphia, and became quieter. After a few days, however, she took a dislike to one of her attendants, smashed a candlestick and barricaded herself in her room, hitting Theodore Newington in the face when he came to see her. Following this incident she was 'put to bed', presumably restrained by a sheet, although no entry to this effect was made in the medical visitation book. Sedated with morphia, she improved to the point where she was allowed to go to church and attend entertainments in the asylum. However, when she smashed a window with her umbrella, her walks were restricted to the grounds of the asylum, until she improved sufficiently to be transferred to one of the smaller houses, Quarry Villa, was allowed to go on day trips to Tunbridge Wells and St Leonards, and was subsequently discharged. Readmitted to Quarry Villa one week later, she became

The fourth generation

excited, throwing stones at Hayes Newington, and was moved to the main building. After she overturned the piano in her room, she was sedated with morphia and purged with calomel; and when she became excited three months later, the furniture was removed from her room in anticipation of the damage she might cause, and she was secluded. Following news of her husband's death shortly after this she spent a week locked in her room on account of excitement. When she managed to pull down a marble mantelpiece and smash it to bits, the Newingtons asked her relatives to remove her.[32]

This system of graduated exclusion or inclusion depending on behaviour represented less of a departure from the original tenets of moral treatment at Ticehurst than the growing disciplinarianism at the Retreat did from Samuel Tuke's therapeutic philosophy. By the 1880s, however, what was at stake was not so much exclusion from contact with the Newington family – although some convalescent patients were invited to dine at Alexander or Hayes Newington's house – but the degree of comfort patients were allowed, and opportunities for outings and entertainment. As at the Retreat, a clearly defined pattern of giving and withdrawing privileges formed one of the main techniques of management in the absence of mechanical restraint. However, despite some routinization in the way in which patients were handled, the generous staffing at Ticehurst meant that the responsiveness of different patients to particular incentives and deterrents continued to be individually assessed. Thus while warm baths, sometimes with cold to the head, were used to soothe patients in a state of hysterical mania, in 1883 a bulimic patient called William Carter, who disliked warm baths, was told that if he vomited after eating he would be given a bath at bedtime, and this encouraged him to retain his food.[33]

A harder question to answer is how far the more organized use of privileges and punishments to manage patients reflected a decline in therapeutic optimism, and a view of the asylum as simply containing. Historians have suggested that the overcrowding of public asylums and apparent increase in insanity made late-Victorian medical psychologists responsive to hereditarian explanations of the cause of mental disease; and although increased space and the death of many long-stay patients at Ticehurst meant a peak of new admissions between 1875 and 1885, only about one-quarter of first admissions between 1875 and 1915 were eventually discharged 'recovered' (see Table 5.1, p. 129 and Figure 4.2, p. 123).[34] In 1884, Hayes Newington published a paper on 'Unverified prognosis' which listed hereditary predisposition as the prime determining factor of the course an outbreak of insanity would ultimately take. While this paper described one four-generational family history taken at Ticehurst as demonstrating 'the tendency to extinction of the race', Hayes Newington also emphasized the difficulty of obtaining a full family history from which to make an accurate prognosis. Thus although hereditarian

177

The fourth generation

beliefs may have lowered therapeutic morale it seems unlikely that they would have been a determining factor in the course of treatment.[35] However, the elision of moral and medical values in degenerationist psychiatry helped to foster a renewed emphasis on the use of discipline in the moral management of the insane.

The increasing emphasis on heredity might have been expected to lead to a renewed interest in the idea of an innate absence of moral sense in patients who were 'morally insane'. In his *Clinical Lectures* Clouston had suggested that while no moral sense had been localized in the brain, and 'There is of course no proof of mental inhibitory centres; . . . there is mental inhibition, and a function always implies an organ of some sort.'[36] Other late-nineteenth-century medical psychologists like G.H. Savage and J. Shaw Bolton (1867–1946) distinguished between an innate lack of moral sense, called 'primary moral insanity' or 'moral imbecility', and an acquired and temporary deficiency of self-control due to some other mental or physical disorder, called '(secondary) moral insanity'. Descriptions of cases of the latter were also informed by evolutionary theory, but emphasized not so much the inheritance of particular characteristics, as a Spencerian hierarchy of instincts and faculties in which moral sense – as one of the most highly evolved faculties – would naturally suffer first from any organic dissolution or disease. It is clear from Hayes Newington's 1887 paper on 'The tests of fitness for discharge from asylums' that he believed not only that some patients suffered from 'a congenital weakness of self-control', but that 'the higher one gets in this scale [from the lower instincts to moral sense] . . . the more readily do we see the emotions fall prey to mental disease'. In 1889 he suggested that the 'morally insane' might benefit from being taken to see wards full of the chronically insane, as though after this moral lesson they would be able to step back voluntarily from the brink of a slippery descent into degeneracy and madness.[37]

At Ticehurst, 'morally insane' and hysterical patients, who were also seen as having some voluntary control over their disorders, were handled with increasing firmness. In July 1881 an hysterical female patient called Georgina Dovrington was started on a 'new treatment':

> Miss Hart has left, also [Mrs Dovrington's] attendant Willis, in their places have been substituted 2 mental nurses from London who have orders to treat Mrs Dovrington with a stricter hand than hitherto. . . . There is no doubt that a great deal of Mrs Dovrington's state of mind is owing to want of self-control, which she is quite able to exercise, so it is thought advisable that those who have the management of her in future should not give way to all her whims and fancies.[38]

In this case, although the patient temporarily improved, a recurrence of her hysterical attacks led her husband to remove her from Ticehurst, perhaps unconvinced that the new approach had been the best treatment for his wife.[39]

The fourth generation

In his article on 'The tests of fitness for discharge from asylums' in 1887 Hayes Newington stressed the importance of the patient's ability to control themselves as one criterion for discharge. Discussing self-control in relation to patients who had been suicidal on admission, he suggested that a clear awareness that suicide was morally wrong, and a restoration of good feeling towards the family, were indications of recovery since, given the evolutionary hierarchy of instincts and moral faculties, the presence of such feelings guaranteed 'that behind these are the other more substantial checks of instinct' – 'love of life and fear of death' – to resist the impulse to suicide.[40] The prevention of suicide may have been a particular concern of Hayes Newington's since 1874, when a female patient of his strangled herself with a sheet while she was secluded at Morningside. Certainly, it is understandable why he chose to focus on the prevention of suicide at this time, since in the early 1880s there had been a spate of suicide attempts at Ticehurst, including two which were successful. In 1881 William Baldwin cut his throat with a dinner knife; and in 1886 Kate Philpott set fire to her nightdress, and died of the burns she sustained. A third patient, Charles Turner, had escaped to France in 1880 and shot himself; and in 1882 Hugh Brodie died from pneumonia after drinking scalding tea, although it is unclear whether this was done with suicidal intentions. Between 1880 and 1886 Sarah Furley attempted suicide by jumping from a window, Captain Walsh precipitated himself head-first from a window sill, Marmaduke Simpson threw himself into the sea at St Leonards, Marion Collier told her husband she had swallowed the pieces of her broken eyeglass and Mary Marshall jumped into the lake near the asylum.[41] Although Sarah Furley and Marmaduke Simpson were on trial discharge when these attempts occurred, and it was how to assess the risk to patients like them that Hayes Newington was concerned with in his article, responsibility for the safety of suicidal patients in the asylum fell on the attendants.

In 1884 G.H. Savage had published an article on 'Constant watching of suicide cases' in which he argued that continual observation encouraged some patients to attempt suicide, and made it more difficult for them to develop self-control.[42] At Ticehurst, however, patients who were believed to be in danger of attempting suicide were never left alone, and falling asleep while on night duty with a suicidal patient was one reason why an attendant could be dismissed from the asylum in the 1880s. Following William Baldwin's death the Lunacy Commissioners asked that knives and forks should be counted before and after each meal, and all knives, scissors and other sharp implements should be accounted for at least once in every twenty-four hours. In 1881 an attendant was dismissed for leaving knives out, although by 1885 another attendant was only given a warning for a similar failure.[43] Hayes Newington was involved in preparing the MPA's *Handbook for attendants on the insane* (1885), which warned attendants of the need for watchfulness with suicidal cases. Amongst means of suicide

179

The fourth generation

which were mentioned were burning or scalding, cutting or stabbing, drowning, falls and precipitation. The *Handbook* advised that suicidal patients should be accommodated on the ground floor, and seated in day rooms as far away as possible from the windows and fireplace. Despite all these precautions, in 1894 a male patient at Ticehurst, S.J., died from injuries he inflicted by dashing his head against a marble mantelpiece.[44] The coroner's inquest cleared the attendants of any blame, but the risk of suicide continued to concern the Newingtons. In *c.*1906 and 1907, two attendants were reprimanded, one for allowing a suicidal patient to be alone while he went to run errands, and the other for leaving a bottle of Jeyes' fluid disinfectant in a ground-floor toilet. The only special commendation of an attendant recorded at Ticehurst was of Henry Watts, for preventing 'a very heavy and powerful man' from committing suicide in 1911. As a reward, Watts's salary was increased; and when he later became ill his sanatorium treatment was paid for by the Newingtons.[45]

In addition to watching suicidal patients, attendants were expected to help create a morally wholesome atmosphere from which the patients could derive strength. Just as Thomas Mayo had suggested that 'the weak take their tone from the strong', Hayes Newington emphasized that the insane needed 'good to imitate, and not bad'. Partly because of this, as well as for the obvious managerial advantages, the Newingtons sought to maintain a strict control over the habits of their employees. Drinking, in particular, was strongly disapproved of; and while attendants being drunk on duty posed a serious safety risk, the Newingtons also sought to regulate off-duty drinking. Thus in 1881 an attendant called George Clegg was given a post at St Leonards 'on agreement to become a Total Abstainer'; and in 1902 an attendant called Henry Vigor, who had twice been reprimanded for drunkenness, was allowed to remain employed 'in view of his long service and family' only if he became a 'Teatotaler' (sic).[46] While drunkenness was the most frequent reason for male attendants' dismissal, other reasons included quarrelling and fighting; betting; 'immoral conduct with a married woman', or any woman 'he being a married man'; discourtesy to patients; stealing food, money and clothes from patients; climbing an escape ladder outside the nurses' dressing-rooms; and being the subject of a criminal investigation. Swearing, smoking and being drunk on duty sometimes led to a reprimand rather than dismissal, with attendants being placed on 'short notice', i.e. under the threat of immediate dismissal if they breached regulations again. In other cases they were deprived of leave or, in one case of stealing food, fined as a punishment.

This style of management makes understandable Alexander's and Hayes Newingtons' comment in 1900 that they liked to recruit male attendants:

The fourth generation

principally from the services. . . . We make a considerable point of their having been officers' servants or mess-waiters, because, in addition to having acquired a sense of discipline and duty, they start with the great advantage of knowing how to speak to gentlemen. We do not appreciate any fancied superiority . . . among our attendants, as it is apt to be galling to our patients.[47]

In 1881 an attendant called W. Walter was reprimanded for a 'want of respect towards Patients in repeatedly wearing his hat indoors in their presence'; and in 1909 James Rigby was dismissed for 'repeated breaches of discipline in not saluting ladies'. Despite the firm handling which the Newingtons believed some patients required, they viewed attendants primarily as 'body servants' or 'valets' whose moral influence was exercised by treating patients with the deference their social standing commanded in ordinary life, rather than through a strong assertion of authority.[48]

There were surprisingly few cases of attendants being dismissed for undue roughness, or violence, in handling patients. Two male attendants, F. Wright and Sydney Hill were dismissed for assault and rough treatment of a patient in 1888 and *c.*1896, respectively; and George Wenbau was reprimanded in 1915 after he had been seen by the resident medical officer, Colin McDowall, behaving 'roughly' towards a patient. One difficulty is that the Newingtons may not have been aware of other incidents of violence. In 1885 H. Baker and J.J. Sibbald were dismissed for not reporting 'ill-usage [crossed out] an accidental fall of Mr H. Wilson', a patient in the asylum. Entries on injuries in the medical visitation books sometimes recorded that they had been caused by attendants attempting to restrain patients, as when Mr M. received a bruise below the eye from his attendant, 'whose brains he [Mr M.] was going to knock out', and Mrs H. had her hand bruised 'in a struggle with two nurses whom she had attacked'; but many minor injuries entered in these books were described as self-inflicted following the attendants' account of the incident. Thus in 1898 Miss M. had a 'slight black eye (right) believed to have been self-inflicted', and in 1906 Miss B. also had a black eye which was said to have been 'caused by knocking herself against the bedstead'. Although injuries to patients were investigated, in most cases the benefit of the doubt was given to the attendants. In one case the patient, a Mr Pulteney, who had received bruises in a struggle with his attendants, '[blamed] himself for this and [acquitted] the attendants of any undue violence'; but patients who complained of ill-treatment were rarely taken seriously. Even after the Newingtons had dismissed F. Wright for assault, the Lunacy Commissioners suggested that the patient whom he had assaulted was 'prone to exaggeration, and [they could not] attribute much weight to his complaints'.[49] While the Newingtons were clearly anxious that their staff should use only the minimum of necessary force, some patients at

The fourth generation

Ticehurst were extremely violent, and it would be understandable if attendants who had heard stories of how, for example, Mary Berryman threw her attendant downstairs and then fell on top of her, or L.B.T. threatened her attendant with a knife, reacted with their maximum strength to prevent injury to themselves.

In theory, attendants were encouraged to call others for help when a patient became violent, to outnumber, intimidate and pacify the patient, and administer a sedative if it was thought necessary; but in practice, even with generous staffing, as the asylum expanded in size the time-lag before other attendants could reach them meant that they often had to act to restrain the patient by themselves. In 1904 a female patient who a few weeks previously had 'Seized her attendant by the hair & pulled out a big bunch', 'attacked her attendant, got her down on the floor & during the struggle the patient received a black eye (Rt.) but it was not ascertained what struck it'. If the attendants were thus placed in an ambiguous position of being in service but nevertheless sometimes having to use force to control patients, it was a dilemma which was shared by the asylum doctors. In conversation, Hayes Newington's grandson observed that his grandfather's physical stature and strength had been an asset in his work at the asylum, and that when a male patient became violent once towards Hayes Newington, he had been able to 'peg him up against the wall' with a chair until assistance arrived. The only use of force which the Newingtons sanctioned was that used in self-defence, and they attempted to weed out attendants whose volatile tempers might make them prone to violence under stress: thus apart from dismissing attendants who got into fights with each other, in 1891 an attendant who had not actually assaulted anyone was dismissed for 'Assuming an aggressive attitude' towards a patient.[50]

In addition to their preference for ex-service personnel, the Newingtons noted the ability to play a musical instrument or being a keen sportsman as assets when considering whether or not to employ men who had applied to become attendants. Regular exercise and entertainments continued to be an important aspect of asylum life. The asylum band played twice-weekly, and in the winter there were weekly dances, as well as occasional special entertainments. Walter Newington saw his first silent film in the entertainments hall of the asylum. In addition to archery, billiards, bowls, cricket, golf, running with the harriers, tennis and trips out in horse- and donkey-drawn carriages, some patients went riding with Theodore Newington, who was a keen horseman, and 'tricycle tandems' were bought in 1891 to enable patients to go cycling without risk of being separated from their attendants. A new game introduced in the 1890s was bicycle-polo, which Alexander and Hayes Newington described as 'a really valuable agent, as it needs such skill and direct attention to the game that [patients'] mental idiosyncracies have little scope for action for the

182

The fourth generation

time-being'.[51] In a similar way, Hayes Newington's paper on 'Some mental aspects of music' emphasized that the complex co- ordination of functions required to play an instrument, or even to sing, was only fully achievable in a state of mental health; but he encouraged patients to play the piano with him, or accompanied them on the piano while they played another instrument. Lady and gentleman companions continued to be employed to foster patients' interest in reading, drawing, painting and sewing, and it was partly because of their presence that the Newingtons felt happy to restrict the attendants' role to one of personal service.[52]

The emphasis on attendants as personal servants also makes it clear that, despite the renewed assertion of a strong moral authority over patients, the asylum was perceived as providing a service to patients and their families in which the wishes of the asylum's clientele were sometimes the paramount consideration. As the appointment of a French chef in 1893 confirmed, the prototype for the asylum continued to be that of a costly country hotel. Although attendants did not wear uniform, domestic staff, such as footmen, were dressed in livery. Smartness and neatness of dress were regarded as assets when the Newingtons were considering whether or not to employ someone. One letter of reference in 1882, from a person who had previously visited Ticehurst to see a patient, expressed the opinion that the attendant, G.H. Brown, was 'hardly a sufficiently smart man for your place. He looks fairly strong – not very good-looking. . . . He is not so presentable a man as the Attendant who was looking after Mr. Rolles when I was at Ticehurst'; and although Brown was given one month's trial, he was not offered a permanent appointment. In 1888, when L.B.T. was first admitted to Ticehurst, she mistook the asylum for an hotel; and in order to characterize the kind of service which his grandfather had provided at Ticehurst, Walter Newington explained that Hayes Newington tried to make the asylum as much like a good quality hotel as possible. Although the Newingtons had persisted in their strict treatment of Georgina Dovrington until her husband removed her, in some cases they allowed relatives' and patients' wishes to influence treatment. Thus in 1884, when William Carter's wife asked that he should not be weighed because it worried him, the Newingtons agreed. After three days, however, afraid that Carter's visible loss of weight meant that he was taking advantage of walks in the grounds to make himself vomit, they began weighing him again.[53] While this example would suggest that, as in Samuel Newington's time, Alexander and Hayes Newington were prepared to be respectful of relatives' feelings only in so far as they did not interfere with effective treatment, they told a meeting of the MPA in 1900 that one reason why medical treatment was not more active at Ticehurst was that 'at times refusal or resistance may force us to modify what seems most applicable'.[54]

Nevertheless, the 1880s–90s had been a period of increased medical intervention, including more frequent use of chemical sedation. Although

183

The fourth generation

Table 6.2   Diagnoses of first admissions to Ticehurst, 1885–1915

Diagnoses	1885–95	1895–1905	1905–15
Mania	38	35[i]	28
Melancholia	22[ii]	26	14[iii]
Delusional insanity*	10[iv]	8	25[v]
Dementia	7	6	13
General paralysis	7[iv]	7	5
Other insanities*	3	2	4
Moral insanity	1	2[vi]	1
Dementia praecox			1
None given	1	10	10

*Before 1895 'delusional insanity' includes some patients who were diagnosed as suffering from 'hallucinations' or 'delusions'; 'other insanities' include 'senile insanity', 'hysterical insanity', 'insanity of adolescence', etc.

i includes   4 '& delusions', 1 '& hystero-epilepsy';
ii includes   1 '& delusions';
iii includes   1 'hypochondriasis';
iv includes   1 '& partial dementia';
v includes   1 '& hypochondriasis';
vi includes   1 'insanity of conduct'
Sources: See Table 6.1

this paralleled an increase in admissions who were described as suffering from 'mania', a similar, slightly earlier, increase at the Retreat, suggests that it may also have been part of a wider trend (see Tables 5.5 (p. 154) and 6.2). From the early 1880s fewer patients were listed in the medical visitation book as being treated for 'debility', and increasing numbers were prescribed medication for 'excitement', 'insomnia' and 'restlessness'.[55] At the Retreat, chloral hydrate and potassium bromide were the main sedatives used. However at Ticehurst, although both of these were used, together with chloroform, valerian and other milder means of calming patients such as mustard baths, in contrast to long-standing practice, morphia began to be used freely as a sedative, and hyoscyamine, a purer and more powerful extract from the hyoscyamus which Thomas Mayo had recommended, was used as a hypnotic.

The strength of sedation was graduated to correspond to the degree of restlessness and violence manifested by the patient. In cases of hysteria and moral insanity, mild sedatives were prescribed, with tonics and cathartics if the patient was also debilitated or amenorrhoeic. Thus in 1883 Mary Phipps, who had been diagnosed as suffering from 'moral insanity', supposed cause 'suppression of period', was prescribed a tonic of aloes and iron, a cathartic magnesium sulphate, and potassium bromide, tincture of valerian and spirit of chloroform simultaneously as sedatives. In 1882 Rachel Groom, diagnosis 'hysterical mania', supposed cause 'disappointment over marriage', was given an enema before being

The fourth generation

prescribed the sedatives potassium bromide, tincture of hyoscyamus, and chloroform; and when despite this she still had a restless night, she was given 'syrupi chloralis', morphia and chloroform. In cases of acute mania, like that of Emma Osborne described above, supposed cause 'uterine hysteria', stronger sedatives and purgatives were given, the purgative being prescribed prophylactically to counteract morphia's known side-effect of constipation as well as to cleanse and decongest the system. From the early 1890s, morphia and hyoscine were injected hypodermically, and the rapidity with which patients could thus be quietened made these drugs an attractive option, even in cases of hysteria. Thus in a paper on 'The diagnosis of hystero-epilepsy from status epilepticus' published in the *Lancet* in 1898, Ticehurst's resident medical officer Wilfred Robert Kingdon, described the case of D.D., a young female hysteric in the asylum, who had slept for five hours after being injected with hyoscine hydrobromate. As Kingdon stressed, the drug's rapid action and effectiveness when hypodermically injected made it 'much less tedious than the old chloroform method' of sedation.[56]

Understandably, at a time when the motives of private asylum proprietors were being scrutinized, chemical sedation seemed preferable to increased mechanical restraint, the use of which was closely monitored by the Lunacy Commissioners. Dissatisfaction with psychological medicine in the 1880s spread more widely than the attacks made on private asylums by the lunacy reform movement. Pressure on the rates from overcrowded county asylums wanting to expand at a time of economic depression, in the absence of impressive cure rates, led to criticism in the press. Within the medical profession, the bacteriological discoveries of the 1870s–90s made asylum medicine seem relatively lacking in research sophistication and therapeutic resources. As Batty Tuke observed in 1889:

> The public seeks in vain for any manifest indication that the speciality which professes the treatment of insanity has kept abreast in the onward march of medical science . . . asylum physicians have failed to stay the progress of the disease by . . . their art, and have but partially succeeded in bringing their speciality within the pale of medical science.[57]

While a hereditarian understanding of the causation of insanity offered no new therapeutic directions, except the possibility of prevention through the early identification and prophylactic treatment of those most at risk, asylum doctors cast around for possible remedies, and were ready to look to abandoned treatments of the past as well as to new methods suggested by scientific medicine.

In 1881, the observation that an acute intercurrent bodily illness sometimes seemed to relieve insane patients of their mental symptoms led G.H. Savage to observe that cases like that of a general paralytic patient who became well enough to go home after developing a large carbuncle

The fourth generation

on his neck 'make one review the old blistering and seton treatment, and cause doubts to cross one's mind whether with heroic treatment also passed away valuable remedies for some dangerous diseases'.[58] In the 1880s–90s at Ticehurst, counter-irritation was prescribed in cases of acute mania, and to inhibit masturbation. Thus in 1885, after a consultation with Henry Maudsley, Marmaduke Simpson was given cold shower baths every night and morning in the hope of allaying his excitement. When little change had occurred in his condition a week later, his head was shaved and croton oil applied to blister his scalp.[59] In cases like this, the eruption of blisters was believed to be beneficial because it might relieve the blood of toxic materials which were thought to be causing the patient's symptoms. In the case of counter-irritation to discourage masturbation, however, the rationale was rather that masturbation might be a reflex response to local irritation, which could be relieved by providing an alternative, stronger source of irritation.

Speaking at a meeting of the MPA in 1886, Hayes Newington opposed the idea put forward by Robert Percy Smith (1853–1941), that 'even the grossest lesions of the female genital apparatus are not sufficient of themselves to produce insanity'. Arguing that 'very small lesions in females often [cause] a very serious state of mind', Hayes Newington suggested that an irritation of the os uteri could produce 'a distinct class of mental alienation' in which menopausal women became compulsively obscene, and began to masturbate as 'a kind of counter-irritation to relieve the uterine trouble'. Although female patients who masturbated at Ticehurst were douched with alum to soothe any irritation, the use of the blistering agent liquor epispasticus to discourage masturbation in male patients commenced after Hayes Newington's arrival at Ticehurst. The idea that masturbation in men could also be caused by local irritation was clear in the case-history of C.J., a chronic masturbator who was circumcised at Ticehurst in 1895 because it was believed that his 'prepuce ... was abnormally long & allowed secretion to collect, forming a source of irritation'. Although the percentage of female patients whose mental disorders were attributed to gynaecological and obstetrical problems on admission declined after 1885, it is clear that Hayes Newington continued to believe, like Skae and Clouston, that 'the whole of insanity specially associated with the female sex was more or less connected with the sexual relations'; however, the rationale behind the belief that amenorrhoea could lead to mental disturbance was now toxaemic rather than hyperaemic, the fear being that an absence of periods meant that degenerated uterine tissues were retained within the body as a potential source of poisoning.[60]

The belief that toxins in the body could cause insanity was evident in Skae's interest in alcohol and lead poisoning. In his 1873 paper on syphilis, Hayes Newington referred to 'foreign material', left behind after an acute syphilitic inflammation, causing the patient's symptoms. Reiterating the

The fourth generation

point that mental disorders could be caused by 'retention of abnormal material in the blood', in 1887 Hayes Newington suggested that since one patient had improved mentally after an attack of haematuria, if his condition worsened 'it would perhaps be desirable to try the effect of bleeding him'. Although in 1886 a paper on the value of bleeding in epilepsy had met with some favourable comments at a Scottish meeting of the MPA, a revival of venesection ultimately posed more problems than therapeutic promise. It was the example Alexander and Hayes Newington gave as a case in point when they suggested that the 'resistance and refusal' of patients was a major obstacle to 'active' medical treatment, and no patients at Ticehurst were venesected after 1895, when an epileptic patient, Lt Col G., had twelve ounces of blood removed from his arm by Alexander Newington.[61]

The belief that toxins could cause inflammation or irritation of the nervous system or brain also provided a rationale for the use of enemas. Thus in 1900 Alexander and Hayes Newington argued that enemas were preferable to purgatives because they cleansed the bowel more thoroughly of any residual faeces, preventing it from '[producing] a reflex irritation, or perhaps even a more direct action on the nervous system by absorption into the blood of injurious faecal degeneratives'.[62] It was indicative of the poverty of therapeutic resources available to late-Victorian asylum doctors that the heroic treatments of the late-eighteenth and early-nineteenth centuries should have been revived under a rationale of toxaemia rather than hyperaemia; but it is understandable why they looked to a toxicological analysis of the blood for a new initiative in the treatment of insanity. In the late 1860s–80s morphological studies of the blood helped lead to the bacteriological breakthroughs of the germ theory, which yielded a rich prophylactic harvest of antitoxins for the prevention of physical disease through inoculation. If microscopic analysis had failed to fulfil Bucknill's and Tuke's 1858 hope that it would make perceptible an organic pathology of the brain and nervous system which was imperceptible to the naked eye, in the 1880s–90s chemical physiology seemed to offer an alternative route to a more sophisticated understanding of mental disorders which left no structural alteration of the brain and nervous system.

Nor was this hope without promise of fulfilment. Victor Horsley's (1857–1916) work on myxoedema in the late 1880s led to successful trials in the early 1890s of the use of thyroid extract in treating myxoedematous insanity. In 1895, L.C. Bruce suggested that the effect of thyroid extract in raising body temperature and quickening the pulse might make it more generally useful in the treatment of insanity as a pyretic. As Clouston argued in one of the later editions of his *Clinical lectures on mental diseases* the effects of thyroid secretion appeared to be similar in action to a toxin circulating in the blood, holding out the hope that psychiatrists might:

187

The fourth generation

'some day be able to inoculate some septic poison and get a safe manageable counter-irritant and fever, and so get the alterative effect of such things and the reaction and stimulus to nutrition that follow febrile attacks'.[63] If Julius Wagner-Jauregg's (1857–1940) use of malarial infection to halt the progress of general paralysis of the insane ultimately realized some of Clouston's hopes in 1917, Hayes Newington was almost certainly attracted to the use of thyroid extract for its alleged stimulative effect in cases of stupor rather than its potential as a fever-inducing agent. In the late 1890s thyroid extract was prescribed to two stuporous patients at Ticehurst with only temporary beneficial effects, and by 1900 the Newingtons were ready to conclude that 'no special benefit [arises] from thyroid treatment', despite continuing interest amongst other members of their profession.[64]

Stuporous patients were also treated with electricity in an attempt to stimulate their nervous systems. Thus D.D., the hysterical patient whose case-history was published by W.R. Kingdon, had her spine massaged with a faradic current which was said to have produced a 'very considerable moral effect, and for a short time she is able to answer questions and appears much brighter'. In 1900 Alexander and Hayes Newington noted that electro-magnetism helped convince some patients with globus hystericus that they could open their throat and swallow, thus avoiding the necessity of force-feeding. One patient who was treated in this way was William Carter, who was given regular electro- magnetic massages in 1883. The Newingtons also cited an exceptional recovery, when 38-year-old Leon Lazarus, who had been subject to cataleptic fits since he was 16, became well enough to go home after being galvanized in 1883, and had remained well since.[65]

After 1900 the principles of treatment applied by the Newingtons remained much the same as in the latter decades of the nineteenth century. As the proportion of patients described on admission as being in a state of mania declined, so too did the number of patients who were prescribed medication for 'excitement' and 'restlessness'. However, this decline in chemical sedation was paralleled by an increase in the number of incidents of bruising and other minor injuries caused in struggles with attendants. The reduction in the prescription of morphia, particularly its hypodermic administration, may have been influenced also by concern over the drug's addictive properties. Early studies of the barbiturate veronal, introduced into the English market by Fischer and von Mering in 1903, stressed its alleged non-addictiveness as an advantage. Since the 1890s synthetic narcotics like sulphonal, and later trional, had been used in preference to morphia in cases of chronic or recurrent mania. Initially, veronal was tried at Ticehurst on patients of this type, since, being about twice as powerful as trional, it could be administered in stronger doses without ill-effects. Thus in 1904, J.B., a chronic maniac, was prescribed veronal during a period of excitement, rather than trional with which she had hitherto been

The fourth generation

sedated; however, the veronal '[did] not have much effect', and when she became excited again she was sedated with trional. While published studies of veronal's effectiveness suggested it was best used as a narcotic in cases of hysteria and sleeplessness caused by melancholia, rather than as a sedative in cases of acute mania, the Newingtons conducted their own trials by substituting trional for veronal to see which was more effective. Thus in 1904 when L.B.T., who had been diagnosed as suffering from 'hysterical insanity' in 1888, was readmitted as a voluntary boarder she was prescribed veronal, then trional, and then veronal again because the 'Trional did not seem to answer so well'.[66]

However, these experiments were primarily concerned with the problem of how to manage troublesome patients rather than with therapeutic results. The insecurity of the 1880s had led to an increased heroicism in medical treatment, but the Newingtons' willingness to let their interventionism be curtailed by the opinion of patients' families revealed the social pressures and lack of deep therapeutic conviction which had underlain this enhanced activity. The strong sedation of patients, and pervasive lack of therapeutic optimism, led to a decline in the percentage of patients who were discharged 'recovered', which fell to an all-time low of around 15 per cent of first admissions between 1895 and 1905, rising again to around 25 per cent between 1905 and 1915, but remaining below the rates of the late 1850s–70s. The percentage of patients who were discharged 'relieved' also declined, suggesting that this change did not simply reflect the Newingtons' perceptions of how much they were able to achieve (see Figure 4.2, p. 123). Following the protection of existing private asylums under the Lunacy Act of 1890, pressure on asylum doctors to intervene more actively, whether or not they had therapeutic resources at their disposal, was reduced, and this may be one reason why the Newingtons were not tenacious in pursuing the potential of new therapies, such as thyroid treatment. Apart from the introduction of barbiturates, there were no new therapeutic developments at Ticehurst in the last seventeen years for which Hayes Newington was medical superintendent.

In 1917, Charles Mercier described Hayes Newington in an obituary in the *British Medical Journal* as:

> a Tory both in politics and in medicine. He would have said, like the late Duke of Cambridge that he was ready to welcome any innovation that was an improvement; but like the late Duke, he never considered an innovation an improvement.[67]

There was a deeply reactionary thrust in Hayes Newington's treatment of patients at Ticehurst in the late nineteenth century. If Mercier's comment exaggerated to some extent Hayes Newington's unwillingness to try new forms of treatment, it captured the apparent lack of enthusiasm and persistence with which he carried out any experiments he made.

189

The fourth generation

Nevertheless, if Hayes Newington lacked therapeutic initiative and determination, the new trust he created placed Ticehurst on a sound business footing. In addition, as the next chapter describes, his most significant achievement was his contribution to the successful campaign to secure the future of private asylums under the 1890 Lunacy Act.

Notes

1. George Montague Tuke was no known relation to the Tukes of York, or Manor House; after leaving Ticehurst he went into general practice in Staplehurst (see *Medical Directory*).

2. Letters of administration to Eleanora Newington re Charles Edmund Hayes Newington MD, 5 March 1863; probate Samuel Newington, 19 December 1882; probate Alexander Thurlow Newington, 12 July 1898; Ticehurst asylum audit, 1875.

3. *Alumni Cantab*, entries on Alexander Samuel, and Theodore Newington.

4. Rhys Williams visited Ticehurst for example, CB24, p. 132; Savage referred twenty-seven admissions to Ticehurst between 1888 and 1916 (RA1881–90; RP1890–1906; and CR1907–19).

5. Robert Barnes had been one of the medical members of the Alleged Lunatics Friends Society; see N. Hervey, 'Advocacy or folly: the Alleged Lunatics Friends Society 1845–63', *Medical History*, 1986, 30, note 66.

6. Ticehurst asylum audits 1875 and 1881.

7. Tape of conversation with Walter Newington.

8. H.F.H. Newington, 'Hospital treatment for recent and curable cases of insanity', *JMS*, 1889, 35: 312.

9. Tape of conversation with Walter Newington.

10. See C. MacKenzie, 'A family asylum', London University PhD thesis, 1987, p. 496.

11. Between 1890 and 1910 cases in single care rose from 446 to 593; private beds in county asylums increased threefold in the same period, from 1,027 to 3,366 (*LCR*, 1890, p. 135 and *LCR*, 1910, p. 247).

12. RA1881–90, RP1890–1906 and CR1907–19; and see MacKenzie, op. cit., note 10 above, p. 509.

13. VB1869–87, 14 April 1882; VB1887–1904, 1 December 1887, 22 May and 29 November 1888, 30 November 1889 and 24 May 1893; A.S.L. Newington and H.F.H. Newington, 'Some incidents in the history and practice of Ticehurst asylum', *JMS*, 1901, 47: 65.

14. Ticehurst asylum audits, 1880–95; Accounts, 1895–1920, *passim*.

15. For Skae's system of classification see T.S. Clouston, *Clinical lectures on mental diseases*, London, J.& A.Churchill, 1883, p. 45.

16. H.F.H. Newington, 'Notes of a case of insanity dependent on syphilis', *JMS*, 1874, 19: 558.

17. See, for example, *idem.*, 'Hemiplegia in relation to insanity', *Edinburgh Medical Journal*, 1874, 20: 23.

18. *Idem.*, 'Some observations on different forms of stupor, and on its occurrence after acute mania in females', *JMS*, 1874–5, 20: 374.

19. *JMS*, 1875, 20: 656–8.

20. W.F. Bynum, 'Alcoholism and degeneration in 19th century European medicine and psychiatry', *British Journal of Addiction*, 1984, 79: 63.

21. Apart from *Clinical lectures on mental diseases*, London, J.& A. Churchill, 1883

The fourth generation

and *Unsoundness of mind*, London, Methuen & Co., 1911, T.S. Clouston's main publications were: *Female education from a medical point of view*, London, J.& A.Churchill, 1882; *The neuroses of development*, Edinburgh, Oliver & Boyd, 1891; *The hygiene of mind*, London, Methuen & Co., 1906; and *Before I wed*, London, Cassell & Co., 1913.

22. M.S. Thompson, 'The mad, the bad and the sad: psychiatric care in the Royal Edinburgh Asylum (Morningside), 1813–94', Boston University PhD thesis, 1984, pp. 121–7.

23. Morningside accommodated some middle- and upper-class patients in its East House, but most inmates were working-class. Clouston built an additional house for private patients, Craig House, in 1894, which took upper-class patients, ibid., Thompson, pp. 86–9, 95.

24. Newington, op. cit., note 16 above, p. 557; and op. cit. note 18 above, pp. 385–6.

25. Op. cit., note 18 above, pp. 384–6.

26. 'Miss X.Y.' can be identified as Elizabeth Beeching, RA1845–81, case 375; H.F.H. Newington, 'Case of an extraordinary number of convulsions occurring in an epileptic patient, with remarks on nutrient enemata', *JMS* 1877, 23: 89–95.

27. Ibid., pp. 92–3.

28. T. Newington, 'Feeding by the nose', *Lancet* 1879, i: 83.

29. See, for example, CB29, p. 47; CB38, pp. 143, 288.

30. F. Wilton, 'A case of obstinate constipation and inactivity of the liver', *JMS* 1880–1, 26:67–9; A. Digby, *Madness, morality and medicine*, London, Cambridge University Press, 1985, p. 130; notes on L.B.T. in CB40, p. 162; J. Perceval, *A narrative*, London, Effingham Wilson, 1840, pp. 99, 391.

31. Digby, op. cit., note 30 above, pp. 85–7; for transfer within the asylum, see CB27, p. 146; on seclusion and restraint see medical visitation books, *passim*; on mustard packs, see Newington and Newington, op. cit., note 13 above, p. 71.

32. CB25, pp. 335–64; 26, pp. 229–34.

33. CB27, p. 356.

34. See Bynum, op. cit., note 20 above, p. 63.

35. H.F.H. Newington, 'Unverified prognosis', *JMS*, 1887, 32: 225–7.

36. T.S. Clouston, *Clinical lectures*, 2nd edn, London, Bailliere & Co., 1887, pp. 317–18.

37. See G.H. Savage, 'Moral insanity', *JMS*, 1881, 27: 147–55; and J.Shaw Bolton, 'Amentia and dementia: a clinico-pathological study', *JMS*, 1905, 51: 523–7; H.F.H. Newington, 'What are the tests of fitness for discharge from asylums?', *JMS*, 1887, 32: 497, 500; H.F.H. Newington, 'Hospital treatment for recent and curable cases of insanity', *JMS*, 1889, 35: 307.

38. CB26, pp. 247–8.

39. Ibid., p. 248.

40. Newington, op. cit., note 37 above, 1887, p. 497.

41. *Royal Edinburgh Asylum Reports*, 15 November 1874; CB25, pp. 215, 240, 327; CB27, p. 29; CB28, p. 216; CB30, pp. 101, 161; and CB31, p. 14.

42. G.H. Savage, 'Constant watching of suicidal cases', *JMS*, 1884–5, 30: 19.

43. AB, pp. 10, 219, 257; PB1846–1904, 12 February 1881.

44. *Handbook for the instruction of attendants on the insane*, London, Bailliere & Co., 1885, p. 57; CB35, p. 270.

45. AB, pp. 89, 412, 414.

46. Ibid., pp. 30, 226, 401.

47. Ibid., pp. 4, 10, 13, 28, 31, 38, 70, 73, 89, 92, 93, 155, 232, 247, 381; Newington and Newington, op. cit., note 13 above, pp. 68–9.

48. Ibid., p. 69; AB, p. 405 and loose letter.

The fourth generation

49. Ibid., pp. 83, 380, 410, 412; MVB1884–6, 25 May 1885; MVB1895–8, 17 January 1898; MVB1905–10, 16 April 1906 and 6 July 1908; VB1887–1904, 22 May 1888.

50. CB28, p. 233; CB38, pp. 203–4; and CB40, p. 163; tape of conversation with Walter Newington; AB, p. 374.

51. Newington and Newington, op. cit., note 13 above, p. 72; VB1887–1904, 18 November 1891; CB29, p. 56.

52. H.F.H. Newington, 'Some mental aspects of music', *JMS*, 1897, 43: 704–21.

53. AB, pp. 225–6; CB28, pp. 200–1; CB32, pp. 5–6; tape of conversation with Walter Newington.

54. Newington and Newington, op. cit., note 13 above, pp. 69–70.

55. Digby, op. cit., note 30, p. 129; MVB1877–82, MVB1882–4, MVB1884–6 and MVB1846–9, *passim*.

56. CB27, pp. 63–4 CB29, p. 343. For examples of sedation with chloral hydrate: CB28, p. 94; CB29, p. 47; CB30, p. 158; CB33, p. 269; with potassium bromide: CB29, p. 47; CB30, pp. 156, 158; CB33, p. 269; with mustard baths: CB26, pp. 129, 283; with chloroform: CB25, p. 286; CB29, p. 343; with hyoscyamine: CB26, p. 129; CB27, p. 63; and with morphia: CB25, p. 335; CB29, p. 47. Hypodermic injections had been used at Ticehurst since the late 1860s, but were much more frequently used in the late 1880s–90s; for the hypodermic injection of morphia see, for example, the case of C.J. (CB36, pp. 17–18); W.R. Kingdon, 'The diagnosis of hystero-epilepsy from status epilepticus', *Lancet*, 1898, i: 320.

57. Quoted in Newington, op. cit., note 37 above, 1889, p. 296.

58. G.H. Savage, 'Marked amelioration in a general paralytic following a very severe carbuncle', *JMS*, 1880–1, 26: 566.

59. CB30, p. 102.

60. CB36, p. 17; *JMS*, 1886–7, 32: 298–9; MacKenzie, op. cit., note 10 above, pp. 505–6.

61. Newington, op. cit., note 16 above; *JMS*, 1886–7, 32: 304–5; and 1887–8, 33: 161; CB36, p. 258.

62. Newington and Newington, op. cit., note 13 above, p. 70.

63. *JMS*, 1895, 41: 636; Clouston quoted in R. Eager, 'An investigation as to the therapeutic value of thyroid feeding in mental diseases', ibid., 1912, 58: 427.

64. CB36, pp. 226–32 and CB37, p. 284; and Newington and Newington, op. cit., note 13 above, p. 69.

65. Newington and Newington, op. cit., note 13 above, pp. 71–2; CB28, pp. 13, 199 and CB38, p. 135; and Kingdon, op. cit., note 56 above.

66. MJ1898–1901, MJ1901–5, MJ1905–10 and MJ1910–15, *passim*; reports on veronal were published in the *BMJ*'s epitome on therapeutics, 1903–4; CB36, p. 286; CB38, pp. 331–2 and CB40, pp. 64–5.

67. Obituary of H.F.H. Newington in *BMJ*, 1917, ii: 201.

7

The protection of private care

One of the most usual claims about late-nineteenth-century British medical psychology is that it was ineffective politically. For Kathleen Jones, the 1890 Lunacy Act represented a 'triumph of legalism', partly because it involved a magistrate, as well as two doctors and a family representative or friend, in the certification process.[1] Andrew Scull's account of psychiatric professionalization concluded that, 'At the close of the nineteenth century, the professional status of asylum doctors remained distinctly questionable.'[2] Certainly, asylum practice carried a relatively low status within the medical profession; and private asylums were viewed as particularly liable to abuses and malpractice. Nevertheless, this chapter argues that private practitioners were able to organize effective lobbying against proposed lunacy reforms, which secured the continuance of private care into the twentieth century.[3]

A corporate identity

Parry-Jones's survey of private asylums suggested that 'One of the failings of the private-madhouse system was that it never achieved any effective corporate organization or identity'.[4] In the eighteenth century, the College of Physicians had operated in a concerted way to protect the interests of its members in private madhouses in London; and after the Madhouses Act of 1828, they continued to exert some influence on the Metropolitan Lunacy Commission through medical representatives.[5] Until the 1840s, provincial proprietors may have served their interests best by maintaining cordial relationships with local magistrates and visiting physicians. However, the introduction of central inspection from 1842 weakened the power of these relationships, in a way which could have been damaging to the interests of provincial madhouse-keepers.[6] Nevertheless, evidence from Ticehurst suggests that Nicholas Hervey is right to detect the existence of an 'extensive and cohesive network' of asylum proprietors and private practitioners, which extended beyond London, and provided concerted opposition to any rigorous policing of private practice by the Lunacy Commissioners.[7] Indeed, the existence of such a freemasonry between established private practitioners may provide one explanation of

193

The protection of private care

the slowness with which some private asylum proprietors responded to the creation of the more formally constituted Association of Medical Officers of Asylums and Hospitals for the Insane in 1841.

This network included members of the College of Physicians whose families had long-standing interests in metropolitan madhouses, like Edward Thomas Monro (1794–1856) and Alexander Sutherland. In addition, as Hervey has argued, Alexander Morison's Society for Improving the Condition of the Insane (founded in 1842), which presented the case for unregulated single care, and the need for some use of mechanical restraint, provided another formal nexus of this group.[8] The Newingtons had links with Morison, and several other members of his society, notably Alexander Sutherland and his son. It was Morison who transferred the Earl of Carlisle's son, Revd W.G. Howard, to Ticehurst from single care in 1846.[9] Alexander John Sutherland (1811–67) certified several admissions to Ticehurst in the 1840s–60s, and other patients were transferred to Ticehurst from his private asylums, Blacklands House and Otto House. Other admissions had spent time in private lodgings for single lunatics in Alpha Road near Regents Park to which Sutherland, like Morison, supplied patients whom he then took responsibility for medically attending.[10]

In February 1851, the Lunacy Commissioners criticized Charles Hayes Newington for not notifying them of the transfer of a patient called William Raikes from Alpha Road to Ticehurst in December 1850; somewhat implausibly, he pleaded ignorance of the law. Later certificates which recorded admissions from private lodgings – like those endorsed by the prominent lunacy physician Forbes Winslow in St Leonards – rarely gave a full address of the private lodgings in which patients had been confined.[11] Doctors who were members of the Society for Improving the Condition of the Insane in the 1840s continued to send patients to Ticehurst until the early 1880s; and violent or noisy patients whom the Newingtons were unwilling to admit to Ticehurst were referred to Brooke House, Clapton, which was run by the Monro family. Patients were also transferred from Ticehurst to Brooke House and the Priory, which belonged to another former member of Morison's society, W. Wood.[12]

As Hervey has pointed out, the Lunacy Commissioners' lack of tenacity in enforcing their powers to regulate private practice was partly due to the presence of medical Commissioners on the board who had personal or professional links with that private practice. The former Metropolitan Lunacy Commissioners, John Robert Hume (1781–1857) and James Cowles Prichard (1786–1848) were friends of Morison and Alexander Sutherland; and another former Metropolitan Lunacy Commissioner, Henry Herbert Southey (1783–1865), certified admissions to Ticehurst with the Sutherlands: one with Alexander Sutherland before the board was established, and two after Southey had resigned from the board, with

The protection of private care

Alexander John Sutherland.[13] Although Samuel Gaskell and James Wilkes (1811–94) were less tractable medical Commissioners, from 1857 the Newingtons had an ally on the board in Robert Nairne (1804–87). A contemporary of Charles Hayes Newington at Trinity College Cambridge, on graduating Nairne became physician at St George's, a hospital with strong Evangelical connections, where Charles Hayes had studied for his LRCP. Just as Charles Newington had fostered the continuing goodwill of the magistrates through gifts from the estate at Ticehurst, Samuel Newington sent presents of fruit grown at Ticehurst to Robert Nairne and Robert Lutwidge (1802–73) at the Lunacy Commission.[14]

Although many private practitioners were slow to join the Association of Medical Officers of Asylums and Hospitals for the Insane (AMOAHI), Alexander Morison and some other members of the Society for Improving the Condition of the Insane did join; and Alexander John Sutherland became president of the association in 1855. Forbes Winslow's *Journal of Psychological Medicine and Mental Pathology* (1848–61), which supported the interests of private practioners, proved relatively short-lived once the AMOAHI began producing its own journal in 1854, edited by John Charles Bucknill, who was then medical superintendent of Devon County Asylum.[15] It was not until 1862 that Charles Hayes and Samuel Newington joined the Medico-Psychological Association (MPA) (as it had by then become); but increasingly in the 1850s–60s private practitioners looked to the association, rather than Morison's society or Winslow's journal, to represent their views.

At one level, this is understandable, since many county asylum doctors engaged in some private practice, or ran private asylums after retiring from the public sector.[16] Nevertheless, there were times when private practitioners must have feared that the MPA would fail to represent their interests with sufficient force. For example, during the critical period of the 1877 Select Committee, the editor of the association's *Journal of Mental Science* was Henry Maudsley, who favoured the closure of private asylums; and this was one factor in forcing Maudsley's resignation as editor in the same year.[17] As this example suggests, however, one reason why private practitioners may not have felt a continuing need for a separate organization is because they were adept at dominating the politics of the MPA; and this was crucial to their success in modifying proposed lunacy legislation, since they had only limited support from the medical profession as a whole.

Asylum practice and the medical profession

In the 1870s–80s, the *Lancet* and the *British Medical Journal* both supported calls for lunacy reform. A series of articles in the *Lancet* by Mortimer Granville on asylums and asylum treatment, in 1875–7, had contributed to the mounting pressure for a government inquiry into the lunacy laws

The protection of private care

which led to the 1877 select committee. Granville was particularly concerned with the effectiveness or otherwise of medical treatment in asylums, and criticized excessive use of 'chemical restraint', or strong sedation. When no legislation followed publication of the select committee report, James Wakley mounted an increasingly radical editorial campaign in the *Lancet* attacking private asylums. In May 1879, he called for their immediate abolition, arguing that 'hotel-keeping' was incompatible with professional ethics, because proprietors had a vested interest in their patients' non-recovery. Eighteen months later, he made the same point; and went on to compare private asylums to zoos, stressing that their function was custodial, and ridiculing moral treatment as a system of management and containment rather than therapy and cure.[18] Together with Bucknill's articles in the *British Medical Journal*, these editorials helped to sustain pressure for lunacy reform; and suggested that asylum practitioners could expect little support from their general medical colleagues.

The insecurity of asylum doctors *vis-à-vis* the rest of the medical profession led several prominent medical psychologists to consider the question of how psychological medicine related to general medicine. In 1884, G.H. Savage's presidential address to the psychology section of the BMA called for more physiological measurements of the insane to be taken routinely in asylums, in the hope of discerning a new physical pathology. More importantly, he argued for an expansion of the importance of psychological medicine to the profession as a whole, through an exploration of the mental symptoms of ordinary physical disorders.[19] This was important, since one of Wakley's points had been that a knowledge of insanity did not form a routine part of medical training, so that it was difficult for doctors who were not lunacy specialists to sign certificates of insanity with confidence.[20] In 1886, T.S. Clouston's presidential address to the same section raised the question 'How may the medical spirit be best maintained in our asylums?', and suggested that the separation of acute and chronic cases, with more active treatment of the former in a hospital wing, would help reassert the medical and curative, rather than custodial, nature of asylums.[21]

By the mid-1880s, the *Lancet* was concentrating its fire on lunacy administration, rather than asylum practice. In 1884, the editor sympathized with the Lord Chancellor's Visitors' criticisms of the Lunacy Commission, which he described as an 'effete body'; and, in the wake of the scandal surrounding the case of Georgina Weldon, argued that if medical men went on 'strike', and refused to sign certificates of insanity, it would make little difference, since it was already so easy to confine someone to an asylum.[22] Perhaps surprisingly, the *Lancet* later criticized the MPA for seeking to subordinate the judiciary to medical opinion in the certification process; but this too emphasizes the *Lancet*'s sympathy with the Lord

196

The protection of private care

Chancellor's Visitors. Whereas Lord Shaftesbury had opposed the involvement of the courts in the certification of private patients, because he thought it would deter families from referring patients for treatment, the Lord Chancellor's Visitors naturally favoured a system which would bring the certification of all private patients closer to the procedure in Chancery cases.[23]

In 1886, the editors of the *Journal of Mental Science*, Savage and D.H. Tuke, were stung to learn that, during a debate on the proposed lunacy legislation, Lord Coleridge had remarked:

> that it had come to his knowledge that the proprietors of private asylums are not regarded in an altogether favourable light by other members of the medical profession . . . we [Savage and Tuke] regret to observe the continual use by peers during this debate of the terms 'incarceration' and the 'keepers' of private asylums in an obnoxious sense.[24]

Although the proposed legislation of 1886 was dropped, a new bill was being drafted in 1887–9, and the medical respectability of asylum practice continued to be of major concern to those who hoped lunacy practitioners' powers would be protected, rather than curtailed, in the new Lunacy Act.

How could such respectability best be assured? In February 1888, a storm of protest was raised in the MPA over the appointment of a Dr C.E. Saunders, who had no experience of psychological medicine or asylum management, as medical superintendent of Sussex County Asylum. Under rules drawn up in 1870, the Sussex superintendent had to be a graduate of a British university, and a member of one of the two British colleges of physicians. Unable to find a suitably qualified candidate amongst those with experience of asylum work who applied for the post, the Sussex committee of visitors appointed Dr Saunders instead. However, as Dr Murray Lindsay, the medical superintendent of Derbyshire County Asylum, pointed out to the MPA:

> Out of a total of 54 superintendents in 52 county asylums, only nine . . . are medically qualified and eligible according to the Sussex rule. . . . Out of a total of 12 borough asylum superintendents, only three . . . are medically qualified and eligible . . . the three Senior Medical Commissioners in Lunacy for England, Scotland, and Ireland, one of the Lord Chancellor's Visitors in Lunacy, and half the Council of the Medico-Psychological Association, are all medically unqualified and ineligible.[25]

Medical psychologists in the late 1880s were thus a relatively low-status branch of the medical profession in terms of qualifications. The only prerequisites to sitting the MPA's certificate in psychological medicine – which was not, in any case, required for asylum appointments – were that candidates should be medically licensed, and have some experience of

The protection of private care

working in an asylum. At the next annual meeting of the Association, G.H. Savage proposed a resolution that the Medical Council should be asked to register the MPC, 'and that the importance of this guarantee of practical experience of lunacy be impressed upon the Government in introducing any new Lunacy Bill', a motion which was unanimously carried.[26] Yet, as Murray Lindsay may have been aware, one sector of asylum practice already included a majority of university graduate MRCPs: thirteen of the twenty-four medical proprietors of metropolitan licensed houses had both these qualifications, including those like Henry Monro, Henry Sutherland, Henry Forbes Winslow and William Wood, who were direct descendants of the pre-association network of private practitioners.[27] Despite differences of opinion between the MPA and the general medical profession, these continuing links between asylum medicine and the College of Physicians were important to the effectiveness of private practitioners' lobbying against restrictions on private care.

The MPA and lunacy reform

Although Maudsley had resigned as editor of the *Journal of Mental Science*, conflicting attitudes to private asylums continued to divide the MPA. In 1880, an editorial in the *Journal* suggested that there were significant levels of support for the closure of private asylums within the association.[28] Nevertheless, by 1884–6 the MPA's parliamentary committee was lobbying against any restriction of private practice, as well as criticizing the 'anti-medical' character of proposed legislation. The main reason for this shift was the fact that private practitioners were able to secure a majority on the parliamentary committee created to review the proposed lunacy legislation in 1884. Hayes Newington was one of the private asylum proprietors whose opposition to the lunacy reform movement carried him onto this committee; and he continued to be a member until after the 1890 Lunacy Act became law. The lunacy bill presented in 1887 retained many of the principles of the bill proposed in 1886: a magistrate would be involved in the certification of private patients; no new licences would be issued for private asylums, and existing institutions would not be allowed to increase their numbers; single care would be limited to Chancery cases; and the Secretary of State would be given powers to amalgamate the offices of the Lord Chancellor's Visitors and the Lunacy Commission.[29]

While this bill was being debated in 1887–8, some county asylum superintendents complained that the MPA's parliamentary committee was mainly composed of asylum doctors who worked in the private sector. Apart from Hayes Newington, five members of the committee of fourteen had links with metropolitan licensed houses, including William Wood; one was joint-proprietor of Fisherton House in Salisbury; three were medical superintendents of registered hospitals, including Frederick Needham

198

The protection of private care

from high-class Barnwood in Gloucestershire and G.H. Savage from Bethlem; leaving only four members of the committee who worked in asylums funded by local government – Thomas Clouston, and three other district and county asylum superintendents. Of prime concern to county asylum superintendents was the fact that the parliamentary committee had failed to persuade Salisbury's government to include pensions for former county asylum superintendents amongst statutory requirements to be provided by the new county councils created by the Local Government Act; and that so far the new lunacy bill's only recommendation concerning pensions was that any pension rights included in county asylum medical officers' contracts of service should be transferable within one county.

The parliamentary committee's published recommendations for amendments to the new bill – opposing the clause which would have prevented medical practitioners from receiving non-Chancery cases as single patients, insisting that Chancery patients ought to be able to be sent on temporary leave from asylums like other patients, and criticizing compulsory questions on admission concerning 'whether any near relative has been afflicted with insanity' – primarily reflected the concerns of private practitioners, although they also recommended that county asylum superintendents' pensions should be transferable from one county to another, as well as within one county. Few county asylum members of the association can have been pleased, therefore, when they arrived at the annual meeting in Edinburgh in August 1888 to learn that, at a time when new negotiations seemed possible because the lunacy bill had been postponed to the next parliamentary session, the MPA's council were recommending Hayes Newington to succeed Clouston as president of the MPA in 1889–90.[30] The selection of a university-educated, although not graduate, MRCP from one of the oldest families of private asylum proprietors in the country represented all the vested gentlemanly interests the insecurely professionalized county asylum superintendents felt they needed to oppose.

Although Hayes Newington's selection was not openly contested, several members of the MPA raised objections to the system of election under which the council recommended nominees who were then invariably approved by the full membership of the association. Ordinary members had the right to propose alternative nominees, but in August 1888 David Yellowlees, from Gartnavel Asylum in Glasgow, described the electoral procedure as a 'solemn farce, since no one would think of erasing any of the names proposed by the Council'.[31] Clouston pre-empted any immediate alteration in the system of election by appealing to the rules of the association, which stated that advance notice had to be given to members of motions which were to be discussed at the annual meeting, and suggested that Yellowlees should propose a different electoral system at next year's meeting. A motion proposed by the medical superintendent of

The protection of private care

Hanwell, Dr Henry Rayner, that the ordinary membership of the council of the association should be increased from twelve to eighteen, making a total of twenty-eight council members including those who held special offices, was unanimously carried. Amongst those who spoke in favour of this motion was Alexander Urquhart, a former assistant medical officer at Ticehurst under Hayes Newington and now physician superintendent at Perth Royal Asylum, and the MPA's Scottish secretary; Urquhart complained that since quarterly and committee meetings were held in London and the association could not afford to refund travelling expenses, 'it was thought by some in the country that London influence predominated too much in regard to the business and the selection of officers', a fault which he hoped the council's increase in size would help to correct. At the same time as Hayes Newington was elected president, ten new members, four of whom replaced retiring councillors, were voted onto the council, including nine who were superintendents of county, borough or district asylums.

In addition, after further discussion of members' concern that county asylum superintendents were under-represented on the parliamentary committee at a time when the restructuring of local government might lead to major financial problems, as rate-bound elected representatives replaced county magistrates on the committees of visitors, Henry Rayner proposed a second motion that the parliamentary committee should be empowered to draft in more members, in the hope of securing a fuller representation of county asylum superintendents' views; and this was approved.[32] When news of the death of John Alfred Lush, joint proprietor of Fisherton House through his marriage to W.C. Finch's daughter, and a former Liberal MP for Salisbury in 1868–80, reached the parliamentary committee, a district asylum superintendent, Dr T. Oscar Woods, was appointed to the committee; but it seems unlikely that he would have travelled all the way from Co. Kerry in Ireland to attend committee meetings in London. No other county asylum superintendents were drafted onto the parliamentary committee, and the new lunacy legislation, which incorporated some of the MPA's suggested amendments, but made no change to the bill's original clause on county asylum superintendents' pensions, had passed its second reading before the parliamentary committee could be radically restructured at the next annual meeting of the association in July 1889.[33]

It is unclear how far the death of Dr Lush, who had been a member of the Select Committee of 1877, and, as his obituary in the *Journal of Mental Science* expressed it, retained 'his loyalty to the ex-Premier' Gladstone, helped ease negotiations with Salisbury's government, and made them more willing to incorporate some of the MPA parliamentary committee's suggested amendments at the standing committee stage. By refusing to press the question of the security of county asylum superintendents'

200

The protection of private care

pensions, focus was brought to bear on the restrictions the bill would have imposed on private practice and important concessions were gained; particularly when the standing committee reversed the bill's prohibition on medical practitioners receiving non-Chancery cases into their own homes. Although new licences for private asylums would be issued only in exceptional circumstances, the Lunacy Act permitted medical practitioners to receive single patients into their homes, and included the amendment that 'Under special circumstances the Commissioners may allow more than one patient to be received as single patients into the same unlicensed house.'[34] In lobbying for this change, the MPA's parliamentary committee had the support of the College of Physicians, who once again came to the fore in protecting private lunacy practice. Ironically, one of the College of Physicians' delegates to lobby the Home Secretary in 1889 was Henry Maudsley, who had of course been a long-time advocate of single care in preference to private asylum treatment.[35]

With undisguised pleasure, and some disingenuity concerning their own role as members of the MPA's parliamentary committee in helping to secure this change, Savage and Hack Tuke suggested in the *Journal of Mental Science* that:

> It is not a little amusing, and is surely the very irony of fate, that a Bill brought in with the avowed purpose of abolishing Private Asylums should deliberately introduce a clause, at the last moment, and under no pressure whatever from without, which restores Private Asylums to all intents and purposes, without a licence, and more important still, without the supervisory visitation required in the case of Licensed Houses.[36]

On the one hand, restrictions on the issuing of new licences legally underwrote the cartel of private practitioners which had to some extent remained unchanged since the early 1840s, at a time when the crisis in British psychological medicine threatened their future survival; ensuring that as private asylums filled with chronic cases, demand from consumers would always exceed the number of places available. In this sense, the 1890 Lunacy Act represents an early example of late-Victorian Conservatives' increasingly protectionist economic policies during a period of economic decline, which led to the levelling of high tariffs on imports under the slogan of 'fair trade' rather than 'free trade'. One of the MPA parliamentary committee's criticisms of the lunacy bill as it was originally drafted was that, if medical practitioners were not allowed to take private patients in Britain, the relatives of upper- and middle-class lunatics would simply send them abroad.[37]

On the other hand, the twilight area of 'special circumstances' under which more than one patient could be received into unlicensed houses also left room for expansion in a less regulated market if demand rose to a sufficiently high level. Care in an unlicensed house still offered the greatest

The protection of private care

privacy to patients' relatives; although, even when a patient was admitted into single care, medical and legal certification was required, medical journals had to be kept, and patients would be visited annually. One amendment which the MPA's parliamentary committee had failed to secure was Hayes Newington's recommendation that there should be no question on the admission papers concerning any insanity amongst the patients' close relations; but the revised bill incorporated the MPA's parliamentary committee's proposal that Chancery patients should be allowed to go on trial discharge as other patients were.[38]

One clause which was first introduced into the lunacy bill after the MPA parliamentary committee's proposed amendments had been published in July 1887 was section 45, which stressed that 'Mechanical means of bodily restraint shall not be applied except for surgical or medical treatment, and to prevent the lunatic from injuring himself or others'.[39] This amendment may have been included partly as a result of a series of letters from J.C. Bucknill to *The Times* in September and October 1888, which alleged that Savage had used excessive mechanical restraint and strong sedation at Bethlem, which caused an unusually high death rate of 14.4 per cent (as opposed to 7.8 per cent of asylum inmates nationally); and that, in June 1887 18 out of 264 patients had been mechanically restrained at Bethlem, compared to a total of 25 cases of mechanical restraint recorded in all other asylums in Britain during the same month. Despite defending his use of restraint in the *Lancet*, but not *The Times*, Savage resigned as resident physician at Bethlem.[40]

Under Maudsley's editorship, the *Journal of Mental Science* had provided little space to members of the profession who would have preferred the use of mechanical restraint to be less closely regulated by the Lunacy Commissioners. Even after the murder of one of the Lunacy Commissioners by a violent patient in 1873, and subsequent appeal by the president of the MPA in 1874, T.L. Rogers, for the regulation of restraint to be liberalized, during Shaftesbury's lifetime the Lunacy Commissioners remained determinedly opposed to any increase in its use. However, under the editorship of Savage and Hack Tuke, the question of whether mechanical restraint might be beneficial for some patients was reopened and sympathetically debated, particularly after 1888. At the Scottish quarterly meeting of the MPA in November, David Yellowlees defended Savage's position, pointing out that the fact that the Scottish Lunacy Commissioners did not count the use of gloves as mechanical restraint meant that ten out of Savage's eighteen cases of restraint in June 1887 would not have been counted in Scotland. Most subsequent speakers concurred that a limited use of physical restraint was an indispensable part of their resources as asylum doctors; including Clouston, who suggested that 'In some exceptional cases . . . restraint was the only remedy, the most humane resource, and the most scientific application of the principles of modern brain therapeutics'.[41]

The protection of private care

While section 45 was intended to clarify what the Lunacy Commissioners would regard as a reasonable use of mechanical restraint in a restrictive way, it inscribed in law the original belief of members of the Society for Improving the Condition of the Insane that some use of instrumental restraint was both necessary and valuable. Initially, Savage and Hack Tuke criticized the introduction of this clause as 'interference with the action of the medical superintendent', but by the time the bill became law they were hailing it as:

> the first time in the history of lunacy, mechanical restraint has been formally recognised by an Act of Parliament. The medical superintendents of asylums will now have legal authority for applying 'instruments and appliances' in the treatment of patients without the doubts and misgivings they have long suffered from as to whether mechanical restraint is or is not a legitimate form of treatment.[42]

Although they allowed further debate to take place in the *Journal of Mental Science* between Alexander Robertson, physician of Glasgow City Parochial Asylum, and David Yellowlees, whom Robertson accused of being 'the leader in Scotland of . . . a distinctly retrograde movement', Savage and Hack Tuke used their editorial position to encourage a broad interpretation of the Act's meaning, suggesting, for example, that patients who kept removing their clothes, but were not suicidal or dangerous ought to be restrained, 'for to clothe such lunatic and keep him warm is certainly medical treatment, and prevents him injuring himself by bringing on fatal pneumonia through exposure'.[43]

In cases like this, the use of strong clothing, rather than a complete restriction of physical movement, was what was being recommended. Nevertheless, like the proposed return to blood-letting, and increased use of counter-irritation, the advocacy of a greater use of mechanical restraint reflected the therapeutic and managerial despair of asylum superintendents whose medical philosophy gave them little reason to hope for any improvement in recovery rates, who were becoming wary of the extensive use of strong narcotics as 'chemical restraint', and who felt unsupported by national and local governments' refusal to provide substantial financial incentives and funding for medical practitioners who worked in asylums. The advantages of sulphonal over other sedative drugs were discussed as enthusiastically at these meetings as the use of mechanical restraint.[44]

The 1890 Lunacy Act and private practice

Whose interests were represented in the 1890 Lunacy Act? The Lord Chancellor's Visitors no doubt welcomed the involvement of the courts in the certification of all patients; and they may have hoped their powers would be extended by any future amalgamation of their office with the

The protection of private care

Lunacy Commission. In contrast, although the Lunacy Commissioners had finally achieved greater regulation of single care, the Lord Chancellor now had almost unlimited powers to 'give such directions as he may think fit for the reconstitution of the Commissioners, and for the exercise and performance of the powers and duties of the Commissioners'.[45] In fact, these powers were never used.

Although some members of the medical profession may have objected to the subordination of doctors to the courts in the certification process, many lobbied for medical signatories to be protected against legal action by patients who believed they had been wrongfully confined. The government responded to this wish by making one of the stated objectives of the 1890 Lunacy Act the intention 'to protect medical practitioners and others in the performance of their duties'.[46] As Nikolas Rose has argued, the involvement of the courts in the certification process, and the exemption of medical practitioners from prosecution unless bad faith was proved, 'freed doctors from the accusation of wrongful confinement and minimized the contentious nature of commitment decisions'.[47] Nevertheless, although Savage and Tuke welcomed the protection of the medical profession from 'frivolous' and 'vexatious' litigation, they also, like the *Lancet*, criticized the restriction on new licences for private asylums for creating a monopoly amongst existing proprietors.[48]

In forbidding the issue of new licences, the long-term objective of the Lunacy Act was, in the words of Baron Herschell in 1886, to 'produce a gradual cessation of the number of licensed houses, and thus prepare the way for public asylums'.[49] Direct abolition had been decided against mainly because the government was unwilling to compensate private asylum proprietors. The delegation from the College of Physicians to the Home Secretary in 1889 similarly argued that an expansion in single accommodation for private patients was desirable because it would help to expedite the 'gradual abolition of private asylums'.[50] Nevertheless, private practitioners were evidently relieved not to be faced with the closure of their businesses. Some may have welcomed the creation of an effective monopoly; and there were opportunities for expansion in single and 'double' care. By gaining control of the MPA's parliamentary committee, and the continuing support of the College of Physicians on some issues, private practitioners had been able to defend themselves first against the closure of private asylums and then against restrictions on single care. Although the status of medical psychologists within the profession remained low, private practitioners had secured the future of private lunacy practice.

The 1890 Lunacy Act was only partially successful in achieving the objectives outlined by Baron Herschell. Private accommodation in county asylums was permitted in the Act; and the provision of suitable accommodation was encouraged by a clause which required any profit from private patients to be paid to the local authority. From 1890, these

The protection of private care

Table 7.1 Distribution of private patients, 1890–1910

Year	County, borough or district	Registered hospital	Licensed houses	Single care	Total
1890	936 (12.0%)	3,408 (43.6%)	3,035 (38.8%)	446 (5.7%)	7,825*
1910	3,188 (30.5%)	3,775 (36.1%)	2,897 (27.7%)	593 (5.7%)	10,453*

* Not including private patients in naval, military and criminal asylums
Sources: LCRs 1890 and 1910

asylums increased their share of the private market. Not surprisingly, given the restriction on any expansion of licensed houses, the number of patients accommodated in private asylums did not increase. Nevertheless, the decrease of numbers of private patients in licensed houses after 1890 was less than that between 1880 and 1890; and the number of patients recorded as being in single care rose in line with the overall increase in numbers of private patients (See Table 7.1). By 1910, several of the family businesses founded in the eighteenth or early-nineteenth centuries remained open. In the provinces, Brislington House and Ticehurst were still run by the Foxes and the Newingtons; and, although it was no longer operated by the Finch family, Laverstock House was still open. In London, the Monros, the Sutherlands and the Woods were still running Brooke House, Otto House (and Newlands in Tooting), and the Priory.[51] What remains to be explored is the impact which the 1890 Lunacy Act had on private patients and their families.

Edwardian choices of private care

But in that red brick barn upon the hill
  I wonder – can one own the deer,
And does one walk with children still
  As one did here –
  Do roses grow
Beneath those twenty windows in a row –
  And if some night
When you have not seen any light
They cannot move you from your chair
  What happens there?
  I do not know.

  So, when they took
Ken to that place, I did not look
  After he called and turned on me
  His eyes. These I shall see –

(Charlotte Mew, 'Ken')

The protection of private care

By making the certification of private patients a matter for the courts, the 1890 Lunacy Act gave some credence to lunacy reformers' fears that patients were sometimes confined from corrupt motives. Nevertheless, like the 1877 Select Committee Report, the 1890 Lunacy Act recommended that, whenever possible, patients should be referred by a near relation; or, if they were married, by their husband or wife.[52] This suggests that the drafters of the legislation believed that worried families might be susceptible to self-interested advice from lunacy doctors, rather than that they suspected families of confining patients from corrupt motives. Certainly, if admissions to Ticehurst are representative, the recommendation that patients should be referred by a near relation merely inscribed common practice in law. What was new was that the Act made voluntary admission of private patients possible for the first time. However, at Ticehurst, more than half the voluntary boarders from 1890 to 1914 were convalescents or readmissions; and only about one in twenty new admissions came as voluntary boarders (see Table 7.2).

Shaftesbury believed that the routine involvement of the courts in the certification of private patients would deter families from referring the mentally disturbed to asylums. Nevertheless, the number of private patients confined in asylums continued to rise, albeit more slowly than the number of pauper patients. The gradual trend away from confinement in licensed houses, in favour of registered hospitals and private beds in local authority asylums, was already well established when the 1890 Lunacy Act was passed (see Table 4.2, p. 000). Nevertheless, the continuance of this trend suggests that criticism of private asylums may have influenced families' decisions about care. County asylums and registered hospitals were relatively free of the taint of allegedly corrupt motives which were associated with licensed houses; and, despite their success in influencing legislation, private asylum proprietors were only gradually able to improve their public reputation.

As in the Victorian period, middle- and upper-class Edwardian families regarded certification as a last resort. When doctors advised separation

Table 7.2 Voluntary boarders admitted to Ticehurst, 1890–1914

Patients admitted 1 January 1890–31 December 1914
Numbers in brackets represent readmissions

	Men	Women	Both
From certificates in Ticehurst	8	5	13
Former inmates admitted from home	1 (1)	2 (3)	3 (4)
New patients	6 (1)	7	13 (1)
Total	15 (2)	14 (3)	29 (5)

Sources: VB1890–1930

The protection of private care

from the family, travel abroad was still seen as preferable to certification. Just as Merivale had been treated at a hydropathic establishment near Koblenz before being admitted to Ticehurst, in 1904, despite suffering from agoraphobia, Ford Madox Ford travelled to Germany when his doctor recommended that a separation from his family might benefit his nerves. As Ford wrote later: 'years ago . . . I was seized upon by one German nerve-specialist after another and sent further and further towards Central Europe in one hydropathic establishment after another . . . I all but died.'[53] Nevertheless, he eventually recuperated sufficiently to return home.

As this example suggests, patients and their families frequently explored other treatment options before considering asylum care. Although asylum doctors were willing to attribute their patients' mental disorders to miscellaneous physical causes, Edward Shorter is probably right to suggest that patients and their families preferred treatment in hydropathic and other private clinics for physical disorders, because this made it less obvious to others that a problem was mental or nervous.[54] If this was so, it is a trend which can only have been reinforced by the need to apply to a court in order to certify a private patient. Certainly, advertisements for private nursing homes, sanatoria, inebriate asylums and hydropathic establishments proliferated alongside those for private asylums in the *Medical Directory* from the 1880s; and some private asylums changed their name to one which incorporated 'home' or 'sanatorium'. For example, West Malling Place (formerly William Perfect's madhouse) became 'Kent Sanatorium', but continued to be licensed as a private asylum. There is widespread evidence of patients being admitted to unlicensed nursing homes and sanatoria in preference to licensed houses; and of medical psychologists supplying patients and acting as consultant physicians to such institutions. In fact, doctors who attended patients in nursing homes in this way maintained precisely the kind of separation between profit from boarding patients and profit from medical attendance, which the *Lancet* had advocated when it criticized private asylums in the 1880s.[55]

When John Cowper Powys's sister Katie suffered a nervous breakdown after an unhappy love affair in 1912, she was sent to a sanatorium in Bristol rather than a private asylum.[56] Similarly, despite the fact that there were periods when she was suicidal, Virginia Woolf was referred by G.H. Savage to Burley, a nursing home in Twickenham. In a letter to Violet Dickinson, Woolf described how Burley was full of 'several not altogether like other people women. One of them leapt with fright when one looked at her, and shook her fork in one's face'.[57] More bluntly, she told Vanessa Bell that Jean Thomas, who ran the home, was one day: 'in a highly wrought state, as the lunatic upstairs has somehow brought her case to court. . . . The utmost tact is shown with regard to our complaints; and I make Miss T. blush by asking if they're mad.'[58]

Admission to a nursing home or sanatorium rather than a private

The protection of private care

asylum protected the patient and their family from the stigma of certification; and it is possible that standards of care were similar to those in many private asylums. However, institutions like this were not subject to the Lunacy Commissioners' regulations, although inebriate asylums were the subject of separate legislation. Patients were admitted voluntarily to nursing homes and sanatoria, but it is clear that, once they were inmates, their letters and access to family and friends were controlled sometimes in a way which was strictly illegal.[59]

Nursing homes and sanatoria filled the gap in the market created by the stricter regulation of private asylums and single care. The possibility of wrongful confinement in an asylum had been lessened by the new certification procedures for private patients. In 1895, the socialist and feminist Edith Lanchester was committed to Wood's asylum, the Priory, by her father and brothers on an urgency order, signed by the lunacy physician, G. Fielding Blandford. Before her admission, she had been living with a railway clerk in Battersea, and Blandford argued that her 'opposition to conventional matrimony made her unfit to take care of herself'.[60] Under the 1890 Lunacy Act, a patient could be confined on an urgency order for a maximum of seven days before a judicial hearing; and, in this case, Lanchester was released by the Lunacy Commissioners after only five days.[61] Overall, however, there is more evidence of families delaying or seeking to avoid the patients' removal from home than there is of attempted wrongful confinement.

It was not long after a stay at Burley in 1913 that Virginia Woolf attempted suicide by taking an overdose of veronal which had been prescribed by Savage. Despite the fact that for the next two years she suffered from recurrent bouts of anorexia and sleeplessness, and at times the Woolfs had as many as four nurses living in to take care of her, she spent only one more week in a nursing home, while they were moving house.[62] Similarly, Roger Fry employed two nurses to care for his wife Helen at home. Although Helen Fry had suffered periods of mental ill-health since 1898, in which she was sometimes separated from her family, it was only after she became violent and was declared incurable in 1910 that she was certified and committed to an asylum. When this decision was taken, her consultant, Henry Head, comforted Fry by telling him 'You have certainly fought hard to help your wife, and shown a devotion I have never seen equalled. Unfortunately, the disease has beaten us.'[63] As this letter suggests, the decision to have a relative confined to an asylum continued to provoke guilt and grief, which the absence of therapeutic optimism in the Edwardian period may have sharpened.

Paying for private care imposed a financial burden which even the relatively well-off, like Roger Fry, found difficult.[64] Charlotte Mew struggled to find the money to pay for private attendants for her brother Henry and sister Freda, despite the fact that Freda was confined as a

The protection of private care

fee-paying patient in Whitelands Hospital in Carisbrooke, rather than a private asylum. The poem 'Ken' is believed to express Mew's feelings when Henry was certified. More broadly, it suggests that the decline in therapeutic optimism, and growing sense that those admitted to asylums were unlikely to return, cannot be equated with a decline in feeling for the insane. In another poem, 'On the asylum road', Mew demonstrated an awareness of degenerationist views of madness when she referred to the insane as 'the incarnate wages of man's sin', but this did not lessen her continuing regret that her sister and brother were confined.[65] Mew's poems suggest that, by the early twentieth century, asylums were perceived as institutions which offered relatively impersonal systems of care; they were 'red brick barns', which grouped patients in 'long galler[ies]'.[66] Although private asylums might reasonably claim to offer more individual care than the private wards of county asylums, the fact that they were not more effective in attracting patients is a measure of the public disillusion with licensed houses. Advertisements for private asylums emphasized the fact that they offered treatment in home-like surroundings, but were increasingly in competition with nursing 'homes' and the 'home treatment' promised in sanatoria and asylums for inebriates.[67]

Initially, despite the prevalence of hereditarian ideas, some families may have referred patients for treatment hoping for a cure. In 1909, when Helen Fry was removed temporarily from home, Roger Fry expressed his grief and hopes about the separation:

> Oh, I feel like crying at having to leave you and yet you see it must be for a while because I can do you no good while you resent all those wretched restrictions and limitations of your freedom that are still necessary to save you and make you well again. . . . Oh Nell, my own Nell, all happiness lies before us if only you can yield your own personal will and accept the wisdom of those who know, who have spent their lives in learning what is wise and what will help those who are ill in mind and spirit.[68]

When Virginia Woolf was in Burley in 1913, her biographer Quentin Bell suggests that she and Leonard Woolf 'Again and again . . . expressed to each other the hope that somehow the cure would work, that somehow they would yet be able to make a happy life together'.[69] These hopes made private patients and their families willing to comply with their physicians' advice, even when it went against their feelings. When she was at Burley in 1910, Woolf confessed to her sister how much she hated 'all the eating and drinking and being shut up in the dark' required by the rest cure Savage had prescribed; but in the same letter she promised 'I will abide by Savage'.[70] In a letter to Helen Fry, her husband lamented how much he and the children were missing her, but explained 'Dr Chambers advises my not coming just yet'.[71] When treatment proved unsuccessful, patients

The protection of private care

might decide to seek alternative advice, as the Woolfs did when they consulted Henry Head and Maurice Wright after Virginia's condition deteriorated following her stay at Burley in 1913. Nevertheless, in this case, the advice given by Head and Wright was the same as that given by Savage.

As Bell observes, although:

> The doctors with their prescriptions of rest and food, 'Robin's Hypophosphate', and mulled wine at night, could at least relieve the symptoms of Virginia's disorder. It was something of which they understood almost as little as did their greatgrandfathers.[72]

Late-Victorian and Edwardian medical psychologists were painfully aware of their lack of real therapeutic resources; and, in the face of rapid advances in other areas of medicine, most notably immunology, they struggled to reassert their scientific credibility. In 1889, it was just over seventy years since Thomas Mayo had gone into print 'To vindicate the rights of [his] profession over insanity', but in his presidential address to the MPA, Hayes Newington felt a need to re-emphasize the 'fact that we all admit, nay, that we are all fighting for, which is that insanity is primarily and essentially an expression of disease of the body'.[73] Like Clouston, he recommended that acute and chronic patients should be separated in asylums; and that acute cases should be given 'hospital treatment' by a medical team which would include a general physician and a neurologist as well as a medical psychologist.[74] Yet this recommendation did little more than to endorse the division between acute and chronic patients which was already common in asylums which were built on the villa system; and, although asylums might acquire the infrastructure of a more scientific medicine, this was not matched by any new understanding of mental disorders or disease. Medical psychologists also strove to enhance their professional prestige by establishing a university-taught Diploma in Psychological Medicine from 1911, which they hoped would be state-registered.[75] Jones and Scull may have exaggerated the political ineffectiveness of medical psychologists in the late nineteenth century, but in the early twentieth century the MPA were unable initially to achieve this state registration, or the status of a royal college.[76]

In the absence of an improved understanding of mental disorders, and the real possibility of cure, an emphasis on a more clinical, hospital-like atmosphere may have been off-putting to relatives seeking long-term care for patients with whom they could no longer cope at home. Particularly since, in asylums which were funded by local authorities, doctors recommended that resources should be concentrated on patients who were perceived as curable.[77] Private asylums were not subject to the same resource constraints, but increasing competition from private wards in county asylums meant that some private asylums lowered their fees by 1900 to as little as 25s. per week.[78] This must have had an impact on staffing levels in private asylums, and increased the likelihood that mechanical and

The protection of private care

chemical restraint would be used routinely. Fees at Ticehurst remained high, but nevertheless the care offered to patients deteriorated with the growth of therapeutic pessimism. In 1926, the Royal Commission on Lunacy and Mental Disorder questioned the restriction on new licences for private asylums because it had created a virtual monopoly among private licensees, leading to poor incentives to maintain standards, or seek new therapeutic initiatives. Against the express intentions with which it had been introduced, the 1890 Lunacy Act had to some extent protected licensed houses; but it had done little to improve standards of care for private patients and their families.

Notes

1. K. Jones, *A history of the mental health services*, London, Routledge & Kegan Paul, 1972, Chapter 7.
2. A. Scull, *Museums of madness*, London, Allen Lane, 1979, p. 258.
3. N. Rose has argued more broadly that the 1890 Lunacy Act represented a 'reframing and reorganization' of psychiatry's power, in P. Miller and N. Rose (eds), *The power of psychiatry*, London, Polity Press, 1986, pp. 203–4.
4. W. Ll. Parry-Jones, *The trade in lunacy*, London, Routledge & Kegan Paul, 1972, p. 90.
5. N. Hervey, 'A slavish bowing down: the Lunacy Commission and the psychiatric profession, 1845–60', in W.F. Bynum, R. Porter and M. Shepherd (eds), *The anatomy of madness*, vol. II, London, Tavistock Publications, 1985, p. 101.
6. For example, Charles Newington sent game from the estate at Ticehurst to one of the visiting magistrates, see C. MacKenzie, 'A family asylum', London University PhD thesis, 1987, p. 145.
7. Hervey, op. cit., note 5 above, p. 116.
8. Ibid., p. 115.
9. Ibid., p. 127, note 127; RA1845–81, case 67.
10. Ibid., cases 11, 13, 77, 79, 83, 84, 97, 107, 131, 134, 139, 148, 275, 325.
11. Certificates for William Raikes, 25 February 1851; and certificates for Henry Shepherd, 18 August 1855, who had been 'since 1841 with Mr Mayer at Highgate, Mr Helling at Clifford, Mr Duft at St John's Wood and Seymour St, and Mr Edwards at Brompton and Richmond', QAL/1/4/E6.
12. G.M. Burrows (Clapham Retreat), G.W. Daniell (Southall Park), H.W. Diamond (Twickenham House), E.T. Monro (Brooke House) and W. Wood (Kensington House and later the Priory, Roehampton) all certified admissions to Ticehurst; patients certified by other doctors were referred from some of these madhouses and others run by members of Morison's society, such as Bailbrook House run by J.B. Daniel (RA1845–81, cases 50–517).
13. Ibid., cases 13, 46, 97.
14. V.&.A./48 E32, letter from Bryan Procter to John Forster; I am grateful to Nicholas Hervey for this reference.
15. See M. Shepherd, 'Psychological medicine redivivus: concept and communication', *Journal of the Royal Society of Medicine*, 1986, 79: 639–45; see also Scull, op. cit., note 2 above, p. 165.
16. For example, J. Connolly had interests in several private asylums while he was medical superintendent of Hanwell.

The protection of private care

17. Murray Lindsay seconded Harrington Tuke's call for Maudsley's resignation by alleging that under Maudsley's editorship the *JMS* had not advanced the interests of the association (*JMS*, 1877, 23: 28–9).
18. *Lancet*, 1875–7; 1879, i: 780; 1880, ii: 902 and 1881, i: 750.
19. G.H. Savage, 'The pathology of insanity', *BMJ*, 1884, ii: 239.
20. *Lancet*, 1877, i: 429.
21. T.S. Clouston, *BMJ*, 1886, ii: 581–3.
22. *Lancet*, 1884, ii, p. 153; 1885, i: 118.
23. *Lancet*, 1887, i: 1289.
24. *JMS*, 1886–7, 32: 75.
25. *JMS*, 1888–9, 34: 149.
26. Ibid., p. 454.
27. *Medical Directory*, 1888.
28. *JMS*, 1880–1, 26: 74.
29. The abolition of single care for non-Chancery cases had been proposed in 1886 (*JMS* 1886–7, 32: 75).
30. *JMS*, 1887–8, 33: i, 324–5; appended 'Observations and suggestions on the Lunacy Acts amendment bill by the parliamentary committee of the Medico-Psychological Association', pp. 5–7.
31. Ibid., p. 450.
32. Ibid., and p. 452.
33. *JMS*, 1889–90, 35: i: 441; the new parliamentary committee had nine county, borough and district asylum members, seven members who had links with private asylums, one who worked at a registered hospital, and one who was a private consultant.
34. *JMS*, 1888–9, 34: 471, 497.
35. *Lancet*, 1889, ii: 33.
36. *JMS*, 1888–9, 34: 397.
37. *JMS*, 1887–8, 33, appended 'Observations . . .', p. 5.
38. See discussion in ibid., p. 326; and *JMS*, 1889–90, 35: 510–11.
39. Ibid., p. 499.
40. For a discussion of the controversy which led to Savage's resignation see S. Trombley, *'All that summer she was mad'. Virginia Woolf and her doctors*, London, Junction Books, 1981, pp. 146–9.
41. *JMS*, 1888–9, 34: 624, 625–6 and 628–9.
42. *JMS*, 1889–90, 35: 220, 399.
43. Ibid., pp. 142, 220.
44. Ibid., pp. 133–4.
45. 53 Vict., *c.* 5, section 337 i.
46. See *JMS* 1888–9, 34: 479.
47. Rose, op. cit., note 3 above, p. 203.
48. *JMS*, 1886–7, 32: 228; and *Lancet*, 1887 i: 1289.
49. *JMS*, 1886–7, 32: 74.
50. *Lancet*, 1889 ii: 33.
51. *Medical Directory*, 1910.
52. 53 Vict., *c.*5, section 5 i.
53. A. Mizener, *The saddest story. A biography of Ford Madox Ford*, London, Bodley Head, 1971, pp. 93–5.
54. E. Shorter, 'Private clinics in central Europe, 1850–1933', *Social History of Medicine*, 1990, 3, 2: 190–2.
55. *Medical Directory*, 1900; see, for example, *Lancet*, 1887, i: 1289.
56. R.P. Graves, *The brothers Powys*, London, Routledge & Kegan Paul, 1983, p. 92.
57. Trombley, op. cit., note 40 above, p. 250.

212

The protection of private care

58. Ibid., pp. 255–6.
59. Ibid., p. 258
60. E. Showalter, *The female malady*, New York, Pantheon Books, 1985, p. 146.
61. Ibid., p. 147.
62. Q. Bell, *Virginia Woolf*, vol. 2, London, Paladin, 1972, pp. 13–26.
63. D. Sutton (ed.), *Letters of Roger Fry*, London, Chatto and Windus, 1972, pp. 30–1.
64. Ibid.
65. P. Fitzgerald, *Charlotte Mew and her friends*, London, Collins, 1984, pp. 44, 72.
66. 'On the asylum road' refers to the 'long gallery' of insane people.
67. *Medical Directory*, 1890–1910.
68. Sutton, op. cit., note 63 above, pp. 323–4.
69. Bell, op. cit., note 62 above, p. 13.
70. Trombley, op. cit., note 40 above, p. 256.
71. Sutton, op. cit., note 63 above, p. 291. 'Dr Chambers' was probably Dr James Chambers, a lunacy physician who was medical superintendent of Woods' asylum, the Priory.
72. Bell, op. cit., note 62 above, p. 13.
73. *JMS*, 1889–90, 35: 300, 302.
74. Ibid., p. 313.
75. See MacKenzie, op. cit., note 6 above, p. 447.
76. See *JMS*, 1910, 56: 373–5; the MPA received a royal charter in 1925.
77. See, for example, H.F.H. Newington, 'The plans of a new asylum for East Sussex', *JMS*, 1900, 46: 684.
78. See, for example, the advertisement for Peckham House private asylum, *Medical Directory*, 1900.

Conclusion

The beginnings of mental disorder are usually noticed first in the family. Irritability, sleeplessness, violence, self-neglect, obsessions, irrational fears and hallucinations, are all likely to become evident in the first instance to the relatives and friends who spend most time with a person. It is they who are likely to face the decision of whether, when and where to refer someone for care and treatment. In the eighteenth century, the increasingly high evaluation of gentility, and close family relationships, helped to create a market for private asylum care. If this represented a change, which rapidly accelerated development of the trade in lunacy, this study has also revealed striking continuities in families' subsequent responses to mental disorder. When relationships were close, insanity in the family made the relatives of sufferers feel helpless and distressed. On the one hand, they wanted to seek help; on the other, they were wary of poor standards, corrupt motives and alleged cruelty in private madhouses. It was these fears which many Georgian asylum proprietors were able to overcome, by emphasizing their kindness and skill in managing the insane. The provision of genteel and comfortable accommodation and facilities for private patients helped to ease families' guilt and fears about confinement.

Nevertheless, there is evidence that, despite this, certification was viewed as a last resort by upper- and middle-class families throughout the Victorian period. Sharp deteriorations in a person's behaviour, such as violent episodes or suicide attempts, made care away from home more likely; but even then certification might be avoided. There is little evidence that Victorian families were convinced that treatment in an asylum necessarily offered the best chance of recovery. As consumers, they were eclectic in their willingness to try other forms of therapy, before referring patients to private madhouses. In the late nineteenth century, the allegations of the lunacy reform movement, and the growth of therapeutic pessimism, enhanced doubts and fears about the trade in lunacy, and helped to precipitate a trend away from private asylum care.

Given the central role of the family in choosing forms of care, it is surprising that, with the exception of Tomes's study of the Pennsylvania Hospital for the Insane, it is a dimension which has been relatively neglected in histories of the asylum movement.[1] Scull was mainly

214

Conclusion

concerned to document the expansionist claims of asylum doctors; but he did suggest that, once the alternative of the asylum became available, the family and the community played a significant role in widening the definition of intolerable behaviour and insanity. Evidence from Ticehurst, as well as diaries and autobiographies, made it possible to document the limits of tolerable behaviour in Victorian and Edwardian families. However, the same sources provide poignant testimony to the conflict and distress caused by the decision to certify. Scull's own argument, in favour of a progressive diminution in family tolerance, wavers when he describes the pauper families who contributed most inmates of the expanding asylum movement as 'less able to resist pressures from others to incarcerate ... intractable individuals', implying that, for pauper families, asylum admission was sometimes a negative choice.[2] If this was so, it was a choice which families who could afford private care were less likely to be compelled to make. Before private asylum proprietors could capitalize on social trends which narrowed the bounds of acceptable behaviour, such as the growth of the moral reform movement, they needed to convince middle- and upper-class families that asylum care was the best alternative available.

From this study, three factors have emerged as being of importance in influencing families' choices of care. Except for the very richest families, cost was a factor which had to be taken into consideration. However, there is evidence that some families were prepared to economize on other areas of expenditure, and even come close to bankruptcy, in order to obtain what they believed to be the best treatment available. This was true particularly of some middle-class families when the main breadwinner was the person affected by mental disorder. The second, and arguably the most important, factor influencing choices of care, was the extent to which families felt confident that their insane relatives would enjoy comfortable facilities and courteous attention. For those families who saw asylum care as a last resort, many of whom no longer expected their relatives to recover, quality of care was more important than any promised effectiveness of treatment. Thirdly, families favoured practitioners who responded sensitively to their fears and preferences: respecting their desire for confidentiality; neglecting to ask embarrassing questions about a family history of insanity; allowing regular visitors, except those disapproved of by the family; and withdrawing or failing to implement treatments which were distasteful to patients or their relatives.

The relationship between private lunacy practitioners and their clients has been a central focus of this study. In some respects, the interests of families and private practitioners coincided. For example, the high premium placed on confidentiality by patients' families supported lunacy practitioners in their efforts to resist the extension of government inspection. Although licensed houses were subject to central visitation from

215

Conclusion

1845, the Lunacy Commissioners failed to establish effective powers over single patients until 1890. Similarly, doctors and patients' families shared a common preference for individual and somatic explanations of mental disorder, which influenced diagnosis and the identification of supposed causes of insanity.[3] In other respects, however, there was tension between the interests of private practitioners and patients' families. For example, private asylum proprietors sometimes advised families against visiting patients; presumably because they found these visits as intrusive and inconveniencing as formal inspection. Similarly, the desire of patients' families to influence treatment decisions restricted doctors' clinical autonomy. In both these cases, lunacy practitioners argued that the families' wishes were against the patients' best interests; but in both cases, in private practice, they were forced sometimes to defer to their fee-paying clientele.

To be successful, private lunacy practitioners needed to fulfil their clients' exacting expectations; closely following the wishes of patients' families, rather than the patients themselves. It was this which Georgian madhouse proprietors did so effectively in the late eighteenth century, and which the Newingtons continued to do throughout the nineteenth century. As entrepreneurs, private asylum proprietors needed to respond flexibly to changes in the market, particularly the sharp reduction in the number of pauper lunatics confined in private madhouses by the 1850s. Some proprietors of licensed houses were ill-equipped to attract a middle- and upper- class clientele, and the number of private madhouses began to decline. However, as a group, private lunacy practitioners succeeded in protecting their position. They continued to attract clients, despite repeated allegations by the lunacy reform movement about abuses in licensed houses; and they mounted an effective political campaign against the closure of private asylums, and outlawing of single care. Where they were not successful was in changing the grim public image of private asylums in the late nineteenth century. Although some private asylums enjoyed good individual reputations, the allegations of the lunacy reform movement, and the development of therapeutic pessimism, meant that late-Victorian and Edwardian asylums were widely seen as places for incurables, which offered dubious standards of care. Increasingly, in a trend which began before the 1890 Lunacy Act restricted further expansion of private asylums, families chose to refer patients to the private wards of county asylums, rather than licensed houses.

Ticehurst's history was not typical of nineteenth-century private asylums, but its story confirms a number of the general conclusions outlined above. Good standards of physical care secured the Newingtons' initial reputation; but their continuing success depended on their ability to attract an increasingly high-class clientele. They were able to do this partly because, in the 1830s, they presented their work as part of the

216

Conclusion

movement for moral reform. However, in the mid-Victorian period their reputation rested on the facilities, nursing and entertainments they provided for patients, rather than any claims of an extraordinary ability to cure mental disorder. Like Tomes, I see the mid-Victorian period as representing a high point in the care of the chronic insane; and, even by Victorian standards, the Newingtons were able to be exceptionally persistent in the efforts they made to nurse chronic, incurable cases.[4] By the 1870s, Ticehurst's reputation was such that, as doctors, the Newingtons enjoyed the luxury of being able to be highly selective about which patients they treated; and, on occasions, could choose to respond negatively to the requests of patients' families. Despite this, like other private asylums, Ticehurst was affected adversely by the allegations of the lunacy reform movement, and the growth of therapeutic pessimism. Like other proprietors of licensed houses in the 1880s, Hayes Newington found that it was necessary to enter the arena of public debate to protect his family's business.

During the period in which this book was written, the role of private medicine in present-day Britain has become the subject of intense political controversy. To a lesser extent, the effectiveness of community care for the mentally ill has also been debated. I would not see this study as having any substantial policy implications, since it aimed to demonstrate that the history of Ticehurst and other private asylums, up to 1917, resulted from a particular set of historical circumstances.[5] Throughout this period, the economic and social relationship between private lunacy practitioners and the families who paid for their insane relations to be cared for did not change, although practitioners became subject to increased government regulation. Similarly, although the class of patients admitted to Ticehurst altered over time, the Newingtons were never subject to severe resource constraints. Nevertheless, moulded by changes in public opinion and expectations, as well as medical attitudes to mental disorder, the quality of care available to patients and their families underwent significant shifts.

Notes

1. N. Tomes, *A generous confidence*, Cambridge, Cambridge University Press, 1985.
2. A. Scull, *Museums of madness*, London, Allen Lane, 1979, p. 240.
3. E. Shorter, 'Private clinics in Central Europe 1850–1933', *Social History of Medicine*, 1990, 3, 2: 162 comments on doctors' and patients' preference for diagnoses which suggested an underlying organic cause.
4. Tomes, op. cit., note 1 above, p. 321.
5. T. Turner, 'The past of psychiatry: why build asylums?', *Lancet*, 1985, ii: 709–11 suggested the range of provisions available to Ticehurst's clientele in the mid-Victorian period might provide one model for a balance between community and small-scale institutional care.

Bibliography

Manuscript sources

Accession numbers beginning QAL and QO refer to records kept at East Sussex Record Office, Lewes. Other accession numbers refer to records belonging to Ticehurst House Hospital, and deposited in the Wellcome Institute for the History of Medicine Western Manuscripts collection, London.

Licences

QO/EW30 Quarter Sessions order book, 1790–3
QAL/1/1/E1 Applications for licences for Ticehurst Asylum and House
QAL/1/2/E2 Applications for renewal of licences for Ticehurst Asylum and House

Visitation records

QAL/1/3/E10   Visitors' Reports, 1828–32
6254–6258 Visitors' Books, 1833–1923
6260–6261 Patients' Books, 1846–1929

Admissions, discharge and death

QAL/1/3/E7 Register of Admissions (Asylum), 1828–32
QAL/1/4/E5 Notices of Admission, Discharge, Removal and Death (House), 1833–52
QAL/1/4/E6 Notices of Admission, Discharge, Removal and Death (Asylum), 1837–58
6284   Account of Patients Admitted, 1828
6285   Admission of Patients, 1842–5
6286   Registry of Admissions, 1845–81
6287   Registry of Admissions, 1881–90
6288   Register of Patients, 1890–1906
6293   Register of Voluntary Boarders, 1890–1930
6290   Civil Register, 1907–19
6297   Medical Register, 1907–30
6301   Letters Book, 1857–73 (unnumbered applications)

Bibliography

6317 Registry of Discharges and Deaths, 1845–90
6318 Registry of Removals, Discharges and Deaths, 1890–1906
6319 Register of Discharges and Transfers, 1907–30
6321 Register of Deaths, 1907–30

Medical records

6361–6414 Case Books, 1846–1917
6420–6421 Daily Case Books, 1866–9
6263–6264 Medical Visitation Books, 1843–5
6265–6266 Medical Journal and Weekly Reports, 1845–53
6267–6273 Medical Visitation Books, 1853–94
6274–6279 Medical Journals, 1895–1921
6281–6282 Registers of Mechanical Restraint, 1891–1925

Financial and business

6554–6560 Bill Books, 1792–1846
6561–6571 Patients' Bill Books, 1846–1918
6604–6611 Ledger B: Patients' Accounts, 1870–1923
6580 [Patients'] Accounts, 1895–1920 (fees)
6589–6597 Ledger A: Business Accounts, 1854–92
6627–6628 Ledger D: Rent Accounts, 1863–1918
6632–6636 Ledger E: Family Finances, 1854–1917
6637–6639 Ledger F: Miscellaneous, 1859–61
       Provisions and Necessaries, 1870–5
       Provisions, 1875–83
6654–6666 Cash Books, 1854–1917
6644–6647 Journal Books, 1875–1917
6649 Private Journal Book, 1898–1918
6677–6702 Annual Audits, 1869–95
6523 Attendants' Book, 1881–1914 (confidential staff book)

Other manuscript sources

V.&.A./48 E32 Forster papers, Victoria & Albert Museum
MH51/735 79595 Country Register, Public Record Office

Parliamentary papers

A return of the number of houses in each county or division of the county licensed for the reception of lunatics, PP1819 (271.)xvii.131
Abstracts of population returns for 1811, PP1812(316.)(317.)XI.1–.
Lunacy Commissioners' Reports, 1846–1915.
Population . . . according to the census of 1821, PP1822(502.)XV.1–.

219

Bibliography

Report from the committee on madhouses in England, PP1814–15(296.)IV.801–.
Report from the select committee appointed to consider of provision being made for the better regulation of madhouses in England, PP1816(227)VI.249–.
Report from the select committee on lunacy laws; together with the proceedings of the committee, minutes of evidence, and appendix, PP1877 XIII.1–.
Statistical appendix to the report of the Metropolitan Commissioners in Lunacy to the Lord Chancellor... PP1844(621.)XVIII, 1–.

Newspapers and journals

British Medical Journal
Journal of Mental Science
Lancet
Sussex Weekly Advertiser
The Times

Books and articles

Ticehurst private asylum for insane persons, 1828, (accession no. 6783).
W. Battie, *A treatise on madness*, London, Whiston & White, 1758.
W. Berry, *Pedigrees of the families in the county of Sussex*, London, Sherwood, Gilbert & Piper, 1830.
J.S. Bolton, 'Amentia and dementia: a clinico-pathological study', *Journal of Mental Science*, 1905, 51: 523–7.
W.B. Carpenter, 'Review of R.B. Todd's *Physiology of the nervous system*', *British and Foreign Medico-Chirurgical Review*, 1850, 5, i: 1–50.
T.S. Clouston, *Female education from a medical point of view*, London, J. & A. Churchill, 1882.
—— *Clinical lectures on mental diseases*, London, J.& A. Churchill, 1883 (2nd edn published by Bailliere & Co., 1887).
—— *The neuroses of development*, Edinburgh, Oliver & Boyd, 1891.
—— *The hygiene of mind*, London, Methuen & Co., 1906.
—— *Unsoundness of mind*, London, Methuen & Co., 1911.
—— *Before I wed*, London, Cassell & Co., 1913.
H. Coombs and P. Coombs (eds), *Journal of a Somerset Rector 1803–34*, Oxford, Oxford University Press, 1984.
T. Denman, *An introduction to the practice of midwifery*, London, J. Johnson, 1801.
R. Eager, 'An investigation as to the therapeutic value of thyroid feeding in mental diseases', *Journal of Mental Science*, 1912, 58: 424–7.
(Mrs) Epps, *Diary of the late John Epps, MD Edin . . .*, London and Edinburgh, Kent and Co., 1875.
B. Faulkner, *Observations on the general and improper treatment of insanity . . .*, London, H. Reynell for the author, 1789.
J. Forbes *et al.* (eds), *The cyclopaedia of practical medicine*, vol. II, London and Sherwood, Gilbert & Piper, 1833.
S. Greg, *A layman's legacy*, London, Macmillan, 1877.
W.R. Greg, 'On the failure of natural selection in the case of man', *Frasers' Magazine*, 1868, 78: 353–62.
—— 'Life at high pressure', *Contemporary Review*, 1875, 25: 623–38.
Handbook for the instruction of attendants on the insane, London, Bailliere & Co., 1885.
E. Hudder, *The life and work of the seventh Earl of Shaftesbury, K.G.*, London, Cassell & Co., 1886.

Bibliography

T.W. Horsfield, *The history, antiquities and topography of the county of Sussex*, vol. I, Lewes, Sussex Press, 1835.

W.R. Kingdon, 'The diagnosis of hystero-epilepsy from status epilepticus', *Lancet*, 1898, i: 320.

L. Lowe, *The bastilles of England; or the lunacy laws at work*, London, Crookende, 1883.

M.A. Lower, *The worthies of Sussex . . .*, Lewes, printed for subscribers only by G.P. Bacon, 1865.

T. Mayo, *Remarks on insanity; founded on the practice of John Mayo, M.D.*, London, T. & G. Underwood, 1817.

——*An essay on the influence of temperament in modifying dyspepsia or indigestion*, London, B. Fellowes, 1831.

——*An essay on the relation of the theory of morals to insanity*, London, B. Fellowes, 1834.

——*Elements of the pathology of the human mind*, London, J. Murray, 1838.

[H.C. Merivale], *My experiences in a lunatic asylum, by a sane patient*, London, Chatto & Windus, 1879.

H. Maudsley, 'Presidential address', *Journal of Mental Science*, 1871–2, 17: 311–34.

W. Munk, *The gold-headed cane*, London, Longmans & Co., 1884.

A.S.L. Newington and H.F.H. Newington, 'Some incidents in the history and practice of Ticehurst asylum', *Journal of Mental Science*, 1901, 47: 62–72.

C. Newington, 'An instrument invented for administering food and medicine to maniacs by the mouth during a closed state of the teeth', *Lancet*, 1826, 10: 845–6.

H.F.H. Newington, 'Notes of a case of insanity dependent on syphilis', *Journal of Mental Science*, 1874, 19: 555–60.

——'Hemiplegia in relation to insanity', *Edinburgh Medical Journal*, 1874, 20: 119–23.

——'Some observations on different forms of stupor, and on its occurrence after acute mania in females', *Journal of Mental Science*, 1874–5, 20: 372–86.

——'Case of an extraordinary number of convulsions occurring in an epileptic patient, with remarks on nutrient enemata', *Journal of Mental Science*, 1877, 23: 89–95.

——'Unverified prognosis', *Journal of Mental Science*, 1887, 32: 223–33.

——'What are the tests of fitness for discharge from asylums?', *Journal of Mental Science*, 1887, 32: 491–500.

——'Hospital treatment for recent and curable cases of insanity', *Journal of Mental Science*, 1889, 35: 293–315.

——'Some mental aspects of music', *Journal of Mental Science*, 1897, 43: 704–21.

——'The plans of a new asylum for East Sussex', *Journal of Mental Science*, 1900, 46: 673–86.

S. Newington, 'A new remedial agent in the treatment of insanity and other diseases', *Lancet*, 1865, i: 621.

——'On a new remedial agent in the treatment of insanity and other diseases', *Journal of Mental Science*, 1865, 11: 272–5.

T. Newington, 'Feeding by the nose', *Lancet* 1879, i: 83.

W. Pargeter, *Observations on maniacal disorders*, Reading, for the author, 1792.

[J. Perceval] *Narrative of the treatment experienced by a gentleman during a state of mental derangement . . .*, London, Effingham Wilson, 1838.

J. Perceval, *A narrative of the treatment experienced by a gentleman during a state of mental derangement*, London, Effingham Wilson, 1840.

W. Perfect, *Methods of cure, in some particular cases of insanity, the epilepsy, hypochondriacal affections, hysteric passions and nervous disorders*, Rochester, T. Fisher for the author, 1778.

——*Select cases in the different species of insanity*, Rochester, Gillman, 1787.

Bibliography

——*A remarkable case of madness, with the diet and medicines used in the cure*, Rochester, for the author, 1791.

——*Annals of insanity*, London, for the author, 1809.

J.C. Prichard, *A treatise on insanity and other disorders affecting the mind*, London, Sherwood, Gilbert & Piper, 1835.

G.N. Ray, *The letters and private papers of William Makepeace Thackeray*, 4 vols, London, Oxford University Press, 1945.

J. Read, *An appeal to the medical profession, on the utility of the improved patent syringe . . .*, London, W. Glendinning, 1824.

G.H. Savage, 'Marked amelioration in a general paralytic following a very severe carbuncle', *Journal of Mental Science*, 1880–1, 26: 566–7.

——'Moral insanity', *Journal of Mental Science*, 1881, 27: 147–55.

——'Constant watching of suicidal cases', *Journal of Mental Science* 1884–5, 30: 19.

——'The pathology of insanity', *British Medical Journal*, 1884, ii: 239–43.

C. Seymour, *A topographical, historical and commercial survey of the cities, towns and villages of the county of Kent . . .*, Canterbury, for the author, 1776.

D. Sutton (ed.), *Letters of Roger Fry*, London, Chatto and Windus, 1972.

S. Tuke, *Description of the Retreat*, York, W. Alexander, 1813.

D. Verey (ed.), *The diary of a Victorian squire. Exracts from the diaries and letters of Dearman and Emily Birchall*, Gloucester, Alan Sutton, 1983.

C. White, *A treatise on the management of pregnant and lying-in women . . .*, London, for E. & C. Dilly, 1773.

F. Wilton, 'A case of obstinate constipation and inactivity of the liver', *Journal of Mental Science* 1880–1, 26: 67–9

S. Winkworth, *Letters and memorials of Catherine Winkworth*, 2 vols, Clifton, for the author, 1883 and 1886.

A. Wynter, *The borderlands of insanity and other allied papers*, London, R. Hardwicke, 1875.

Secondary sources

M. Anderson, *Approaches to the history of the western family, 1500–1914*, Studies in Economic and Social History for the Economic History Society, Houndmills, Hants and London, Macmillan Education, 1980.

R.H. Balme, 'Early medicinal use of bromides', *Journal of the Royal College of Physicians*, 1976, 10, 2: 205–8.

J.A. Banks, *Prosperity and parenthood. A study of family planning among the Victorian middle classes*, London, Routledge & Kegan Paul, 1954.

M. Barton, *Tunbridge Wells*, London, Faber & Faber, 1937.

G. Bateson, *Perceval's narrative. A patient's account of his psychosis, 1830–1832*, New York, William Morrow & Co.Inc., 1974.

G. Battiscombe, *Shaftesbury*, London, Constable, 1974.

Q. Bell, *Virginia Woolf*, vol. 2, London, Paladin, 1972.

I. Bradley, *The call to seriousness: the Evangelical impact on the Victorians*, London, Cape, 1976.

P. Branca, *Silent sisterhood. Middle-class women in the Victorian home*, London, Croom Helm, 1975.

S. Burman (ed.), *Fit work for women*, London, Croom Helm, 1979.

J. Burnett, *A history of the cost of living*, London, Penguin, 1969.

W.F. Bynum, 'Rationales for therapy in British psychiatry, 1780–1835', *Medical History*, 1974, 18: 317–34.

——'Alcoholism and degeneration in 19th century European medicine and psychiatry', *British Journal of Addiction*, 1984, 79: 59–70.

Bibliography

W.F. Bynum, R. Porter and M. Shepherd (eds), *The anatomy of madness*, vol. II, London, Tavistock Publications, 1985.

J. Chandos, *Boys together. English public schools 1800–64*, London, Hutchinson, 1984.

J.C.D. Clark, *English society, 1688–1832*, Cambridge and New York, Cambridge University Press, 1985.

G.D.H. Cole and R. Postgate, *The common people, 1746–1946*, London, Methuen & Co., 1971 edn.

N.G. Coley, ' "Cures without care", "chymical physicians" and mineral waters in seventeenth-century English medicine', *Medical History*, 1979, 23, 2: 191–214.

L. Davidoff and C. Hall, *Family fortunes. Men and women of the English middle class, 1780–1850*, London, Hutchinson, 1987.

A. Digby, *Madness, morality and medicine. A study of the York retreat, 1796–1914*, Cambridge, Cambridge University Press, 1985.

K. Doerner, *Madmen and the bourgeoisie: a social history of insanity and psychiatry*, Oxford, Basil Blackwell, 1981.

H.T. Engelhardt, 'The disease of masturbation: values and the concept of disease', *Bulletin of the History of Medicine*, 1974, 48: 234–48.

W.V. Farrar, K.R. Farrar and E.L. Scott, 'The Henrys of Manchester. Part 2. Thomas Henry's sons: Thomas, Peter and William', *Ambix*, 1974, 21: 188–207.

G.B.A.M. Finlayson, *The seventh Earl of Shaftesbury*, London, Eyre Methuen, 1981.

P. Fitzgerald, *Charlotte Mew and her friends*, London, Collins, 1984.

M. Foucault, *Madness and civilisation. A history of insanity in the age of reason*, London, Tavistock Publications, 1967.

A. Gauld, *The founders of psychical research*, London, Routledge & Kegan Paul, 1968.

P. Gay, *The bourgeois experience. Victoria to Freud. Vol. I, Education of the senses*, Oxford, Oxford University Press, 1984.

I. Gibson, *The English vice. Beating, sex and shame in Victorian England and after*, London, Duckworth, 1978.

R.P. Graves, *The brothers Powys*, London, Routledge & Kegan Paul, 1983.

E. Grierson, *Storm bird. The strange life of Georgina Weldon*, London, Chatto and Windus, 1959.

B. Haley, *The healthy body and Victorian culture*, Cambridge and London, Harvard University Press, 1978.

P.J.N. Havins, *The spas of England*, London, Hale, 1976.

N. Hervey, 'A slavish bowing down: the Lunacy Commission and the psychiatric profession, 1845–60', in W.F. Bynum, R. Porter and M. Shepherd (eds), *The anatomy of madness*, vol. II, London, Tavistock Publications, 1985.

——'Advocacy or folly: the Alleged Lunatics' Friends Society, 1845–63', *Medical History*, 1986, 30: 245–75.

L.J. Hodson and J. Odell, *Ticehurst: The story of a Sussex parish*, Tunbridge Wells, 'Courier' Co., 1925.

P. Honan, *Jane Austen. Her life*, London, Weidenfeld & Nicolson, 1987.

W. Houghton, *The Wellesley index to Victorian periodicals, 1824–1900*, vol. II, Toronto, University of Toronto Press, 1972.

R. Hunter and I. Macalpine, *Three hundred years of psychiatry, 1535–1860*, London, Oxford University Press, 1963.

——*George III and the mad business*, London, Allen Lane, 1969.

S.W. Jackson (ed.) Revd W. Pargeter, *Observations on maniacal disorders*, London, Routledge, 1988 reprint.

K. Jones, *Lunacy, law and conscience, 1744–1845*, London, Routledge & Kegan Paul, 1955.

——*A history of the mental health services*, London, Routledge & Kegan Paul, 1972.

J. King, *William Cowper. A biography*, Durham, Duke University Press, 1986.

Bibliography

C. Lamb, *The essays of Elia*, London, Everyman.

P. McCandless, ' "Curses of civilisation": insanity and drunkenness in Victorian Britain', *British Journal of Addiction*, 1984, 79, 1: 49–58.

M. MacDonald, 'Insanity and the realities of history in early modern England', *Psychological Medicine*, 1981, 11: 11–25.

——*Mystical Bedlam. Madness, anxiety and healing in seventeenth-century England*, Cambridge, Cambridge University Press, 1981.

——'Religion, social change and psychological healing in England, 1600–1800', in W. Shiels (ed.), *The church and healing*, Oxford, Basil Blackwell, 1982, pp. 101–26.

——'Lunatics and the state in Georgian England', *Social History of Medicine*, 1989, 2: 299–313.

N. McKendrick (ed.), *Historical perspectives. Studies in English thought and society*, London, Europa, 1974.

N. McKendrick, J. Brewer and J.H. Plumb, *The birth of a consumer society: the commercialization of eighteenth-century England*, London, Europa, 1982.

C. MacKenzie, 'A family asylum: A history of the private madhouse at Ticehurst in Sussex, 1792–1917', London University PhD thesis, 1987.

P. Miller and N. Rose (eds), *The power of psychiatry*, London, Polity Press, 1986.

A. Mizener, *The saddest story. A biography of Ford Madox Ford*, London, Bodley Head, 1971.

R.J. Morris, 'The middle class and the property cycle during the industrial revolution' in T.C. Smout (ed.), *The search for wealth and stability*, London, Macmillan, 1979.

W. Ll. Parry-Jones, *The trade in lunacy. A study of private madhouses in England in the eighteenth and nineteenth centuries*, London, Routledge & Kegan Paul, 1972.

——'The model of the Geel lunatic colony and its influence on the nineteenth-century asylum system in Britain', in A. Scull (ed.), *Madhouses, mad-doctors and madmen*, London, Athlone Press, 1981.

T.M. Parssinen, 'Professional deviants and the history of medicine: medical mesmerists in Victorian Britain', in R. Wallis (ed.), *On the margins of science: the social construction of rejected knowledge*, Keele, Keele University Press, 1979.

R. Porter, 'Was there a moral therapy in the eighteenth?', *Lychnos*, 1981–2, pp. 12–26.

——*English society in the eighteenth century*, London, Penguin, 1982.

——*Disease, medicine and society in England 1550–1860*, Studies in Economic and Social History for the Economic History Society, Houndmills, Hants, and London, Macmillan Education, 1987.

——*A social history of madness. Stories of the insane*, London, Weidenfeld & Nicolson, 1987.

——*Mind-forg'd manacles. A history of madness in England from the Restoration to the Regency*, London, Penguin Books, 1990.

'E.R.' (ed.), *The letters of Charles Lamb*, London, Everyman, 1909.

L. Ray, 'Models of madness in Victorian asylum practice', *Archives of European Sociology*, 1981, 22: 261–2.

D. Roberts, *Paternalism in early Victorian England*, London, Croom Helm, 1979.

D. Rothman, *The discovery of the asylum*, Boston, Little Brown, 1971.

A. Scull, *Museums of madness. The social organization of insanity in nineteenth-century England*, London, Allen Lane, 1979.

——'Moral treatment reconsidered: some sociological comments on an episode in the history of British psychiatry', *Psychological Medicine*, 1979, 9: 421–8.

——'The domestication of madness', *Medical History*, 1983, 27: 233–48.

M. Shepherd, 'Psychological medicine redivivus: concept and communication', *Journal of the Royal Society of Medicine*, 1986, 79: 639–45.

Bibliography

——*The psychosocial matrix of psychiatry. Collected papers*, London, Tavistock publications, 1983.

E. Shorter, *The making of the modern family*, London, Collins, 1976.

——'Private clinics in central Europe, 1850–1933', *Social History of Medicine*, 1990, 3, 2: 159–95.

E. Showalter, *The female malady. Women, madness and English culture, 1830–1980*, New York, Pantheon Books, 1985.

R.H. Shryock, *The development of modern medicine*, New York, Knopf, 1947.

L. Stone, *The family, sex and marriage in England, 1500–1800*, London, Weidenfeld & Nicolson, 1977.

L. Strachey, *Eminent Victorians*, London, Chatto and Windus, 1918.

M.S. Thompson, 'The mad, the bad and the sad: psychiatric care in the Royal Edinburgh Asylum (Morningside), 1813–94', Boston University PhD thesis, 1984.

N. Tomes, 'The persuasive institution: Thomas Story Kirkbride and the art of asylum-keeping, 1841–83', University of Pennsylvania PhD thesis, 1978.

——*A generous confidence. Thomas Story Kirkbride and the art of asylum-keeping, 1840–83*, Cambridge, Cambridge University Press, 1985.

S. Trombley, *'All that summer she was mad'. Virginia Woolf and her doctors*, London, Junction Books, 1981.

R. Trumbach, *The rise of the egalitarian family; aristocratic kinship and domestic relations in eighteenth-century England*, New York, Academic Press, 1978.

T. Turner, 'A diagnostic analysis of the case books of Ticehurst House Asylum, 1845–1890', University of London, MD thesis, 1990; and *Psychological medicine* (supplement), in press for 1992.

——'The past of psychiatry: why build asylums?', *Lancet*, 1985, ii: 709–11.

J.H. Warner, 'Therapeutic explanation and the Edinburgh bloodletting controversy: two perspectives on the medical meaning of science in the mid-nineteenth century', *Medical History*, 1980, 24: 241–58.

J. Woodward, *To do the sick no harm. A study of the British voluntary hospital system to 1875*, London and Boston, Routledge & Kegan Paul, 1974.

G. Zilboorg, *A history of medical psychology*, New York, W.W. Norton, 1941.

Index

Acts of Parliament: 1714 6, 18, 25;
  1744 6, 18; 1774 9, 10, 11, 13, 17,
  47, 53, 55; 1808 66; 1828 18, 67,
  75, 79, 90, 193; 1845 97; 1862 107;
  1888 199; 1890 168, 169, 176,
  189–90, 193, 198, 201, 203–6, 208,
  211
Addington, A. 11, 12
Addington's madhouse, Reading 11,
  12
admissions: pauper 13, 14–15, 41, 50,
  61, 66, 75, 91, 114; private 2, 10,
  15, 19; rate 15, 121–4; to Ticehurst
  39, 41, 45, 50–1, 65, 66, 129 *see also*
  voluntary admission
advertisements 9, 11, 12, 21, 23, 26,
  35, 37, 39, 40, 42, 62, 207, 209
alcohol 140, 147, 152, 154, 155, 156,
  173, 186
Alleged Lunatics' Friends Society
  (ALFS) 107, 124
amusements 19, 85, 137, 146, 147,
  148, 174, 182 *see also* exercise;
  music; reading
Anglicans 7, 28, 29, 37, 44, 67, 128
animal magnetism 87, 100
Anstie, F.C. 155
apothecaries 11, 12, 37, 45
aristocracy 29, 37, 83
Arnold, Thomas head of Rugby 63,
  83, 84
Arnold, Thomas physician 12, 25
Arnold's madhouse, Leicester 12, 13
Association of Medical Officers of
  Asylums and Hospitals for the
  Insane (AMOAHI) 194, 195
asylum superintendents: of county
  asylums 130, 152, 195, 197,
  198–200, 203; of registered

hospitals 27, 137, 166 *see also*
  proprietors
asylums: county 18, 47, 55, 61, 66, 97,
  108, 121, 133, 152, 168, 185, 195,
  197, 204, 206, 209, 210, 216;
  metropolitan private 10, 14–15, 18,
  66, 133, 194–5, 198; private
  chapter 1 *passim*, 47, 55–6, 61, 66,
  67, 79, 89–91, 97–8, 107–9, 113–4,
  124, 158, 193–8, 201, 204–9, 211;
  provincial private 11, 12, 13, 15,
  18, 193
attendants: 13, 14, 15, 21, 27–8, 70,
  71, 84, 99, 103, 109–10, 137, 138,
  141, 143, 144–5, 146, 147, 148,
  149, 150, 176, 178, 179–83, 188,
  208, at Ticehurst, H. Baker 181;
  G.H. Brown 183; George Clegg
  180; Sydney Hill 181; Robert
  Minchin 109–10; James Rigby 181;
  J.J. Sibbald 181; Henry Vigor 180;
  Henry Watts 180; George Wenbau
  181
Austen, George 22
Austen, Jane 22

Bakewell, S.G. 25
Bakewell, Thomas 28
Balsdean, Sussex, asylum at 66
Baptists 7, 11, 16
Barnes, Mary *see* Newington
Barnes, Robert 166
Barnwood, Gloucestershire 110, 113,
  133, 137, 199
baths 141, 155, 177, 184, 186
Battie, William 10, 12, 14, 16, 25 *see
  also* Wood's Close
Beatson, Georgiana *see* Newington
behaviour: before certification 17,

226

Index

20–1, 44, 50, 62, 86, 89, 103–5,
116–7, 173, 208, 215; and treatment
27–8, 42, 143–4, 145, 148–51,
176–7 *see also* sexual behaviour;
violence
Bell, Quentin 209, 210
Bell, Vanessa 207
Bethlem 6, 10, 25, 52, 166, 169, 175,
199, 202
Birchall, Dearman 104, 110, 113, 124,
136–8, 153
Blacklands House, Chelsea 134, 194
see also Sutherland
Blandford, George Fielding 116, 208
blistering 27, 64, 143, 186
blood-letting 24, 25, 27, 29, 42, 64,
79, 139–40, 154, 155, 156, 186–7
Bodmin Asylum, Cornwall 134
Box, Wiltshire: madhouse at 11, 13, 26
Brislington House, Bristol 7, 12, 21,
27, 39, 44, 55, 67, 71, 83, 88, 90–1,
97, 104, 141, 205 *see also* Fox
British Medical Journal 106, 110–11,
116, 189, 195, 196
Brooke House, Clapton 10, 12, 134,
194, 205 *see also* Monro
Brown-Séquard, C.E. 156
Bucknill, John Charles 108, 110–11,
117, 119, 155, 187, 195, 196, 202
Burley, Twickenham 207, 209 *see also*
Thomas
Burman, Thomas 12, 39
Burman's madhouse,
Henley-in-Arden 12, 39
Burnett, John 19
Bynum, W.F. 26, 44, 63, 173

Camberwell House, Camberwell 134
care: acute 108, 124, 149, 196, 210;
long-term 15, 18, 19–20, 22, 23,
55, 104, 108, 124, 135, 168, 196,
201, 210; physical 44, 56, 62, 86,
90, 91 *see also* single care
Carpenter, William B. 143, 154
certification 10, 13, 16, 17–18, 20–1,
50, 79, 86, 101, 102–6, 107, 109,
110, 111–12, 113, 115–6, 117, 119,
124, 143, 150, 153, 169, 193, 194,
196, 197, 198, 202, 203, 206–7,
208
Chambers, Dr James 209
Chancery Court *see* Court of Chancery
Chancery lunatics 106, 107, 109, 110,

111, 113, 119, 124, 136, 197, 198,
199, 201, 202
Clarke's madhouse, Clapton 10
Cleeve Hill, near Bristol, madhouse at
7, 12 *see also* Fox, Edward Long
clientele: of private asylums 13, 14,
20, 24, 28, 30, 44, 47, 56, 83, 89,
97, 100, 114, 168; of Ticehurst 8,
14, 37, 45, 74–5, 79, 124, 128, 130,
135, 138, 145, 158, 183
Clouston, Thomas Smith 166, 173–4,
178, 186, 187, 196, 199, 202, 210
Coleridge, Lord 197
College of Physicians *see* Royal College
of Physicians
Collegium Insanorum, St Albans 11,
14, 23 *see also* Cotton
comfort 22, 23, 24, 40, 42, 117, 137,
174, 177
commercialization 6, 29
commission of lunacy 136 *see also*
Chancery lunatics
Commissioners in Lunacy *see* Lunacy
Commissioners
confidentiality 20, 22, 23–4, 147, 90,
107, 130 *see also* privacy
confinement 8, 12, 22, 40, 47, 62, 84,
98–9, 108, 114 *see also* certification;
wrongful confinement
Conolly, John 111, 150
consumers 8, 12–13, 14, 30, 139, 201
Cooper, Anthony Ashley, 7th Earl of
Shaftesbury 98–9, 101–2, 106, 107,
108, 112, 113, 117, 121, 158, 197,
202, 206
Cooper, Maurice 98–9, 101–2
Cooper, 'Minny', Lady Shaftesbury 99
Cotton, Nathaniel 11, 14, 22, 26, 28,
29 *see also* Collegium Insanorum
Court of Chancery 17, 102, 109, 114,
136
Courthope, George 53
Cowper, William 23–4, 28–9
cure 10, 16, 19, 22, 52, 61, 62, 63, 82,
88, 89, 99, 101, 104, 108, 117,
119–21, 123–4, 136, 137, 168, 173,
185, 196, 209, 210

deaths: 52, 88, 120; death rate 88, 89
Defoe, Daniel 9, 10
diagnosis 50, 89, 91, 102, 115, 124,
153, 154, 184–5
Dickinson, Violet 207

227

Index

diet 23, 25, 35, 42, 64, 101, 140, 154
Digby, Anne 28, 81, 88, 89, 121, 146,
    151, 152, 157, 176
discharge 19, 20, 40, 51, 52, 67, 88,
    89, 90, 99, 102, 104, 105, 107, 108,
    109, 110, 119, 120, 121, 124, 128,
    129, 133, 135, 137, 138, 142, 148,
    149, 150, 176, 177–9, 183, 189, 202
Dissenters 7, 28, 37, 74
doctors, at Ticehurst: local, certifying
    admissions – Thomas Bishop 50,
    Charles Crouch 50, Charles
    Herbert Fazan 169, William
    Mercer 169, John Taylor 169,
    Robert Watts 50, 53, Robert
    Montague Wilmot 50, Augustus
    Woodroffe 169 see also Mayo,
    Newington (2) medical officers –
    Thomas Belgrave 149, 152,
    Wolstan Dixie 209, James Henry
    Earls 166, Arthur Edis 156,
    Wilfred Robert Kingdon 185, 188,
    Colin F.F. McDowall 167, 181,
    Alexander Urquhart 200, Francis
    Wilton 150, 175 see also Mayo;
    Newington
Doerner Klaus 6
domestic economy see household
    economy
Droitwich Asylum, Worcestershire 11,
    13, 23
drugs see medicines
Duncan, Matthews 116
D'Vebre, Deborah 9

eclecticism see animal magnetism;
    homoeopathy; hydropathy
entertainments see amusements
enthusiasm 7, 28, 29
entrepreneurism 8, 11–12
Epps, Ellen 87
Epps, John 87, 100
Evangelicalism 23, 29, 62, 67, 82, 84,
    90, 91, 101, 152, 195
exercise 24, 25, 27, 43, 64, 71–5, 85,
    140 see also horse-riding; running;
    walking

families, of patients see relatives
family: changes in 9, 14, 21, 23, 25–8,
    33, 35; life 22, 23, 29, 56, 89, 97,
    124
Faulkner, Benjamin 10, 16, 26

Faulkner's madhouse, Little Chelsea
    10
fees 14, 15, 18–20, 23, 39, 42, 45, 50,
    54, 55, 56, 66, 67, 70, 74, 75, 79,
    83, 86, 89, 90, 102, 114, 128, 130,
    133, 135–7, 138, 139, 172, 208, 210
Finch, W.C. 200
Finch, William 11, 12, 16
Finch, William, M.D. 21, 23–4, 26–7,
    61–2, 90
Finch family 12, 205 see also Fisherton
    House; Laverstock House
Fisher House, Islington 52
Fisherton House, Salisbury 111, 198,
    200 see also Finch
Fishponds, Bristol: madhouse at 7,
    11, 12 see also Mason
Fonthill Gifford, Wiltshire: madhouse
    at 11, 26
force, use of 25, 27–8, 84, 181–2
force-feeding 64, 70, 142, 174, 175–6,
    188
Ford, Ford Madox 207
Foucault, Michel 6, 26, 28
Fox, C.J. 21
Fox, Edward Long 7, 12, 21, 37
Fox, F.K. 21
Fox family 12, 21, 22, 55, 91, 141, 205
    see also Brislington House
friends, of patients see relatives
Fry, Helen 208–9
Fry, Roger 208–9

Gaskell, Samuel 195
Gauld, Alan 115
gentility 14, 20, 23–4, 30, 56, 61, 87,
    90, 135, 142, 175
George III 7, 11, 12, 13, 14, 25, 35,
    37, 43–4
Goold, Mr 97
Goold, Mrs 97
Granville, J. Mortimer 195
Great Foster House, Egham, Surrey
    12
Greatford, Lincolnshire, madhouse at
    7, 11, 12, 39, 43, 45, 47 see also
    Willis
Greg, Samuel 100–1, 152
Greg, William Rathbone 100, 104,
    130, 137, 151, 152
Greg family 100, 104, 152, 155
Guildford, Surrey, asylum at 99 see
    also Irish's madhouse

228

Index

Gull, William 109, 115, 116, 121

Haley, Bruce 153, 157
Hall, John 11 *see also* St Luke's, Newcastle-upon-Tyne
Head, Henry 208, 210
Henry, Charlotte 152
Henry, William 152
Herschell, Baron 113, 204
Hill, George Nesse 64, 79
Holly House, Hoxton 52
homoeopathy 87, 100, 101
Hook Norton, Oxfordshire 11, 12, 88, 89
horse-riding 26, 43, 67, 71, 130, 138, 150, 182
Horsfield, Thomas 75
Horsley, Victor 187
household economy 14, 18–19, 102, 208–9
Hoxton House, Hoxton 10, 11, 14, 26
Hume, John Robert 194
hydropathy 100–1, 155, 207

individualism 21, 22
insanity, causes of 29–30, 63, 82, 84, 116–7, 143, 151, 152, 153, 155, 156, 172, 177, 184, 186, 187, 207
Irish, David 16
Irish's madhouse, Guildford, Surrey 11, 16

Journal of Mental Science 111, 166, 195, 197, 198, 201, 202, 203

Keble, John 63
Kenrick, Sarah 101

Lamb, Charles 39
Lamb, Mary 39, 41
Lancet 116, 185, 195, 196, 202, 204, 207
Lanchester, Edith 208
Laverstock House, Salisbury 11, 12, 14, 21, 23, 55, 61, 67, 90, 91, 205 *see also* Finch
Laycock, Thomas 143
Lindsay, Murray 197, 198
Locock, Dr 156
lodgings for single patients: Alpha Road, Regents Park, London 134, 194; Mr Badcock's, in or near Ticehurst 40; Mrs Bakewell's,

Camberwell 98; W. Balcombe's, in or near Ticehurst 106; Revd Cawithen's, Devon 99; Culham family, Monk Sherbourne 22; Jesse Henry Newington's, Tenterden 134; Samuel Wilmot Newington's, Goudhurst 134; in St Leonards 134; Widow Skinner's, in or near Ticehurst 41
Lord, Revd John 7, 37
Lord Chancellor's Visitors 106, 107, 108, 109, 110, 111, 113, 114, 119, 124, 136, 138, 196, 197, 198, 203
Lord's madhouse, Drayton Parslow, Buckinghamshire 7
Lowe, Louisa 107, 108, 109, 110, 111–12, 115
Lunacy Commissioners 64, 91, 98, 106, 107, 109–10, 111, 113, 114, 117, 119, 137, 139, 142, 143, 145–6, 155, 158, 179, 181, 185, 193–5, 196, 197, 198, 202, 203, 204, 208 *see also* Metropolitan Commissioners
Lunacy Law Reform Association (LLRA) 107–8, 109, 110, 111, 112, 113, 124, 136
lunacy reform 24, 61, 102, 106, 107, 111–12, 113, 185, 193, 195, 196, 198, 206
Lush, John Alfred 111, 198, 200 *see also* Fisherton House
Lutwidge, Robert 195

MacDonald, Michael 7, 17, 44
McLaren, James 173
mad-doctors 7, 8, 11, 16, 20, 21, 22, 23, 25, 27, 28, 30, 35, 37, 44, 106, 107 *see also* asylum superintendents; medical psychologists; proprietors; psychiatrists
madhouse-keepers *see* proprietors
magistrates 6, 9, 13, 18, 53, 55, 66, 71, 85, 90, 98, 110, 117, 119, 130, 141, 144, 193, 195, 200
Manor House, Chiswick 133, 157
Martineau, Harriet 74
Mason, Joseph 7, 11, 12, 16 *see also* Cleeve Hill; Fishponds
Maudsley, Henry 107–8, 110, 172, 186, 195, 198, 201, 202
Mayo, John 53, 55, 62, 81

229

Index

Mayo, Thomas 62–4, 66, 71, 79–87, 89–91, 100, 139, 140, 144, 145, 148, 151, 155, 180, 184, 210
medical profession 6, 63, 82, 86, 98, 108, 110, 119, 121, 130, 139, 146, 169, 185, 193, 195, 196, 197–8, 204
medical psychologists 166, 172, 177, 178, 196, 197, 204, 207, 210 *see also* asylum superintendents; mad-doctors; proprietors; psychiatrists
medical treatment 7, 27, 42, 44, 61, 62, 63, 64, 71, 79, 82, 139, 140, 143, 154, 157, 174, 183–4, 187, 189, 196, 202, 203 *see also* baths; blistering; blood-letting; diet; exercise; force-feeding; medicines; purging; restraint
medicines 14, 25, 27, 29, 37, 39, 42, 62, 63, 64, 71, 81, 155, 156, 157, 174, 175, 176, 184–5, 188–9, 203 *see also* alcohol; sedation; tonics; vomits
Medico-Psychological Association (MPA) 107, 111, 166, 167, 173, 179, 183, 186, 187, 195, 196, 198, 199–202, 204, 210
mesmerism *see* animal magnetism
Metropolitan Commissioners 9, 18, 29, 193
Mew, Charlotte 205, 208, 209
Mew, Freda 208
Mew, Henry 208, 209
Minchin, Mrs Sarah 11, 12
Monro, Edward Thomas 194
Monro, Henry 198
Monro, John 10
Monro family 10, 12, 134, 194, 198, 205 *see also* Brooke House
Moorcroft House, Uxbridge, Middlesex 134
moral insanity 81–3, 84, 85, 89, 91, 105, 124, 153, 158, 172, 178, 184
moral management 26, 30, 62, 85, 146, 157, 178
moral reform 56, 61, 81, 82, 89, 91
moral treatment 26–9, 42, 43, 44, 61, 62, 63, 79, 81, 84, 85, 98, 139, 140, 141, 143, 145, 146, 147, 157, 174, 176, 177, 196
Morel, Benedict 172, 173
Morison, Alexander 194–5
music 27, 43, 71, 139, 141, 146, 148, 182, 183

Myers, Frederic 115

Nairne, Robert 195
nature, healing powers of 63, 140, 157, 172, 173
Needham, Frederick 137, 198–9 *see also* Barnwood
Newington: Alexander Samuel 163, 166; Alexander Thurlow 163; Charles 39, 53, 62, 64–6, 67, 70, 71, 74, 75, 79, 84, 85, 90, 91, 134, 139, 141, 145, 154, 155, 175, 195; Charles Edmund Hayes 139, 143, 145, 146, 148, 150, 153, 154, 163, 194–5; Eliza 67; Eliza (née Hayes) 53, 67, 90; Elizabeth 145; George 39; Georgiana (née Beatson) 163; Helena 163; Herbert Archer Hayes 166–7; Herbert Francis Hayes 109, 163, 166–7, 169, 172–3, 174–5, 176–8, 179–80, 182, 183, 186–8, 189–90, 198, 199, 200, 202, 210; Jesse 39, 53, 62; Jesse Henry 134; John 39; Joseph 39; Martha (née Playsted) 38–9; Mary (née Barnes) 166; Samuel (1) 11, 12, 16, 35, 37, 38–9, 40, 42, 53, 61, 106; Samuel (2) 105, 106, 109, 110, 121, 134, 138, 139, 141, 142, 143, 145, 146–7, 149, 150, 153–5, 156–7, 163, 167, 172, 173, 174, 183, 195; Samuel Playsted 39, 50, 66, 79; Samuel Wilmot 79, 134; Theodore 163, 166, 175, 176, 182; Walter 167, 182, 183; Walter James 163; Zebulon 39
Newington family 35, 43, 50, 53–6, 62, 85, 87, 90, 100, 104, 121, 130, 134, 139, 140, 141, 144, 145, 147–9, 151, 152, 153, 154–5, 156, 157, 158, 163–7, 169, 175, 177, 180–3, 188–9, 194, 195, 205 *see also* Ticehurst
Newlands, Tooting 205 *see also* Sutherland
non-conformists *see* Dissenters
non-restraint 27, 65, 81
Northampton Asylum 131
Northumberland House, Stoke Newington 134

Otto House, London 194, 205 *see also* Sutherland

230

Index

Pargeter, William 16–17, 19, 20, 21, 25, 27, 29
Parry-Jones, William Ll. 88, 89, 193
Parssinen, Terry 100
patients: pauper 6–7, 11, 14, 15, 18, 26, 41, 47, 55, 61, 66, 88, 90, 97, 206; private 9, 13, 14, 15, 18, 22, 23–4, 47, 55, 61, 62, 75, 97, 102, 107, 108, 111, 114, 115, 119, 134, 197, 198, 201, 204, 205–11; single 21, 106–7, 109, 134, 168, 199, 201; at Ticehurst, John Allsopp 74, Thomas Avan 40, Miss B. 181, J.B. 188–9, 'N.B.' 84–6, 87, Miss Baker 53, William Baldwin 179, Arthur Basset 103, Elizabeth Beeching 175, Mary Berryman 182, Miss Bertrand 66, James Bigg 39, Henry Charles Blincowe 74, 128, Mr Boorman 66, 141, Henry Borrer 141, Timothy Charles Brett 145–6, 153, Hugh Brodie 179, James Brook 103–5, 123–4, 136–8, 153, 157, William Carter 177, 183, 188, Revd James Chambers 45, 51, John Chatfield 64, James Coles 145, Marion Collier 179, Mrs Cosham 66, Revd William Cotton 148, Revd William Courthope 53, Henry Crommelin 140, D.D. 185, 188, Marianne Dalton 175, William Debary 141, Stephen Dickenson 74, 128, 130, Prince Ahmed Saaf ed Din 172, Anna Direy 103, Georgina Dovrington 178, 183, Countess of Durham 116, 117, 121, 133, 156, Sarah Farley 179, Anne Farquhar 149, 150, 153, Pauline Folliau 103, Isabella Foster 105, Mary Anne Foster 155, Augustus Gawen 105, Eliza Gipps 104, Henrietta Golding 105, Alexander Goldsmid 74, 86, 128, 138, Frederick Goulburn 143, 156, William Green 147, Lucy Anne Greg 100, 104, 130, 152, 155, Rachel Groom 184, Mrs H. 181, Eliza Hawes 141, 143, Samuel Hill 130, 152, Frances Hoffman 154, Ann Hopkinson 153, W.G. Howard 136, 141, 194, C.J. 186, S.J. 180, Revd Joseph Jefferson 136, Miss Jenney 154, Captain Hope Johnstone 117, 119, Page Keble 74, George Kenrick 100, 101, Lady Beatrix Legge 142, Sophia Lindsell 129, Daniel Lintall 39, 42–3, Edward Lloyd 103, Revd Lofty 45, John Daniel Lucadon 51, 128, Miss M. 181, Mr M. 181, K.M. 175, Louisa Manning 145, Joshua Mantell 86, 87, 100, Mary Marshall 179, Walter Marshall 109, 110, 111, 115, 116, 121, David Martineau 74, 79, Emily Martineau 74, Charles Mawley 105, 149, 150, Revd James Maxwell 136, Herman Charles Merivale 99–100, 101, 102, 107, 111, 121, 124, 128, 147, 157, 207, Charles Nunn 74, William Augustus O'Kelly 141, Emma Osborne 176, 185, Henry Montagu Oxenden 143, Revd John Patterson 103, 148, John Perceval 27, 28, 41, 44, 62, 64, 65, 70–4, 83, 84, 85, 86, 87, 90, 101, 107–8, 128, 138, 144, 154, 157, 176, Kate Philpott 179, Mary Phipps 184, Miss Pilgrim 53, Revd Richard Podmore 40–1, Thomas Preston 109, 110, Frederick Pulteney 181, William Raikes 194, William Harcourt Ranking 150, 153, Charles Rawdon 103, Mr Robinson 66, I.S. 144, Samuel Sands 40, 41, Henry Shepherd 105, Mrs Shrivell 41, 42, Marmaduke Simpson 179, 186, Caroline Simson 128, 138, George Simson 128, Fritz Steiner 150, Revd Henry Sulivan 136, L.B.T. 176, 182, 183, 189, Washington Travers 99, Charles Turner 179, Mary Turney 105, 149, Henrietta Unwin 105–6, 124, 157, Revd Louis de Visme 128, 149, Letitia Walker 149, Capt. Edward Walsh 179, Mrs Welstead 149, 156, Mrs Whitehead 53, Frances Willington 105, Howard Wilson 181, Henry Winkworth 98, 102, 129, 130, Elizabeth Winser 103, George Wood 104, 150, Thomas Wright 104, 150, Sir William Walter Yea 74, 79
Perfect, William 12, 16, 17, 26, 35–7, 83

Index

Perfect's madhouse, West Malling, Kent 12, 13, 35
Phillips, Charles Palmer 110
physicians 7, 12–13, 15, 18, 27, 50, 53, 55, 62–3, 71, 79, 85–6, 88, 99, 100, 102, 107, 109, 116, 121, 134, 138, 139, 145, 147, 152, 156, 157, 163, 166, 169, 172, 174, 185, 195, 197, 200, 202, 203, 207, 208, 209, 210 *see also* Royal College of Physicians
Pilgrim, Mr 53
Playsted, Martha *see* Newington
Porter, Roy 7, 8, 12, 23, 24, 25, 42, 43
Powys, John Cowper 207
Powys, Katie 207
Prichard, James Cowles 82, 194
Priory, Roehampton, Surrey 133, 194, 205, 208 *see also* Wood
privacy 20, 24, 56, 71, 98, 107, 113, 114, 201 *see also* confidentiality
Procter, Bryan 98
proprietors, of private asylums: 7–13, 16–18, 20–30, 42, 44, 75, 90, 91, 97, 100, 107–9, 111, 114, 116, 157, 163, 185, 193–5, 197–200, 204, 206; medical 10, 12, 16, 26, 61, 198; non-medical 7, 16
psychiatrists 65, 120, 172, 173, 187 *see also* asylum superintendents; mad-doctors; medical psychologists; proprietors
psychiatry 24, 173, 178
psychophysiology 139–58
purging 24, 25, 27, 71, 79, 140, 155, 177, 185, 187

Quakers 7, 61, 84, 151

Radcliffe, C.B. 156
Ray, Laurence 121, 124
Rayner, Henry 200
Read, John 64
reading 71, 141, 147, 150, 183
recovery 7, 25, 28, 29, 43, 52, 53, 55, 81, 84–5, 88, 114, 120, 123, 145, 155, 167, 179, 188, 203 *see also* cure
reflex physoiology 143, 153, 174, 186, 187
relatives, and friends, of patients: feelings of 23, 26, 29, 30, 86, 98, 101, 115, 119, 208, 209; visits by 16–17, 21, 87, 116–17, 119, 209
restraint: chemical 81, 157, 196, 203,

211, *see also* sedation; mechanical 24–5, 26, 27, 35, 41–2, 44, 64–5, 81, 84, 85, 140, 141–4, 146, 149, 176, 177, 185, 194, 202–3 *see also* non-restraint
Retreat, York 22, 26–8, 44, 53, 81, 84, 85, 88–9, 121, 129–30, 146, 151, 154, 157, 176, 177, 184
Ringmer, Sussex, asylum at 66
Robertson, Alexander 203
Robertson, Charles Lockhart 108, 111, 203
Rogers, T.L. 202
Rose, Nikolas 204
Royal College of Physicians 9–11, 90, 193–4, 198, 201, 204
Rugby School 83, 84, 135
running 39, 71, 147, 182

St Luke's, London 10, 14, 40, 52, 86
St Luke's, Newcastle-upon-Tyne 11
Saunders, C.E. 197
Savage, George Henry 166, 169, 178, 179, 185, 196, 197, 198, 199, 201, 202–3, 204, 207, 208, 209, 210
Scull, Andrew 6, 7, 8, 24, 26, 61, 119, 121, 124, 193, 210
sedation 27, 79, 81, 140, 157, 184, 185, 188, 189, 196, 202 *see also* restraint
Selborne, Lord 112–3
select committees: 1763 9; 1815–6 26, 41, 55–6, 61–2, 63; 1858–9 107; 1877 101, 108, 109–11, 113, 115, 119, 124, 158, 195, 196; 1925–6 Royal Commission 211
services, growth of 8, 13
sexual behaviour: 105, 143, 148, 150, 186; masturbation 142–3, 152–3, 156, 186
Seymour, Charles 35
Shaftesbury, Lord *see* Cooper, Anthony Ashley
Shillingthorpe, Stamford, Lincolnshire 12, 55, 91 *see also* Willis
Shorter, Edward 21, 207
Sidgwick, Henry 115
Sieveking, H. 152
single care 19, 47, 85–6, 102, 106–8, 109, 111, 114, 119, 124, 136, 168, 194, 198, 201, 202, 204, 208 *see also* lodgings; patients

232

Index

Skae, David 172, 173, 186
Smith, Dr, of Ilkley Wells 105
Smith, Robert Percy 169, 186
Society for Improving the Condition of the Insane 194–5, 203
Southey, Henry Herbert 194
spirituality: and healing 28–9; of patients 117
surgeons 12, 15, 37, 39, 45, 50, 53, 64, 86, 90, 130, 140, 145
Stone, Lawrence 21
Stroud, Mr 12, 39
Stroud's madhouse, Bilstone, Staffordshire 12, 39
suicide 103, 115–6, 152, 179–80, 208
Sussex House, Hammersmith 134 see also Winslow
Sutherland, Alexander John 99, 134, 194–5
Sutherland, Alexander Robert 86, 194
Sutherland, Henry 198
Sutherland family 134, 194–5, 205 see also Blacklands House; Otto House

Tattlebury House, Goudhurst, Kent 79, 134 see also Newington, Samuel Wilmot
Thackeray, Isabella 98
Thackeray, William 98
therapeutic pessimism 172–4, 211
Thomas, Jean 207 see also Burley
Thompson, Margaret Sorbie 175
Thudichum, J.L.W. 155
Ticehurst: 11, 12, 13, 15, 19, 21, 97, 98–106, 109–10, 113, 115, 117, 121, 124, 193–5, 205, 206, 211; Asylum (House) 67, 70, 71, 87; Gables 169, 172; Highlands 53, 66, 74, 87, 90, 102, 145; Quarry Villa 176; Ridgeway 172; Vineyards 37 see also doctors; Newington; patients
Tomes, Nancy 119
tonics 64, 71, 79, 140, 154, 174, 184
Travers, Benjamin 99
treatment see medical treatment; moral treatment
Tuke, Batty 185
Tuke, Daniel Hack 155, 187, 197, 201, 202, 203, 204
Tuke, George Montague 163, 167
Tuke, Samuel 26–8, 42, 43, 53, 84–5, 177
Tuke, Thomas Harrington 134, 157

see also Manor House, Chiswick
Tuke, William 37
Tunbridge Wells 13, 35, 37, 53, 77, 147, 176
Turlington, R. 9, 10
Turlington's madhouse, Chelsea, London 9

venesection see blood-letting
violence 6–7, 21, 22, 25, 27, 30, 39, 40–2, 44, 63, 65, 82, 84, 99, 101, 103–4, 106, 119, 141–2, 143, 149, 157, 176–7, 181, 182, 184, 194, 202, 208
visitors see magistrates
voluntary admission 107, 114, 206
vomits 25, 27, 81

Wagner-Jauregg, Julius 188
Wakefield, Edward 61, 62, 91
Wakley, James 196
walking 71, 74, 142, 145
Warburton, Thomas 14 see also White House, Whitmore House
Warner, John Harley 140
Weldon, Georgina 112, 196
West Malling, Kent, asylum at 47, 129, 134, 207 see also Perfect's madhouse
White House, Bethnal Green 10, 11, 26
Whitelands Hospital, Carisbrooke 209
Whitmore House, Hoxton 10, 11, 26
Wilkes, James 195
Williams, William Rhys 166
Willis, Revd Francis 7, 11, 12, 13, 14, 25, 27, 35, 37, 39, 43–5
Willis, Robert Darling 45, 51
Willis family 55 see also Greatford; Shillingthorpe
Winkworth, Catherine 98, 101, 104
Winkworth, Susanna 98, 101, 102, 104, 130
Winkworth family 102, 135
Winslow, Forbes 134, 194, 195
Winslow, Henry Forbes 198
Witnet, Oxfordshire 88
Wood, W. 134, 194
Wood, William 198, 208
Wood family 205 see also Priory
Wood's Close, Clerkenwell 10
Woods, T. Oscar 200
Woolf, Leonard 208, 209, 210

Index

Woolf, Virginia 207, 208, 209, 210
Wright, Maurice 210
Wright's madhouse, Bethnal Green,
London 10 *see also* White House

wrongful confinement 9, 18, 61, 108,
124, 204

Yellowlees, David 199, 203